Scene&Style

Celebrating 10 Years of Published Boston Fashion Columns

Contents

Chapter One – 2024

Everything I have I owe it to Pasta. - Sopia Lauren

Chapter Two – 2023

"What you wear is how you present yourself to the world, especially today, when human contacts are so quick. Fashion is instant language." — Miuccia Prada

Chapter Three – 2022

"Give a girl the right kind of shoes and she can rule the world." — Marilyn Monroe

Chapter Four- 2021

"One is never over-dressed or under-dressed with a Little Black Dress." — Karl Lagerfeld

Chapter Five – 2020

"Don't be into trends. Don't make fashion own you, but you decide what you are, what you want to express by the way you dress and the way to live." —Gianni Versace

Chapter Six – 2019

"Style is something each of us already has, all we need to do is find it." — Diane von Furstenberg

Chapter Seven – 2018

"Dress shabbily and they remember the dress; dress impeccably and they notice the woman." —Coco Chanel

Chapter Eight – 2017

"My relationship with fashion has always been that each of us stars in our own movies and costumes ourselves to play the part we want. You take blouses and jeans and dresses, and you put them together, and they tell your story." - Marc Jacobs

Chapter Nine – 2016

“After all, computers crash, people die, relationships fall apart. The best we can do is breathe and reboot" - Carrie Bradshaw

Chapter Ten – 2015

“Never use the word ‘cheap.’ Today everybody can look chic in inexpensive clothes—the rich buy them, too. There is good clothing design on every level today. You can be the chicest thing in the world in a T-shirt and jeans—it’s up to you.” - Karl Lagerfeld

Chapter Eleven – 2014

“Fashion fades, style is eternal” - Yves Saint Laurent

Chapter Twelve – 2013

"Fashion is part of the daily air and it changes all the time, with all the events. You can even see the approaching of a revolution in clothes. You can see and feel everything in clothes." —Diana Vreeland

Chapter Thirteen – 2012

“A Women should be two things, classy and fabulous” —Coco Chanel

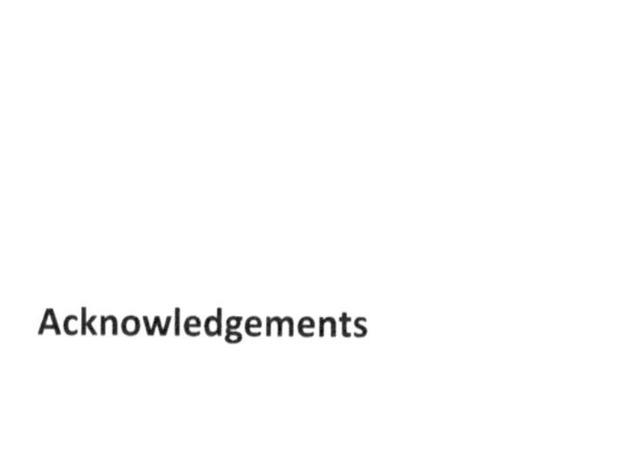

Acknowledgements

I want to thank all the people that helped bring this project to life. Linda Riccio for recommending me at the Boston Post-Gazette in 2011 which has gotten me here today. My former editor Pam Donnarumma and Joanie at the Gazette for taking out the time to dig up my first columns and searching through photos. The fashion designers, media, and those that give me content.

Lastly, Denise Hajjar for being my rock, my friend with honesty, family, a client, and my muse of inspiration.

My Press Pit family

I want to give a special dedication to you all. The ones who grind it out with me have taken me under their wing and who hazed me in the beginning of this journey. I am not a photographer; I do my best to use photos of yours when publishing my cover and article. However, I do rue stealing the light from your flashes.

As much love as I have for you all let's be realistic, it's called a pit for a reason. I remember Archie Bloch hazing me for almost two years telling me to get that damn iPad out of his angle. Iggy Barskov literally branding me "iPad Angela." Robert Paris, we went a few rounds in the early days about who was standing where. I love you all now!

Recently I had Andrew Dunn telling me the first time he ever saw me I was yelling at a photographer during the Joe Malaika show. I laughed, and he said, "I've been dying to know what he said to you." As the story goes, he stole my chair. A respected professional is moving around in the press pit, the runway or stage. Joe had asked me for help, and I had to step away for a minute. When I returned some guy had taken my seat. I didn't know who he was and honestly at that point in my career 2022, I was known and if I didn't know you, not going to end well. Not to mention, I have my guard up I am generally the only female in the pit. As I was that evening and Joe's shows are a huge production.

I asked the guy to get up and his actual response was, "No." Mind you this guy had just shown up after a few sets. I have been there since the beginning. Any photographer knows Joe's shows are lengthy, rarely start on time. Love you Joe, a typical designer and we all end up staying because the amazing content and designs are well worth the wait.

I was HEATED! First off, I'm old school Italian, how the hell are you in good conscious going to steal a woman's chair. He was disgustingly set in his way of taking my chair. Michael Rose offered me his and I politely declined being he's an elder to me. MANORS, God help us all!

The situation took a dark turn when he claimed that it wasn't my chair trying to spare himself the embarrassment. At that point I was all set and intentionally embarrassed him by asking him to hand me my purse and jacket that were under the chair he was sitting in.

I am a woman of class and ease however you get the flavor you ask for from me. Now this was a Sunday, in December which means I had played a high level soccer match and was most likely sore and tired. Yet here I am in heels running around a press pit. Homie stole my chair, so he got what he asked for.

I proceeded to stand directly in front of him, he sat I stood he had no shot whatsoever. Putting the cherry on top of my Italian temper, I began to booty drop right in front of him in my dress and heels. Shouting at his size and that I had just played a soccer match and here I am in heels. Literally creating a spectacle as I dance right in front of him getting my content. He didn't stay long after that. Michael Rose left, I took a seat and Clark Linehan, and I rode out the rest of the evening.

Let me be clear, I don't attend these shows to mingle this is my profession. I have respect for professionals and treat those that are with respect. The rest that have seen this side, sorry not sorry you stepped into the pit and got what you asked for.

On the lighter side, I have so many amazing memories with the true professionals. Right back to the prior December and 2021 Joe Maliaka show. There seemed to of been some hiccups and Brian Pitcher and Robert Paris hopped to it on the wires. Clark, Michael and myself just waited it out. Dan Minucci was celebrating his birthday and being silly, Hill Zhou was making one of his first appearances and we took maybe one of the best Boston Media photos ever.

I would like to give a special shout out to Robert Paris. For not only doing an amazing book cover photo shoot but literally having to come pick me up off the side of the highway, hair half done and was able to get me to zone in as the model I am not and get it done. Also, for the ride back to my now non existent car, lol love you!

You all know who the members of this squad are and mean so much to me. Literally when life has handed me lemons over the last decade, I have been able to check out mentally and check in to a press pit and feel blessed to have you all as my press pit family. Love you all always!

Introduction

All too often during interviews I am asked, "how did you get into fashion?" I have always had the spirit in my soul. My grandmother was inspiration for me early on. She was a grand type of women. A pianist at a hotel chandelier bar. I have memories of being backstage with her as she prepared, put on that matte red lipstick. By the age of five, she had me sewing, painting my nails. For anyone that truly knows me, my nails are always done. I will throw any extra elbow out of anger on the field if I happen to of broken one.

A writer I have always been, won my first award at the age of eight. As for fashion, I rolled my pants, wore crazy socks, shaved my legs in the fifth grade, began coloring my hair about the same time. My passion has always been there, I even found my way through hair dressing school. Although in college I received a degree in journalism and communications.

My Boston Fashion Week fetish began back in 2012. I had decided I wanted to rekindle my writing career after returning on injury from playing professional soccer in Italia. I was writing merely a year for the Boston Post-Gazette when I found my way in.

I had a column called Around Town covering events around the city of Boston. My Editor Pam Donnarumma had suggested I check out a local fashion designer Denise Hajjar whom happen to be having a Boston Fashion Week show on the horizon. I reached out to her press contact and after multiple follow ups was graced with the opportunity to stand in the back of the a sold out show.

When I arrived, there was Denise out front taking care of business at the check-in table. As always, she was personally making sure every detail was set. I was a bit nervous as her energy was so powerful, and in a bold, bossy manor she told me to stay right in a little corner as that space was a gift.

I entered the grand ballroom of the Copley Hotel and my passion was immediately lit. Every seat filled for rows upon rows, chandeliers giving the perfect light upon the runway, press running about the room looking for the perfect place to shoot.

Then the fashion, attire came down the runway that was suitable for a State Street working woman to a Hollywood starlit sitting at the bar with her Manhattan. The models, glamourous professionals gliding through the front row exuding confidence in the pieces put together by the one and only. It was mid-show I literally began to cry from all the beauty, the life, the buzz. I felt like I was at the Oscars and knew, I wanted more. My career as a fashion writer began right there, blessed with standing room only.

For the next thirteen years I made my way, attended any and every show. Throwing elbows in the press pit with photographers, demanding my space. All whom I have grown to love and now steal their flash at those shows with the bad lighting. Finding the nerve to approach the legendary Jay Calderin which happens to be mentioned in an upcoming chapter. I began to grow my name, create a new niche of Scene&Style on site posting live via social media.

Through all the shows, all the years, it was an honor and glamourous thing to get dolled up. As for Boston Fashion Week specifically, that was always a grueling time. Again, for anyone who knows me, I am a footballer as Americans refer to a soccer player. The struggle is real to make a paycheck doing that so I would be mid-season of coaching kids somewhere out in the burbs when the week rolled around.

Few knew I would all too often double park rushing to make a show. Coming straight from soccer, changing in my car, the venue bathroom or backstage. Each year I was literally a traveling dressing room. Making my way from molding young minds to multiple shows in one night.

Nothing was going to hold me back from Scene&Style being on site. When I came to terms that Scene&Style would not be on site for the first time in eight years, I decided to create the first book in 2020, a collection of columns. As I began the process, I became obsessed with the idea of this cover photo. It had to be from my very first fashion show, Denise Hajjar in 2012 and of "Our Girl Linda."

As I continued, I did not even realize it had been so long, my fashion writing career so lengthy. It is an amazing feeling this project as now I celebrate book number two being published. Digging through everything to find my first fashion column in 2012, running around the city trying to find my dream cover photo, putting it all into place.

I have been putting the pen to the paper almost as long as I have been kicking around the ball. I am blessed with an amazing life; parentless at 11, forced to make my own way. Recently I was told it is a miracle I am alive let alone all I have accomplished.

At this point in my career, I have been awarded the Boston Fashion Award for publication twice and this past November crowned the Boston Fashion Icon for Media. It was at this ceremony where so many of us gathered that have created this community. It was also where I was outed.

During my introduction Elizabeth Minor a founder, did her digging on me. It was announced that I grew up in Rapid City South Dakota and the room erupted. Not one person knew, nor does anyone really know that. As I stated in my thank you speech, I tell everyone I am from Medford as it is easier than having to explain yes I grew up with electricity.

I have lived an interesting life, traveled the world by the grace of goalscoring. However, it was a pleasant path. I have not ever dwelled on the hardships of my childhood yet its most certainly why some assume I am crazy. I believe I am, yet that is what makes me damn fabulous.

To clear things up for those in the room that were stunned by my beginnings. My dad's family is all from the Salem area. He chose to drop out on his Northeastern track scholarship and join the air force, he got stationed at Ellsworth Air Force in Box Elder South Dakota. My mother's family is from Chicago. Her father was on the run from an organized "business" and was hiding out in South Dakota. I never met him yet I am sure I would love a guy with a name like Sonny Bellino. There is it two Italian stuck in South Dakota who decided to have me.

My mom decided she had things to do, left when I was five and never looked back. My father did what he could, coached my soccer team until I was eighteen. Yet at eleven, he looked me in the eyes and told me he had to focus on his own life. I had to figure out mine. I had my first cash job in the third grade and paycheck job in the sixth grade, which was illegal. I was reputable, a track star, violinist, writer for the school newspaper, cheerleader, clearly a soccer star. I could not tell anyone what was going on as I guess I continue to still hide to this day.

The first time I was ever homeless was in the sixth grade, I slept in one of those concrete cylinders on the playground. I bounced from a few friends' houses from time to time yet spent most of my childhood sleeping in the girls' locker room at school, the science hall (they never locked it) or my car in my teens. As for food, well we have always had an interesting relationship. Until I was in my twenties, we never had one. In high school I used to pretend I had some stomach issues and when I went out to lunch with my friends I would not eat. I did not have money, anything I ever made went to pay for soccer.

I always giggle a little when I say that my dad had to focus on his own life. Well, that included a piece of my fabulousness. I had asked him when I was seven to coach my soccer team, ours had quit. He may not have put a roof over my head, or even spoken to me but he sure as hell played me. He wanted to win. One of the last times I saw my father was when I rallied my team to win over foe, we played the last game of the season and lost 8-0 and then in the state finals beat them 2-0. One of my last gifts to him was a shiny trophy and two goals.

I then threw the middle finger up to all my Midwest scholarships, bounced around Alaska for a bit and then googled college soccer in Boston. Up popped Bunker Hill, I contacted the coach, sent over my resume and was on a flight to Boston. From there I got a full ride to CCRI won a national championship, found my way to Italy to be the first American women to play in the Seri A and loop back to the beginning of this introduction of returning home on injury to start my writing career.

As I ran through the columns, I wanted to be honest with my development as a writer. I aloud myself to fix any spelling errors as for grammar I thought it best to let my growth as a writer speak for itself as you near the closing chapters.

This is a celebration, 10 years of Published Boston Fashion Scene&Style magazines. Although I have been writing in print columns for 14 years and more yet to be revealed. This past fall fashion season of 2024 is how the book begins, highlights of onsite Scene&Style. In the index listed are when the full articles will be released in upcoming issues as an entirely new personalized format. Stay tuned and enjoy the trip of all the time we have spent together creating our fashion family.

Chapter One – 2024

Everything I have I owe it to Pasta.

-Sopia Lauren

October 2024- Denise Hajjar Sets the Standard for bosFW Scene&Style Magazine Issue #91

As in years past Denise Hajjar set the standard for Boston Fashion Week to begin. Her timeless style, new collections are always a fall must see.

Bold colors and must have accessories were focal in the first set of looks from the Denise Hajjar Boutique FW24 collection. Highlights of fur head bands, silk scarves and covers up in staple season shades. Following were autumn shades for a casual Sunday stroll to the power business meeting the second set of looks down the runway from the DHFW24 collection were impressive. Head to toe the outfits were tailored! Gorgeous fur head bands, flowing printed pants and matching tops, shawls, and jeans all in stunning brown, beiges, and piercing greens.

Another set of looks on the Denise Hajjar Boutique FW24 runway were an array of knitted sweaters, shawls, mid length jackets all in nude shades paired with those gorgeous faux fur head wraps and matching gloves all stunning in simplicity.

Jackets with pop appeared with a statement. From a classic tweed Chanel take, trenches to painted abstract. Either way grab a basic top, a pair of jeans, black leather or a pleated skirt, knee high boots and your outfit speaks with seasonal color.

Classics that sparkle were the final set of looks shown at the Denise Hajjar Boutique FW24 show which featured that iconic black and white chic style. Pieces meant for the red carpet, a night on the town, or that holiday party were pieced together from head to toe. Classy suits with striking sparkle and must have faux fur trimmed gloves. The stunner of the set came in an all-white pant suit and faux fur wrap with hinted details of sheer down the jacket and trouser bottom.

A final walkthrough and warm words from the Hajjar wrapped up the yet again hit runway presentation from a group of models and a designer that have spent decades bringing Boston fashion to the runway in timeless style.

November 2024 Boston Fashion Awards – May 2025 Scene&Style Magazine Issue #98

The awards ceremony was in its nineth year of hosting Boston's most fashionably categories in the vibrant downtown district held at the Marriott Boston Ball Room.

The evening opened with a red carpet cocktail party welcoming in the city's finest. Host Josua Paul, CeCy Del Carmen and red carpet diva Meagan Michelle kept guests engaged through the announcement of winners and live performances by hit band Whiskey Six.

Producer Marlena Garcia kept the runway looking dapper with a top shelf list of designers showing off their unique expressions. Opening was, Casaindashi with eye pooping looks that were bright, bold, and full of playful patterns.

Following was Wavvz Newage with retro representation pulling out all the stops with the "purple haze" dresses adorned in a fantasy floral, the collection showed psychedelic patterns and vibrant colors. Next was a classic couture from Werthebyjem. Stunning placement of sequins, impressive sewing, seductive cuts yet keeping it classy. The formal wear that hit the BFA runway was perfect to complement a black tie event.

Next was a dapper don appeal from The Tailor Fit who never disappoints with his suits and formal fashion. Iconic patterns paired with an urban flavor to give each look a touch of unique flair. Closing out the BFA24 runway was Urban Pigeons with cosmic statements from a designer turning heads with his structured statements, painted leathers, and impeccable hemming to make a true one of a kind collection.

The ninth year closed with a futuristic feel in fashion and was a hit. From aspiring to icons in attendance, the fashion family was out in full force. It's not a fashion show it's a fashion party!

November 2024 Mass Fashion Week Finale – April 2025 Scene&Style Magazine Issue #97

In the past year, a new event started making a name in the scene, Mass Fashion Week. Produced by model and entrepreneur Meagan Michelle. Each time the full week filled affair rolls around there are multiple locations each with a focal theme from street wear to couture. Scene&Style made an appearance at the closing ceremony at The Vault in the chic chandelier lit evening.

The first three designers to show on the Mass Fashion Week runway were for all occasions, gave vibes to every aspect from sexy beach wear, sporty and that classy men's look for the office. First to hit the runway was Laurens Swim. It is always suit season when styled by this diva. Cape Cod inspired chic and sexy.

Pogiis Family followed with Sunday classics showed in a luxury men's collection of dapper suits. Soft grays paired with pastel undertones for a masculine appearance. Blessed Envision, A line of exclusive varsity jackets with a "members only" trend gives that confidence of a CEO paired for a street style look.

More expression through fashion flowed, designing is more than just a dress. The next set of collections exuded pride in ethnicity, all body types, and the importance of that fine piece of jewelry. Art by Dani gave that classy sex appeal, seductive suit dresses, all white head to toe and tapered leathers showed in designer Dani "Self Canvas" collection. It celebrates individuality, merging bold colors, textures, and self-expression in a unique fusion of art and fashion.

Inskyn was focal on luxury Women's and Men's wear. Promoting body positivity, the designs were carefully crafted to flatter and empower diverse shapes and sizes, ensuring that everyone feels confident and comfortable in their garments. Awula K, a fan favorite of the show embraced African art through stunning pattern work in full length gowns celebrating tradition through contemporary fashion. Whirl Wind Jewels, The finesse of the finishing touch makes a solid statement with a good accessory of sparkle. Her pieces never disappoint for a chic accent to top off that outfit.

Color waves of mood were focal from the final designers to hit the Mass Fashion Week Runway and gave a unique expression with playful color pallets. Jeanne Marie Damico took her collection to a new height of sporty stylish. Literal Art from the Heart was canvassed in a trendy and contemporary line. Minikindesignz showed strategic handmade clothing, knit with couture care that's caters to every demographic stunned. The designers mission is to get the world to appreciate a skill that cannot be duplicated with a machine but with the hardworking hands of people all over the worlds. Calle's looks of casual comfort meshed with punk cuts and detailed hemming and sewn in accessories. Calle 11 derives from a kid looking to rove his childhood dreams as an adult. The name derives form the street and number of the home the designer group up in as child in the Dominican Republic. It's a lifestyle "there no heroes on Calle 11." Jeremy has been part of the Mass Fashion Week team since the beginning.

Following was Valentina, a collection that brings a unique voice to fashion with her innovative streetwear and bridal designs specifically created for queer femme individuals while being open to all who identify with her pieces. Her work is all about empowering people to express themselves freely and defy patriarchal norms. By celebrating and embracing authentic femme sexuality, she challenges the idea that women must cover up to be respected, as well as the notion within some feminist circles that dressing sexy is solely for the male gaze.

The closing collection on the mass fashion week runway was pure talent at its finest, literally a fantasy creation from Amazing Gowns and More. The elegant and impeccably tailored ball gowns were a breathtaking representation of high fashion and painted an illusion reminiscent of a royal wedding.

Mass Fashion Week had another hit on their hands. From the packed house, array of designers this is a not to miss event next May of 2025!

November 2024 Boston Fashion Icon Awards Show – March 2025 Scene&Style Magazine Issue #96

A new board of fashionable minds formed in 2024. Founders VaVa Zadi, Racine Bell and Elizabeth Minor began a brand new journey. Their mission was to dig deep into the industry, create new categories and honor those that have put in their time to creating the Boston fashion community.

The inaugural Boston Fashion Icon awards took place in the chic Blanc Spaces and began by welcoming fashions finest with a cocktail hour and red carpet.

The event got underway with a fashion statement of neon shades and structure. The first designer to hit the Boston Fashion Icon runway was Tomy Allen. Showing an everyday collection that can transition to structure statements the unisex clothing line exuded bold colors and popping patterns to give that confidence to be the unique you.

The first award given out went to a woman with grace and gratitude, the beautiful and elegant Elsa Rocha receiving Boston Fashion Icon Award for Model. Following was a man with poise and precision. The Boston Fashion Icon Photographer Award went to the tenacious and keen eye of Monster Jazz Photography, Robert Paris.

The Make Artist Icon award was given to Donna Sousa. Donna has risen to become a celebrity award-winning makeup and hairstylist, earning accolades such as two Boston Fashion Awards for Best Makeup Artist and the prestigious Hall of Fame Award. Her talent shines through her daily work with clients and her highly awarded Luxury Bridal Beauty Business, which has flourished in New England starting in New York, with plans to expand to Palm Beach.

From there the runway reopened with culture in color. The second set of looks to show on the Boston Fashion Icon runway was traditional Indian designer Renu Gupta. The collection was focal on authentic heritage in the bright bold colors used. The line showed tribute to the beauty of ethnicity with wraps, sparkling gems, and hem lines of perfection.

Next to be introduced was a man of innovation. The Icon Designer Award was given to Conrad Lamour. A creator with vision who takes pride in the importance of luxury detail and gives a chic experience with every show.

Following was the man behind the lights. The Boston Fashion Icon Show Producer Award went to Owner of Performer.com Michael Zotos. For over a decade Zotos who had once been behind the camera himself as a photographer is known for his wide spread equipment to guarantee an experience, a radio show and amazing lighting on the runway which Scene&Style has gratefully taken advantage of many times. Also the production of Swim Week, and the upcoming Boston Fashion Awards for its 9th year on November 11th.

The next was a man who needed no introduction for his charisma says it all. The Boston Fashion Icon Ambassador award went to the Don of style on stage Gustavo Leon.

Always dapper from head to toe, can be handed a microphone and without a script own the room and win over the crowd to create a successful show. Gustavo is a Master of Communications as a style writer and idea generator.

Following was a women known for her communications with class and style. The Boston Fashion Icon Media Award went to ME. I was truly honored and blessed as every previous post of winners and more are my inspiration. I won my first writing award at 8 and it's been a journey ever since. The beauty in Boston fashion caught me when my editor at the Boston Post Gazette sent me to my first ever Boston Fashion Week show at the Copley Plaza for Designer Denise Hajjar. The high end couture vibe, the stunning struts of the models, the packed room of fabulous glitterati the energy brought me to tears. I was hooked! I have been published on many topics however, I am a fashion writer. Scene&Style on site doing live runway video with a written review. It's officially been 10 years of published columns and with that ... SAVE THE DATE of December 16th. A book will be born including years of our fashion family shows and memories. Blessed to have amazing creators that give me content.

The last set of looks to hit the Boston Fashion Icon runway came from a creator of the event itself, Vava Zadi in a special dedication of an all-white fantasy. Shimmering lace and satin were focal in the pieces from the White Lion Collection. Stunning pant suits for men and women, dashing dresses with chic cuts, the strategic sewing was breathtaking. The series showed pure couture quality.

The final honoree was the Queen of Glitz and Glamour, The Boston Fashion Icon award for Lifetime Achievement was given to the legendary Yolanda Cellucci. A fashion icon, philanthropist, a tv host, author, designer a wedding dress boutique owner, a woman who spreads glitz and glam wherever she goes. The list of accomplishments goes on with this woman of wonder.

Most people know Cellucci for her iconic Waltham store Yolanda's, where a health spa, beauty salon, dress boutique and more were all under one roof. Yolanda recently celebrated her upcoming 90th birthday at the annual Our Girl Linda dance party by raising more than $90,000 for five local charities - Friends of the Waltham Senior Citizens, Middlesex Human Services Agency, Our Girl Linda Foundation, Waltham Lions Club and The Salvation Army of Waltham.

Yolanda's children have taken on her legacy. Her daughter Linda, who lost her battle with esophageal cancer in 2018 was a blessing to the high end modeling scene and that smile, one of a kind. Also her daughter Sondra is the queen of Swarovski crystals with celebrity her dress designs.

This decorated diva is hardly slowing down! Although family is the most important thing to Yolanda she still can be counted on to be up at 5am with a pant suit on and fully styled. Cellucci continues to host a Waltham cable access show Yolanda Style and Glamour. This icon has given so much to the city of Boston, the fashion community and beyond. Yolanda, thank you!

The evening was an intimate gathering that brought many of the honorees to tears from the presentation to the pride. The inaugural Boston Fashion Icon awards has officially been put on the map and the event ended with a family party continuing late into the night.

October 2024 Boston Caribbean Fashion Week Closing Show – February 2025 Scene&Style Magazine Issue #95

The Caribbean vibes have been coming to Boston for over a decade by Producer/Owner Athea Blackford. Boston Caribbean Fashion Week made its way to the Seaport this year held in the Hampton Inn.

Designer Ann Jodes opened the runway with an eye pooping tangerine and cream look. A seductive dress and daring trench was a highlight from the first set of looks. The collection was focal on autumn toned leather, multi pattern stitching and daring details that were subtle when grabbing attention to the garments.

Outfits with attitude were next to come down the boscfw runway. The line was focused on urban street style with a funk flow. The retro varsity jacket, a painted pattern vest for the ladies and a masculine orange pleather pant paired with a chic oversized charcoal coat.

Casual comfort came down the runway with ease of effortless style that took designer dedication. The entire line featured crocheted pieces from a sexy chic canary yellow crop top and skirt to seasonal carrot color tops and dresses. The collection was true artist work from Oyindas. Strategic stitching showed down the catwalk in suppressed tones from designer Tyson Buggs. The street wear meets high end fashion line appealed to men and women with multiple looks. A female full denim overall suit, a chic pocket placement on men's shorts, unisex vests, and jackets.

During the intermission of boscfw 11th edition the roots were rocking. Between grabbing a cocktail, and a pic on the red carpet, traditional dance took place with costumes so authentic, vibrant, and true Caribbean color from Boston Scoaholics Mascamp.

Continuing the show was Heily Rivas Fashion that was draped in earth ethnicity, a line focal on the natural terrain. Stunning patchwork placement on a hooded dress, chamomile white wraps, showing the softness of a woman. Standing out in the sphere color waves was an eye popping teal sleeveless full length gown with a parachute fabric and painted pattern feel.

Structured cuts and culture made a unique statement down the #bosfw runway was Liza clothing with an old school accessory. The collection stood out with the respect to the Afro patterns and prints. Each piece had its own articulation with draping silks, daring slits up the skirts, traditional simplicity of a full length dress with an assertive pocket placement.

Couture of the Caribbean was the final collection to show on the #boscfw24 runway it was magnificent with African magnitude from the most adorable authentic woman behind the designs. Opening was a set of satin dresses in a ruby red and a royal blue both with traditional headpieces beading and tribal patterns.

Following were seductive two piece suit that gave a little spice to a ladies grace, sleeveless full length dresses, the entire collection was breathtaking with bold and vibrant colors and Afrocentric structure.

Once again, the Boston Caribbean Fashion Week delivered in flying feathers and colors. Visit www.bostoncfw.com for retreats and next year's lineup.

October 2024 bosFW Closing "Glam Slam" Scene&Style Magazine

Boston Fashion Week is in full force and celebrating 30 years. Their annual "Glam Slam" is a story telling event featuring local fashion professionals sharing hilarious, poignant, and sometimes glamourous moments in their career.

The improv type setting of storytelling began with MC for the event Bethany Vandelft a witty, hilarious, honest former model now comedian. In between the story tellers she had the guests rolling in laughter. First to take stage was Kristie Raymond from Humankind Casting. Sharing her extraordinary story working with special needs children and proving that "everybody belongs."

Following came from the heart, Fashion Maven Taneshia Camillo Sheffey spoke on always having passion to push you and slammed the crowd with her inspiration from her mother to being a mother. Misguided to mentor, Designer Carlos Avillamil told his story from pioneering the sustainability market in fashion to now a professor. Carlos paid tribute to those that contributed along his worldly journey.

Boston fashion bonding was brought to the stage by Model, stylist and fashion diva Sonia Garufi who shared industry memories together of laughs and love with other attendees in the room. Also spoke on Sonia 2.0 from photo on the left being her beginning, right the current version and eager to see what 3.0 has to say.

The History of Maggie was truly a treat from now owner Casey of Maggie Inc New England's top modeling agency reminisces about the creation of the company, his entrepreneurial journey and hilarious fashion tell all's of the women behind the beginnings. Closing the evening was, December Thieves Boutique owner Lana Barakat on "the Feeling I Found Myself." She shared customer stories of "the pop in" and the beauty behind being an owner.

Boston Fashion Week wrapped up in an intimate way! The opportunity to see local fashion professionals sharing iconic moments in their careers. The history of the professional models, agents, stylists, boutiques that have created the industry was truly inspiring and eager to see who is in the lineup for bosFW 25.

October 2024 bosFW Everybody Belongs – January 2025 Scene&Style Magazine Issue #94

Humankind Casting welcomed Boston fashion goers to Garage B for an extravagant presentation showcasing models with special needs. Hosted by TV Personality and meteorologist of WBZ, the evening had an arrayment of entertainment. From True Story theatre from Cambridge doing immediate improve to the special guest speakers, musical performances, and a line up of vendors that proved, "Everybody Belonged."

For the fashion, My Skirt Dealer hit the runway was a set of inclusive and reversible looks from designer Kelly Stanzione focal on that sexy flow. The reversible wrap skirts are 100% up cycled Indian Sari and sewn right in Rajasthan. Each piece exuded heritage and traditional print patterns. From the bold turquoise and blues to popping orange.

Next was a collection for freedom of movement focused on improving lives with limited mobility by be free adaptive. The "full zip" styles featured full length zippers that open completely on both sides to make dresser easier, safer, and more comfortable. The fashion was fierce and showed how an everyday look of a cute drop top, a sweater, and a pair of chucks or an adidas original can make an outfit!

The last collection to show on the #everybodybelongs runway for #bosfw24 was a bright and creative statement from Mavvz New Age.

The outfits were head to toe full looks of white leathers, raving neon's, neoprene fits, full trenches, and faux fur. The line was loud and proud with flow and impressive tailoring from this self-taught designer in residence at the Creative Hub in Worcester.

This event was a dear one to Scene&Style, it brought new besties into my life. I love fashion shows, the people I meet, mixing and mingling. I must say this was a brand new experience! As day of production and of course Scene&Style come show time. I ended up putting my Blaine Beauty days to use after a hairdresser backed out. I had an amazing opportunity to spend personal time grooming these amazing models. A chance to make them feel good, a little boost of confidence and instead that is exactly what they gave me.

When it came time for these beauties to hit the runway, I couldn't help but cry. I felt like a proud mom, lol. To see these wonderful souls so happy out there, my makeup was a hot mess! I have never felt so good, so blessed, inspired and open to just be myself. These fantastic people literally changed a piece of my life.

Producer Kristie Raymond set the stage with a perfect event right down to the chic charcutier table. Another unique aspect to the evening was that Raymond did not charge for the event. Donations were encouraged! This Boston Fashion Week show was one for the books!

October 2024 House Fashion Week Closing Show – December Scene&Style Magazine Issue #92

In its third season, House Fashion Week showed what kind of standards they set with being held in a chic European style showroom. The event was a three day affair with three sets of shows each day and Scene&Style was on site for Saturday evening of the closing.

The first collection to show on the House Fashion Week runway was casual in cotton, featuring earthy tones from Designer Cycld. Standing out were a few solid suit pieces in a dynamic midnight black with daring midriff cuts meant for attending that VIP invite basement art exhibition. Beige, autumn browns set the standard for the rest of the line that showed cotton comfort with creative couture expression.

Dark ages meet modern design followed with a mixture of goth and glam from Vo Stewart Baxter. From black pleathers paired with unique head pieces to checked Channel vibes in an oversized jacket made their way down the catwalk. A mesh of 80s vintage rock with sparkle and sequins showed in full length looks of pants, dresses, men's coats to make a statement on a Saturday or can transform a Wednesday work outfit to have a little attitude.

Closing the House Fashion Week catwalk was designer Zonya Campbell with formal and fine heritage literally dripping in rubies and diamonds. Red carpets looks of full length satin dresses sashayed the runway. Pieces pulled full attention to the detail in the dresses of gold glitter, high hems, strategic sewing as each fit was impeccable. A few sneak peaks into the designer's range of talent included a bold blue and yellow African pattern also beautiful bridal dresses. The showstopper of the entire evening was a full gown of diamond colored beading in a chic bustier and the bottom portion a sparkling ruby red. The dress was pure perfection.

The evening was reminiscent of a Paris runway. House Fashion Week closed their annual designer showcase in a stylish setting of a warehouse, perfectly set platform, fabulous fashion, and VIP guest list.

October 2024 NH Fashion Week Debut– November Scene&Style Magazine Issue #91

A new venture was born just outside of Boston in 2024 by Producer Dina Akel also designer of collection Viera Luxe. New Hampshire Fashion Week began its inaugural evening with an art and designer showcase in collaboration with Positive Street Art at The Venues at the Factory.

The opening for New Hampshire Fashion Week came in a chic and sexy vibe from was Vl Couture also the producer for the event. The collection showed high end formal wear with hints of floral, a black dress stunned guests with its off the shoulder cut and sheer sparkle. Each piece was donning daring cuts of seduction while keeping it classy. A few pops of all white bridal gowns with soft hints of glitter made way down the runway. A pair of men's suits gave the line a dapper twist and an all-white jacket having hints of the floral found on one of the gowns.

The second set of looks were all business class, focal for the power businesswoman by Designer Madison Savile. Each look featured a suit jacket showing sensual authority. A basic all back suit killed with its simplicity and hints of sparkle. Soft beiges, winter white top paired with a sleek pant fit that classic look. Stealing the set was an autumn orange gown and a casual coffee colored coat over a bold emerald, green to take charge of the board room.

Next down the NH Fashion Week runway was a modern expression of the big day by Designer Liliana Puertas in an all-white affair. Classic pearl white was the staple in cute crop tops a look finished with cowboy boots, ruffles and sassy flair gave way to a unique

There was what guests thought to be an intermission between designers quickly grew curious to the blank white canvas front and center that turned Hip hop inspired speech into live art. from Artist Lance Johnson a Bronx native now Cleavelandite who wrapped up a residency the day before with the nonprofit Positive Street Art. It took a minute or two with press quickly pivoting and attendee turning their attention to the onsite expression that was created live from an empty textile to powerful speech.

Classic couture ramped back up the runway with a more traditional set of looks made way for a dream wedding day. A bride can never go wrong with an iconic look of satin and lace. Pieces with a simplistic style made an elegant statement from designer boutiqueslie

The final set of looks to close the NH Fashion Week runway were satin suits with flair from LA based designer formalwear pbc. The line featured dignified chic couture suits. Hot pick jackets that were hooded, a hint of masculine glitter and the showstopper was an identical neon ideation head to toe in satin sync was pure romance and red carpet worthy.

The inaugural New Hampshire Fashion Week was classy, chic, and full of creative vibes! The fusion of art and fashion are highly anticipated for 2025.

Designer Vava Zadi's gave a Boston fashion Week preview to showcase a collection at the Liberty Hotels fashionably late.

Casual with a hint of couture was the first set of looks to hit the runway from Designer Vava Zadi that were focal on street wear all in a piecing emerald, green. The line showed an off the shoulder dress, sexy slit to the hip, paired with a vibrant handbag perfect to tuck your laptop on the run. Following was a formal pant suit showing a cute clutch to polish off the ensemble. Next was a solid VZ print ankle length stress fit for the office and topped off with, yet another purse stapled with the designer logo. Closing the set was apparel screaming NYC style. A long sleeve crop top and suit bottom so seductive you almost missed yet again another stunning handbag.

Designer Zadi is known for his men's satin suits and his second set of looks was feminine and fierce formal affair. A lapel kit in a canary yellow strutted the chic hotel runway fished with a full length trench to polish off a perfect red carpet affair. If a sunflower style of yellow isn't your pick following right behind was a Ferrari red version and a pearl white.

Ruffles and roses was the last set of look to hit the Fashionably Late runway from Designer Zadi it was a mesh of formal and sexy fun. A classic bow tie full piece suit stood out with a statement piece of a ruby floral accent on the jacket. Gliding in next was a black satin skirt paired with a tuxedo top, a vintage Vougesque bra look and daring accessories. Dashing in was a similar look with a few strategic tweaks to satisfy particular color pallets with a red skirt and black tie. The show closed in elegant style with a dashing daisy colored outfit. A sheer coat with a business look lapel, skinny solid black tie and staple of a layered ruffled skirt that was the eye grabber of the evening.

October 2024 Fashioning Success: The Intersection of Entrepreneurship and Design Scene&Style Highlight

A group of Boston bred divas sat for an in-depth chat took place in the Boston Design Center on a day of heavily powered panel discussions.

Jaci Conry, Style Editor, Boston Magazine & Editor-In-Chief, Boston Home moderated the panel and picked the minds of amazing women.

Former Vogue fashion editor and co-founder of laligne nyc , Meredith Melling shared her steps to success and the pit stops along the way that gave her thick skin to stive in the fashion industry. Founder and CEO of Gretta luxe, Gretta Monahan gave insight to connecting to a brand, the story and those along the journey which for her include a list of ladies one being the great Yolanda Cellucci.

When asked about " life balance" interior designer Marla Sanford blessed the attendees with the honesty in her journey of entrepreneurship that was pure gold! Her personality filled the room and reminded women, being strong is an asset.

This iconic panel of women had a packed house to hear experiences of their entrepreneurial journeys in the world of fashion and interior design. It was a one of a kind event for aspiring ladies to pick the brains of these trend setters and gather insight to grow their own.

9-20-2024 Our Girl Linda Celebrates Cellucci 10-11-2024 Boston Post Gazette

The fifth annual Our Girl Linda charity dance party had a new act. The evening was also a celebration of Yolanda Cellucci's 90th birthday. Beyond being a fashion icon, an inspiration, a tv host, a wedding dress boutique owner, a woman who spread glitz and glam wherever she goes. Yolanda is a loving mother to Linda Cole Petrosian for whom the annual charity event was founded. Linda was a celebrity model known for her legendary smile, heart of gold, an apple that did not fall far from the Cellucci tree that was lost in 2018 to cancer.

The annual event began with walking into a main hall decorated with glamour shots of Linda, a running video of Yolanda's glitterati interactions over the years. As a good Italian would the room was lined with tables of traditional party treats and a ten tier birthday cake from Montillo's bakery that was sure to feed the five hundred plus guests in attendance.

The brightest sight in the room was Yolanda herself sitting on the Queen's throne welcoming guests with class and charm, donned in all white from top to bottom finished with a feathered headpiece that was far beyond glitz, it was pure glamour.

The evening began with a royal entrance of Yolanda being escorted into the room with her two grandsons Dimitri and Alec on her arms and guided to her VIP seat front and center in her grand throne. The entertainment began with Jeannette A. McCarthy the Mayor of Waltham performed a charming skit appearing as herself to apply as a "Yolanda Girl" and proving a point when returning dolled up exuding the confidence Cellucci gives to all women. With her inspiring story transforming her own life from rags selling wigs out of the trunk of her car to the riches of the high end fashion lifestyle she now leads.

Following was a plethora of local organizations honoring Cellucci with awards such as the City of Waltham, The Waltham Salvation Army where you can see Yolanda every Christmas donating her time. The groups were close to her heart as she is constantly spending time with her local community and making it a brighter place to be.

There were also heartfelt speeches from the family. Her grandsons Dimitri and Alec Petrosian, granddaughter Milan spoke on her "GiGi" and gave insight into being married into the Cellucci clan. Telling the classic story of a typical Tuesday with her husband asking no questions, taking a tour into Brooklyn, and returning to Boston with the fabulous all white thrown Yolanda sat in all night. Her daughter Sondra Celli the iconic Swarovski bling designer honored her legendary life with stories on how she came from nothing, Yolanda mended her own coats over and over to look modern so her and her sister could have a new jacket until the day when her mother spun it all into glitz and glamour.

The entertainment was top class! In true flapper fashion the Waltham Star Dancer gave a tributed all white performance to the birthday beauty Yolanda and fitting for daughter Linda Cole Petrosian herself was sure to be shaking it along with them for the annual Our Girl Linda Foundation dance party. There were politically incorrect moments when Comedian Vinnie Favorito took the stage in a hysterical set. The doo whop band the Watch City Cadillacs opened up the dance floor and guests poured out to twist.

Even with all the birthday celebrations, entertainment this party was started with a cause. It was time to honor the fifth annual Our Girl Linda Foundation with a live auction to raise money for St. Jude's Children's Research Hospital. DJ Jimmy Esposito from 617Events Group took center stage to begin the bidding. Models and designers that were near and dear to Linda sharing runways with that gorgeous smile strutted out the donated items. They ranged from sports tickets, an authentic pink mink coat, five course dinners, wine tours, jewelry and more.

The fifth annual Our Girl Linda charity dance party was host to over five hundred plus in the packed Son's of American Legion – Post 440 in Newton. The night was pure glitz and glamour in a birthday celebration reflective of the legend Yolanda Cellucci is. Also, a heartwarming and extraordinarily successful charity event that her daughter Linda would be so proud of and dancing away in spirit.

The Our Girl Linda Foundation is an amazing team of regulars and part-time volunteers committed to helping others. They take their love of Linda and turn that love into action. They donate all funds to finding a cure for cancer. All contributions are donated to the St. Jude's Children's Research Hospital. They formed the organization to bring together those who loved Linda. All give thanks to the helping hands of the amazing community; the Our Girl Linda Foundation was established in 2018. If you would like to donate, please visit www.ourgirllinda.com

September 2024 - An Infinite Evening of Coco Chanel Scene&Style Magazine Issue #90

OLGA September

A grand fashion gala took place at the elegant ballroom in the Copley Plaza Hotel Boston. "An Infinite Evening of Coco Chanel," produced by Olga Konstanzia Showtime was held in honor of her inspirational trip to a museum in London dedicated to the iconic designer. The event was hosted by Nick Yousif who was true in paying tribute to the celebration of Gabrielle Chanel.

The event began with fashions finest gathered in a royalty interior room with cocktails and red carpet photos. Once guests took their seats in the divine space runway opened.

The first collection of fashion came from the iconic brand Lalla Bee. Designer Melina Cortes Mili married a chic European midnight vibe with lace, velvets, and hand beaded structure. Each piece showed true to the designer's class and couture reputation. Looks were also paired with divine head pieces that complimented the classic eastern appeal from designer Elie Jian Millinery.

Classic formal with pop was next to show on the Coco Chanel inspired runway was Vieira Luxe Couture's collection "Le Fleur" from designer Dina Akel. The looks featured black, white, and bridal formal wear. Each of the pieces has a classic tone with strategic cuts and eye catching encrusted detail. It wasn't all mute tones as a pop of a purple gown, a golden satin dress and all white with floral made their transformative statements.

Following were versatile everyday looks from Designer Tatyana Ayriyan paired with Carla Shaw Fashion Jewelry. The jumpsuit styles had wide leg flow, nude tones for that perfect office outfit. Piercing royal blue representing gowns followed showing sophistication and glamour for that VIP cocktail event. The full length looks were topped off with dazzling head pieces from Ellie Jian Millinery and sustainable jewelry from Carla Shaw Fashion.

Royal culture expression was a highlight on the runway from an emerging designer from the Mass College of Art and Design Zemfira. She showed a collection donning couture stitching, European inspired patterns with a Central Asian fashion flow. The pieces were reminiscent of true Chanel creation and exquisite art that this designer is the future of Boston Fashion. Zemfira was brought to the stage just prior to her collection showing to be honored by Boston Fashion Week Founder Jay Calderin with the Innovation in Fashion Award.

Closing the "Infinity of Coco Chanel" runway was a collection of breath taking bridal gowns from designer Colby John that painted an ivory frosted fairy tale. As seen in the pages of British Vogue, USA, Italy, Ireland, and Canadian boutiques this international sewing superstar shined bright through his work. Each piece was applied to as stunning detail to all white ensembles. The dresses reveled artwork of hand stitched beading, perfectly placed lace with sheet elegance and beauty all by brides aspire to have that special day.

The event was a high fashion celebration with a star studded list of attendees. The evening was a true testament to what Coco Chanel endured, elegance, innovation, and timeless style.

August 2024 Swim Boston on Rooftop Runway - Scene&Style Magazine Issue #89

When the season for open toed heels, board shorts and fruity cocktails and seafood hits New England it is time for the annual Swim Boston fashion show. Performer.com and the crew set up shop on the chic and tucked away Alba restaurant roof deck for the event.

The evening opened with local music talent and iconic radio DJ Money Mav as the MC and special guest host Maegan Michelle, Founder of Mass Fashion Week giving insight to each outfit while on the live Performer.com radio show.

The first set of looks to hit the runway were summer staples! Highlighted sheer fabrics and playful patterns showed from Lauren's Swim collection who paired with Whirlwind Jewels in seductive body jewelry to grab gazes of "I must have" in that summer wardrobe.

The showstopper of the evening came early on. Miketal Swimwear collection painted a summer creamsicle dream in a two piece off shoulder layered look of orange, yellow and a polished white! The entire line had a serious sex apparel of simplistic men's staple red trunks and the ladies amped with strategic cuts for an eye catching style.

Golden is always key; Famed swimsuit designer now magazine mogul Ann Marie LaFauci showed a collection of keeping it simple, in sexy chic with pops of polka dots and a sheer golden one piece grabbing full attention pool side.

Art From the Heart stormed the Swim Boston runway with sleek animal print in heard form with a full piece must have, a vintage tiger stamp in iconic 80s midnight purple. It was followed by a replica in a men's button down and short outfit perfect for that rooftop statement. The complete collection was eye catching from the florals to marble print all donned with flowing shawls.

Timeless pieces that were styled to perfection came from legendary Fashion Designer Denise Hajjar. Attire was pulled from her SS24 collection at her Marina Bay boutique and sent to the Swim stylist team of Marlena Garcia and Liya Kay who proved their keen eye to transition looks is a must have in production of any show. They pulled together a flowing of shawls, eye catching color in full outfits and the sex appeal all in a classy and elegant cascade.

Mesh and that Celtics vibe came from Mav Life Clothing who rocked the Swim Boston runway in true DJ Money Mav fashion with honeycomb cover ups, camouflage, curve popping body suits, and his staple Celtics inspired denim. All year round must haves can be snagged at Bogosplit in Copley Place.

Closing out the annual Swim Boston runway was bloom with attitude in a unique touch of a classic summer staple, flowers. Designer Patti Silver showed a collection of floral and denim patchwork patterns married together in a fun and funky line that had vibrant color and chic trim to the detailed stitching.

The event was a summer night to remember! From the classy kickoff of apps and hors d'oeuvres served, live music and an assembly of Boston sexiest seasonal looks all put on by the performer.com team.

July 2024 bosFW and Boston Bid Present an Open Runway - Scene&Style Magazine Issue #88

Every year Boston Fashion Week pairs up with Downtown Boston BID for an outdoor event showing off the cities next stars in an initiative that provides a platform to fashion designers at every stage of their careers, including student fashion designers.

Open Runway is an open-air fashion show that takes place on the DTX Steps in Downtown Crossing. Using the same premise as an open mic night for singers and comedians, Open Runway provides an opportunity for local fashion designers to show their creations to the public.

The man behind the unique opportunity is Founder and Executive Director of Boston Fashion Week, Jay Calderin. He was host alongside a panel of industry leaders The Stylist Closet, Diana Jaye, and The Seyet. They gave expert critique and praise as they celebrated a diverse collection of unique designs and bold fashion statements created right here in the Greater Boston area.

The show opened with collections from established designers such as Joey Pino, Mark Painter, Love Cashionista, Caity Bug, h.e.r.fashion, Michaela's Market, Headass Honcho, and Hannah Michelle Designs. Their collections showed pieces from butterfly wraps, distressed denims, a work suit for a lady in soft pastels, and crocheted skirts.

Following were fashions future and local aspiring designer as students from Lasell, Mass Art and SFD Boston. The set showed off men's wear with bold colors and strategic pockets and belt, dark violets and ruffles for the gothic trend, stunning patchwork pieces.

One of the two best in show was Designer Zemfira Cholponbaeva with a breath taking tribute to her culture with piercing reds in full trench coats, flawless seems and classic patterns. Also, Designer Vluan Naulv who stole the show with two very extravagant dresses. One was a sheer white body suit with the most elegant over shawl flowing feet from the model, the other appeared to be a white mini dress until a small slip was made and unveiled a popping pink ankle length gown.

Closing out the runway was a dapper line from FNS. The showcase was a feature for the businessman with velvet trimmed jackets, oversized corduroy finding that chic respectable appeal. This event is always an eye grabber in the setting of Downtown Boston and lures with the fashion. It was in part of celebrating Boston Fashion Week 30th anniversary this October.

Mass Art and SFD Boston. The set showed off men's wear with bold colors and strategic pockets and belt, dark violets and ruffles for the gothic trend, stunning patchwork pieces.

One of the two best in show was Designer Zemfira Cholponbaeva with a breath-taking tribute to her culture with piercing reds in

full trench coats, flawless seams, and classic patterns. Also, Designer Vluan Naulv who stole the show with two very extravagant dresses. One was a sheer white body suit with the most elegant over shawl flowing feet from the model, the other appeared to be a white mini dress until a small slip was made and unveiled a popping pink ankle length gown.

Closing out the runway was a dapper line from FNS. The showcase was a feature for the businessman with velvet trimmed jackets, oversized corduroy finding that chic respectable appeal. This event is always an eye grabber in the setting of Downtown Boston and lures with the fashion.

June 2024 Hajjar's Seasonal Must Haves Hit the Marina Bay Runway - Scene&Style Magazine Issue #87

As each season changes there is a fashion presentation to show off the trends set by top designers. In Boston, the Denise Hajjar show is always your mark to get the must haves for your closet collection at the annual EAT DRINK MODEL charity event in Marina Bay.

The chic waterfront boardwalk runway opened with pastels and patterns were the first of looks shown from Hajjar's SS24 featuring psychedelic suits, floral full length dresses, and woven beach bags. Denim and summer sweaters are a highlight each season for Denise. Featured were breathable cable knit cover ups with swanky sayings from "tequila, beach and classic anchor and American flag" emblem to make a summer statement. Each outfit was paired with classic and fringed wide leg denim the look finished with a beaded shoulder strap bag.

The classics of white, black, florals, sheers, sparkle, hats, and bags made their way down the. It is all about how it's paired and the style it is sewn. Hajjar showed multiple looks of power business pieces for the summer to flowing cotton whites for the beach.

Closing out the Denise Hajjar Boutique SS24 collection were flowing pastels in full suits of abstract art. Dresses featuring timeless floral all paired with bright accessories to make that seasonal statement. Simple crocheted shawls, fantastic sombrero, and fedora hats, also woven handbags that made many appearances which is testament they can complement any outfit.

The annual EAT DRINK MODEL fashion show fundraiser to support QCAP went off without a hitch, which is to be expected from Hajjar. Great raffles donated to support charity, decadent dishes from local restaurants served for dinner to seated guests along the docks on the boardwalk and the fashion, always flawless.

The Marina Bay boardwalk boutique always hits the mark each season for all tastes. The Denise Hajjar store is located right in Quincy and has a little something for everyone. Pop in grab your season must haves. Sneak next door to Marina Bay Living and snag some adorable home goods and then take a seat at Café Bari in Terre D'Italia for a cappuccino. Make a day out of it!

April 2024 Living Arts Boston, Fashion's Finest on the Seaport Runway - Scene&Style Magazine

Issue #86

Recently Boston's Convention Center, a statue of the city in the Seaport District, hosted a its third annual Living Arts conference presented by Made Incubator. The 2024 three day extravaganza was filled with sit in speaker sessions, live displays, booths of local craft entrepreneurs and the finale a living art fashion show.

The evening opened with the strings of sensational violinist Rozita Fishta a Berklee College of Music graduate. Her seductive flair covering the top forty hits and draped in a dress by Lidiya Romanchuk to kick off the tribute to fashions finest.

The first collection to show on the Living Arts runway came from Jacque Label. It was a focal metallic maven mesh between Disney princess meets marvel superhero. The unique halter tops made a statement that was softened by the silky skirts.

The brand MOOHDY was next to hit the stage whose staple is tribute to how the emotional states and status one feels in relationships. The collection showed soft pastels and funk patterns with an oversized flow. A teal print made many pops, a focus for a two piece male short suit and a stunning pant for a power walk on a woman.

The next set of looks to hit the Living Arts stage were from Gretta Luxe, a line showing natural tones accented sleeves and pants with a puff look. Simple silk, sheer and denim pieces made their way down the runway and the showstopper of the collection was a beige ankle length dress that flowed and a widespread wing pattern.

Another designer to sashay down the Living Arts Runway was Pattee Silver. Her collection came out upbeat and an emotion which took over the room. The line featured full denim suits with a laced flower pattern and each piece vibing love. The mishmash of attire closed with a stunning layered dress gold fringe and a denim top to make it an everyday look.

Fashion and sport have always complimented one another. Shot Fore Shot showed a collection that gave a bright and bold look to the golfer's game. The line highlighted sleek yet functional pieces.

Making a bohemian statement was the collection This is an Original Work of Art. The line featured conventional looks for the office or a cocktail event with a touch of authenticity to make each piece of a kind and all showed with a work of canvas art. The stunner in this set was a sleeveless beige and subtle striped knee length over coat that screamed chic sexy.

Closing the Living Arts Boston runway was famed designer Melina Cortes Mili of Lalla Bee. Recently she started an everyday line, yet her collections of custom gowns killed the catwalk per usual. The pieces showed detailed touch, vibrant colors, seductive cuts, and that iconic couture glide.

The show was a styled success which the hands of Wave and Woven, Liya Kay and event producer Taneshia Camillo Sheffey. Visit www.livingartsboston.com to see what 2025 has to offer or showcase your Living Art.

March 2024 Retiring Off the Mic, the One and Only DJ Sterling Golden Scene&Style Magazine Issue #85

Boston is a melting pot of business, sports, art, and the highest of education. Then there is one who has radiated in music, fashion and nightlife, DJ Sterling Golden. Recently the iconic radio host retired from his illustrious career. After many appearances on the Sterlingtology Live morning show Scene&Style flipped the mic and got an opportunity to interview the renowned DJ.

Before we get down and dirty with the radio host, it's an honor to look back on his famed career. Sterling has earned a name for himself with a tireless work ethic and unmistakable charisma all his own. A larger-than-life personality, this two-time Best DJ nominee (Boston Nightlife Awards) and two-time SMC Honors winner (2017, 2020) has earned the respect of his peers over the last decade as a Boston radio personality, live DJ, event planner, activist, published writer, podcaster, and founder of 320 Entertainment - a label specializing in promotions and event planning for up and coming recording artists, fashion designers and more.

Sterling's professional journey began in 2009, during the famed "indie sleaze" era, he would encounter longtime independent music promoter Anderson Lynne Mar, who would help pave the way for his entry into the business as a nightclub DJ. His greatest regional notoriety was in the world of independent radio. In this field, Sterling would go on to curate, host and produce several different shows from the long-running STERLINGTOLOGY LIVE morning show, award-winning interview series THE CHOP SESSION, spanning seven seasons. In 2022, Boston Free Radio would honor Sterling's years of radio excellence with the three-hour special GOLDEN AGE OF RADIO: A STERLING ANTHOLOGY.

Now, after a decade and a half Sterling Golden has announced his retirement. Despite this, no matter what life may bring in the future, you can be sure Sterling will continue to live day after day by a simple yet effective credo, "Whatever you do, do it with passion. It's what separates the greats from the ain'ts."

With all these accomplishments it is no wonder Sterling is already missed throughout many industries. Being on the Sterlingtology Live morning show was always a blessing. From kicking back to his playlist, getting in a bit of gossip, and Sterling always getting in his chat about his love for WWF wrestling! I was generally a guest on the show pre or post fashion week.

I thought why not open the in depth session with, "What was your most memorable fashion show?" Sterling replied, "The one that I would point to here is one that we did under unconventional circumstances. It happened during the height of the global pandemic. A virtual event that I curated titled EMBRACE, benefiting the old ONCE Somerville music venue, which was enduring great financial hardship. Part of that EMBRACE presentation included a fashion show featuring the work of Jaclyn Robichaud Doyle, under her Jack Attackk Clothing label."

1. HOW DID YOU GET INTO THE RADIO BUSINESS?

So long before I was in the industry, I actually had an internship offered to me by a local hip-hop station in the New England area, JAM'N 94.5. I never went forward with it.I was given the wrong advice by an important adult figure in my life who I will not name here, to turn down that internship. I was told "Oh, radio's not real work. Go get a regular job, bring money into the house and forget that whole radio vibe." Well, for the next 15 years I worked an endless series of odd jobs. I could never keep one because I didn't play well with others, or didn't take orders from others, so that became an ongoing theme in my life as I was trying to figure out what my calling was. Fast forward to the mid-2000s: I found myself in this horrible situation, a mentally abusive relationship where I turned to depression eating as a way of coping. At my lowest point, I weighed 320 pounds, and I looked like a badly made bed.I knew two things in that moment: I'm depressed.. and one day, I won't be. Eventually, I found the courage to walk away from that relationship. Around 2008, I connected with one of the great nightlife promoters we had in New England, the late Anderson Mar. She helped me get my foot in the door of the nightlife industry. I started out as a nightclub DJ out here, and eventually I was contacted by a gentleman who ran an independent online radio station in the New England area. He suggested I give radio a try, which was interesting because that's where I wanted to start my professional journey in the first place. This turned out to be my gateway to the radio industry, and my first project was hosting and curating weekly radio show titled LEGACY RADIO - basically a promotional vehicle for my monthly LEGACY nightlife event in Allston, Massachusetts. From that point, radio became the focal point of my career, the hat I was best known for rocking.

2. MOST MEMORABLE RADIO EXPERIENCE?

I'll keep it 100 with you, I can't name one particular show or series or guests that stand out as the most memorable of my career, because there were so many of them. So I'll take this one step further and name a few different guests that I deem as memorable to me. There's a few who immediately come to mind: first, John & Gabriel Shipton, the father and brother of the great journalist and WikiLeaks founder, Julian Assange. They pulled up last year (2023) for an interview as part of The Chop Session series, to discuss an independent film titled Ithaka, about Julian's ongoing struggles as the world's most well-known political prisoner.

I also must show love for two of the dopest legends within New England hip-hop, my guys Termanology and Akrobatik. Greats of the community, with artistic reputations that span the globe. Their musical catalogs are unmatched. Both of these guys are two of the most transparent and passionate guests I've ever hosted on any show I've done. There's over 100 episodes of the old Chop Session series available to stream on Spotify, and to this day, whenever anyone asks me which episodes they should start with, I always point them to Term's episode and Akrobatik's episode. Both have amazing stories to tell, two of the best interviews I ever held down.

Another one for you: Bruce Kulick. Iconic lead guitarist of KISS from 1984 to 1996. This one happened in 2016, as part of a radio special I co-produced honoring the memory and the work of the late Eric Carr who was the drummer of KISS for 11 years and sadly passed away in 1991, due to cancer-related complications. Bruce worked extensively with Eric, and he was kind enough to call in to share his memories of working with Eric, what he was like as a human being, and so on. I have great respect for Bruce, for taking the time out to do this interview - and to this day, one of the most memorable days of my career because one of the musical entities that really inspired me growing up was KISS. To have a former band member call into my show, was a dope moment for real. It solidified that I made the right choice to do this as a career.

3. HOW DID YOU GET INVOLVED IN THE WORLD OF FASHION?

To be honest, I never had aspirations of getting involved in fashion. It's something that kind of happened by accident. That journey began over a decade ago, when I found myself pulling up to an old venue in Boston called Splash Ultra Lounge. If memory serves me correctly, Splash wasn't around for long, but in the time they were in business, there was a weekly Thursday night fashion event titled "Style Infusion," which presented local and international fashion designers on the rooftop of the venue. Through that experience I began to connect with some local models, designers, the promoter of the event and so on.

For the next few years, outside of occasionally DJing or emceeing fashion events, I didn't really do much in that world. It was in 2016 when I really found myself immersed in our fashion community. It happened when I kicked off the old Sterlingtology Live morning radio show. I hosted a launch party at a local venue, and to my surprise, all these fabulous local fashion luminaries pulled up to the event. I had not met any of them before. The next thing I know, I was making new connections in that field, and I found this whole new circle of confidants, friends, and professional connections. I was truly honored to meet them all. From there, I became something of a regular at fashion events out here and even ended up hosting and producing several of my own.

4. MOST MEMORABLE FASHION SHOW?

Oh, damn. I have a lot of fashion shows I either emceed or curated, which I deem to be memorable. The one that I would point to here is one that we did under unconventional circumstances: it happened during the height of the global pandemic, for a virtual event that I curated titled EMBRACE, benefitting the old ONCE Somerville music venue, which was enduring great financial hardship. Part of that EMBRACE presentation included a fashion show featuring the work of Jaclyn Robichaud Doyle, under her Jack Attackk Clothing label. As part of this event, Jaclyn and I worked on how to present her fashions in a virtual setting, since every act on the bill from live music performers to DJs fo fashion were working from their own respective closed sets. So up in northern New England, Jaclyn and her team worked on building a runway at an old warehouse It turned out to be a super dope presentation presenting Jaclyn's signature alternative and inclusive fashion vibes. Jaclyn is one of the great designers I respect the most out here, such passion for what she does. She knows herself and she believes in her vision.

5. WHAT'S NEXT IN THE CARDS IN THE LIFE OF STERLING GOLDEN?

Well the honest answer to that question is, continuing to enjoy my retirement. Y'all, your man Sterling has been retired since January 1, 2024, and I'm greatly enjoying this new life of mine. It's well earned. I had a fabulous 15-year run in the industry wearing many hats. I got to live the life I always imagined for myself. I made lifelong connections, created dope memories I shall forever take with me, and I have left behind a lasting body of work that people can go back and revisit on Spotify. Today, my focus is on taking care of family, bonding with my loved ones, traveling, stacking my money, and staying the fuck out of the way. My heart is happy, my circle is small, my blessings are counted, and my life is peaceful.

I'm grateful for everything I got to experience in the industry. The rest of my life began this year, and I'm thankful to everyone who checks in to see how it's been going. To this day, there's so much for me to learn, unlearn and relearn. From this, I plan to continue making a better day for myself, every day going forward. Grateful is what I am. That's the vibe now, always, and forever.

February 2024 Ferrari Red Set the Tone for Fashionably Late Scene&Style Magazine Issue #84

Recently local designers from the Bogo Spilt Boutique collaborated on the Fashionably Late Runway at the Liberty Hotel for an event to preview the upcoming Mass Fashion Week.

Every Thursday from September through May models, Boston and beyond best designers, and the cities in vogue can be found mixing in mingling at a nocturnal hour throughout the hotel's elegant floors until showtime when Dynasty Models finest hit the catwalk.

The show opened with a chic and solid summer look. The bombshell Ferrari shade full piece swimsuit from Lauren Lane Swim oozed sex appeal. This piece, as all outfits were paired with classic eye catching accessories by Whirl Wind Jewels.

Following was a collection of suits and sweats. It was a take on comfort in oversized and muted tones of full hoodie and pant outfits. The showstopper outfit of the evening was seductive cherry red boots pulled together with a ruby hint tiger print bomber jacket. The showstopper outfit of the evening were seductive cherry red boots pulled together with a ruby hint tiger bomber jacket.

Closing the Fashionably Late runway was tailored denim with city style. The collection from MavLife Clothing and designer Money Mav local Boston radio host showed his hometown pride and love for the Celtics just in time for the playoff run in the NBA.

The denim jackets were personalized with jagged cuts and sewn in jerseys to make each piece original. Also was a season must have mustard crop button up paired with an all-white skirt and halter that crept in to offset the last set of looks at the Liberty Hotels fashionably late.

As expected, Bogo Spilt and the Liberty pulled in the cities elite from press to patrons. Also contributing to the event was Model Director Liva Kay and Meagan Michelle founder of Mass Fashion Week.

The occasion was a preview to this springs Mass Fashion Week on May 3rd in Fall River and May 5th in Boston. Tickets can be purchased at Massfashionweek.com

January 2024 Simpson's Collection Shows Vibrant Color Pops - Scene&Style Magazine Issue #83

During this past holiday shopping preparations adidas and Foot Locker paired up to present a fashionable runway on the main floor at the Cambridge Side Mall.

Foot Locker carries many brands however this presentation was an all adidas focus featuring the season's top styles. Most pieces pulled were from the originals collection. Adidas Originals is a subdivision of adidas dedicated to lifestyle, fashion, and heritage products. It is home to many brands' collaborations with fashion designers, celebrities, and cultural figures.

An event aspect was a teaser, to prepare the hype for the launch of the AE1 "With Love" basketball shoe. Anothony Edwards is one of the newest adidas athletes representing the three stripes who is literally making "waves" in the NBA. There will be a launch of a new AE1 colorway each month through May exclusively at Foot Locker and www.adidas.com

The show promoted many looks; a men's ensemble of a hooded puffer jacket styled with OG high tops, adult classic zip ups to top off any outfit, a full beige sweatsuit for the teenager on the go, a camo hoodie paired with black track pants in a youth girl glow, an adorable baby blue and sunflower maxi dress for the mini lady at the playground, and symbolic originals basics of children's tees, shorts.

The showstoppers on the runway were the voguish pairings of the latest drops from "The Simpson's Collection." Matt Groening's "The Simpsons" has transcended its two-dimensional format over the last 34 years, becoming a cultural institution. Since 2021, Homer and his fellow citizens of Springfield have been brought to sneaker form by adidas, further cementing them as part of mainstream fashion.

The first cartoon collaboration to hit the runway was the soft shade of pink "Couch Hoodie." Homer assumes a familiar stance, just as comfortable as you'll be in fleecy soft cotton with ribbed details, a kangaroo pocket, and an adjustable hood. The outfit was matched with staple black track pants and pulling together the color pops with the iconic "Itchy" basketball sneaker. This shoe is implemented in a light blue premium leather upper with orange and white accented panels.

The final look to hit the stage was full focus on Homer! The vibrant yellow tee of his mug, always a must of black track pants, the "Clouds" sky colored hoodie with a bold lemon trefoil logo and finished off with The Simpsons X adidas NMD G1 low "Homer." The latest "Nomad" style features BOOST cushioning underneath a vibrant yellow Prime knit upper à la Homer Simpson.

Post show shoppers were welcome to head up to Foot Locker on the second floor and shop their favorite apparel from the runway. adidas had a shoe customization table setup, with games and pinwheel prizes adding to the event.

The adidas show was a success! Behind the scenes was hair and makeup from glamming by JV and top photographers Monster Jazz Photography and Hill Zhou. The event was a collaboration from local Boston market Foot Lockers from shipping apparel for use, associates walking the runway and managers incorporating their kids into the fashion. If you would like to up your style this season visit your local Foot locker or www.adidas.com

Chapter Two – 2023

"What you wear is how you present yourself to the world, especially today, when human contacts are so quick. Fashion is instant language."
—Miuccia Prada

December 2023 Joe Malaika's Focused Fashion for the Everyday Warrior - Scene&Style Magazine

Issue #82

The annual holiday Excessive Fashion Show by Joe Malaika was held at the A Loft Seaport Hotel. Each year Malaika highlights magnificent high end designs, this collection was focused on glamour for the everyday warrior and proceeds benefitting the A Leg Forever Charitable Foundation.

The evening opened with honor. Artist and songwriter Taylor Deneen notable for working with Missy Elliot, The Eagles set the tone with an incredible rendition of the star spangled banner.

The first set of looks from Malaika were donned by leg amputees and Boston Marathon Survivors. The pieces were classic from the designer tailored with vibrant color, strategic cuts with unique flair.

Following was intermission. Guests can always expect first class entertainment at the yearly runway presentation. On the stage in between each set of looks from the designer were saxophonist Andie Sax, siblings Ester and Ezekiel Mutesasira and Taylor Deneen.

A new interactive spin to the production was a live auction of charitable treasures. The annual Excessive Fashion Show always has a principle to support. This year was a full focus on the A Leg Forever Foundation.

Host of the evening Channel 10 Boston news anchor and professional models took center stage to give attendees the opportunity to bid on authentic artwork from the Congo in a live auction that created honorable banter for a cause adding a few extra thousand to the pot!

Ending the extravaganza was the last set of looks showing bright pastels and cooling blues from Maliaka. The eye popping colors, sharp cuts, with signature sequin's defined couture, designed specifically for amputees and honored everyday warriors with the opportunity to feel the glam!

Closing the evening were heart felt words of gratitude from a mother and CEO of the foundation. Malaika also took the stage and expressed his experience in designing a way he had never. The event was a success and arguably the best show Malaika had ever produced. Class from start to finish.

A Leg Forever Charitable Foundation is a nonprofit charitable foundation established by Liz Norden, Mother of JP and Paul Norden, Boston Marathon Survivors who each lost a leg in the bombings of April 15, 2013. The mission of this foundation is to "pay it forward", by assisting amputees (Massachusetts residents only) who lost limbs under tragic circumstances just as the Norden family was helped in their time of need. If you would like to learn more about the charity or to donate, please visit www.alegforever.coma

LINK TO FULL MAGAZINE https://madmagz.com/magazine/2117551

November 2023 Denise Hajjar Collection Dons Winter Must Haves - Scene&Style Magazine Issue #81

This past Boston Fashion Week legendary fashion designer Denise Hajjar held her annual runway presentation featuring fall and winters styles.

Just across from her boutique the stage was set in the Marina Bay space with rows of chairs perfectly placed to get a glimpse of the iconic models donning elegant outfits.

The first set of looks we're focal on autumn tones; a burgundy flow, stunning mustard, busy classic patterns, and vibrant scarfs to top off each ensemble. Seasonal accessories showed in the second set of looks. Shawls featuring fur trim, plaid coats and neckerchiefs with deep crimson tones and wraps that pair for a winter afternoon, or an evening out.

Hajjar is always keeping it classic; A portion of the DHFW23 collection highlighted the art of a classic black outfit and how the right pairings will make it an eye catcher. Following was a tribute to the New England chill. When it is time to bundle up in Boston, the Denise Hajjar Boutique has your must haves! From fur trimmed over coats, marble colored scarfs, Pom hats, matching gloves, and perfectly paired handbags.

The show closed with edgy and elegant street style. Fall winter fashion is always highlighted with leathers and vintage accessories, The DHFW23 collection nailed it! The boutique brought out its best pieces with metallic jackets, an all olive look that stole the show, pops of lace, and a sequence of chic Bogart hats.

Each season the Denise Hajjar Boutique is the store to hit for all your staple pieces. The boutique is currently open on Saturday and Sunday from 12-5pm.Hit the Marina Bay boardwalk and shop before these exclusive pieces are gone. Be sure to stop into Marina Bay Living and Terre D'Italia for all your home goods and Italian specialties. The same business hours apply, weather permitting. Mark your calendar for the annual "Galentine's Day Market" on Marina Bay from 12-4pm. Pop in and shop!

LINK TO MAGAZINE https://madmagz.com/magazine/2116709

October 2023 United in Style, Fashion for a Cause Hit the Runway - Scene&Style Magazine Issue #80

Boston runway fashion got started this past season at the Shops in Chestnut Hall Mall "United in Style." A charitable collaboration between

Project Smile and Dress for Success Boston for a stimulating fashion show fundraiser hosted by Shayna Seymour & Ramiro.

The event was produced and styled by Kathy Benharris with KB Fashion Productions assisted by Tala Koury & Jacquie Minasian. This runway event was a bit different for Scene&Style as I was surprised to be asked to walk as a local celebrity model. It was truly an honor, and I knew I was in good hands as the only other time I had walked for Boston Fashion Week the queen bee Kathy Benharris was in charge.

I must admit, I rarely find myself nervous approaching a show, however this time around the angle was a bit different. The mastermind of Benharris always makes for a show and decided to have me walk exuding, just who I am. All models were instructed for phones to be away in bags, yet I was backstage getting the general highlights I bring to my live posting. When I hit the end of the runway in my gorgeous Queenia vintage Channel look from Italia, I pulled out my phone and took my press pit selfie with the family I am used to snagging my lighting from.

It was such an amazing experience to be glammed up by Jackie V MUA, mix and mingle with gorgeous models, celebrities and walk for a cause dear to my heart. Yet, I wouldn't have felt like myself unless I captured a collection from the press pit. I snook out before the final walkthrough and caught the last designer to show, J Crew. I had been doing a little backstage coaching with former Celtic Rob Williams and needed to see him strut his stuff down his first runway.

Project Smile and Dress for Success Boston pulled out all the stops to kick off Boston Fashion Week. United in Style was hosted by Shayna Seymour from Channel 5 News Boston and Ramiro from HOT 96.9FM.

The fashion show featured with men & women from the community along with prominent Bostonians, modeling the latest looks from Chestnut Hill retailers. The models included Boston City Council members, Melissa from HOT 96.9, Brianna Borghi from News Channel 5 Boston, Miss Massachusetts, and special guest model Rob Williams formally of the Boston Celtics.

Featured retailers included Ann Taylor, At Cozy, EverEve, Express Edit, Laughing Lotus Jewelry, LMF Fine Jewelry, Marc Cain, J. Crew, Nic+Zoe and Queenia.

A pre and post cocktail party took place and gave guests an opportunity to mingle and enjoy delicious complimentary appetizers & desserts. Complimentary cocktails included with ticket purchase were courtesy of Velo Vodka and Boston Harbor Distillery.

A silent auction- bid took place of local restaurant gift cards, hotel stays, fun activities and more! All proceeds benefited Dress for Success Boston's mission to provide career services and job interview clothing for low income women in the greater Boston area. Also, Project Smile's program, Suits & Smiles, which provides job interview clothing for low income men in the Boston area. Together, these charities help thousands of people in need in our community. Visit www.dressforsuccess.com or www.projectsmile.org to donate!

LINK TO FULL MAGAZINE https://madmagz.com/magazine/2116721

September 2023 Our Girl Linda Dance Party - Scene&Style Magazine Issue #79

Recently the cities top fashionistas and family gathered for the fourth annual "Our Girl Linda" dance party to honor the legendary Linda Cole Petrosian and charity event to support St. Jude at the American Legion in Newton.

The evening began with catered treats and tables of auction items showcasing some of Boston's best businesses. While guests continued to pour in for the sold out event they posed on the step and repeat then took their seats in the banquet room.

The party kicked off with the dance floor open and DJ Jimmy Espo playing rotations that all able to find their groove. After a few spins moves on the floor the event officially began with opening words from the heart. God daughter Milan gave a powerful speech on how Linda had impacted the industry, lives of so many in the community with her spirit that continues to contribute.

She then introduced the live entertainment of the evening; Brenda Arena as Liza Minnelli, Keith Gilbert as Frank Sinatra, and Dan Fontaine as Elvis. From classic Italian hits to the hound dog, it was a rocking good time.

From there the bidding of the live auction began. MC Espo with 617 Event Group who got the crowed upping the ante on the items such as a full dinner for four at the Reel House East Boston, Patriots tickets and apparel, local art, fashion designs and so much more with proceeds going to Linda's favorite charity St. Jude.

The evening ended the way Linda would have wanted. A dance party that brought smiles, love, laughter. A personal impact: The first time I ever saw you, it was my first ever fashion show. I was mesmerized by the grace and energy you brought to the runway. You are a reason I have come as far as I have in this journey.

Your last show I will never forget walking into the Denise Hajjar boutique, upset over silliness, truly letting it affect me. Then there was you smile ear to ear fighting a real battle. You hugged me with a glass of wine in hand. Enjoying everything life was giving and taking.

I stood there again mesmerized, in pure awe of a women so magnificent, strong, and barely enough energy for yourself yet more than enough energy to rule the room and spread a vibe that will live on. You are forever in my heart!

The Our Girl Linda Foundation was established in 2018. It is an amazing team of regulars and part-time volunteers who are committed to helping others. They take their love of Linda and turn that love into action. All contributions are donated to the St. Jude's Children's Research Hospital. You can make donations at www.ourgirllinda.com

Another way to donate to the foundation is by purchasing copies of the entertaining and delightfully illustrated Lindy Lou book series. The books, inspired by Linda's childhood, are written by her mother, Yolanda. ALL proceeds from book sales go to St. Jude's! Shop https://www.amazon.com/Lindy-Lou-her-Dancing-Shoes/dp/1734761601

LINK TO FULL MAGAZINE https://madmagz.com/magazine/2101242

August 2023 Boston Barbie Glittered the Omni Rooftop Runway - Scene&Style Magazine Issue #79

Recently the sparkle of hot pink from Mel the Clothing paired up with Boston Man Magazine to take it poolside at the Omni Hotel rooftop in the Seaport for the 1st Annual Summer Pink Party.

When arriving there was no missing then fact you had just stepped into Barbie's World! Parked out front the chic hotel was Barbie's ride. Designer Mel's dream had come true when to hype up the event Jason Louf from Swampscott Collision had remastered Mel's convertible into a pink dream. Photos next to the classic car were a must, I channeled my inner football barbie look with the pink hot wheel.

Continuing up to Lifted Lounge is where Barbie's Dreamhouse came alive. The city view, pool, cocktails, selfie stations, tasty treats from the Cake Monstah, banging beats from 617 Event Group and fabulous friends gathered for the anticipated 2023 Barbie Collection fashion show from Mel the Clothing and styled by Wave and Woven.

Opening the runway was a hot pink sheer swimsuit cover followed by every girl's idol and every guy's dream Barbie from Tik Tok, business, Boston, tennis barbie, cannabis, and more! Media barbie made her way played by local beauty and business Emcee Jenniffer Mariel Ruiz. Making an appearance was Ken in a Zack Morris beach fit that had all ladies reminiscing. Beat box barbie came rocking out by Gianna Gravalese Kiss 108 radio personality and the pool side show came to a close with mermaid barbie and her sexy seashells on mega model Madeline Adams.

Shortly after Owner of Boston Man Magazine took center stage for a major announcement. He and Amanda Vargus of Wave and Woven will be bringing the first ever Boston's Runway Ball on December 3rd for a night of community, culture, and fashion in the grand ballroom at the Park Plaza Hotel. Proceeds will benefit "Toast to St. Jude" and St. Jude Children's Research Hospital, visit their social media for more information and tickets.

The evening ended with a new age performance on the electric violin from Rozita Fishta vibing in sync with DJ Jimmy Espo from 617 to all the beats and fireworks to make an iconic Barbie dance party.

The first annual summer pink party was a sparkling smash! Guests got to live out their Barbie fantasy and a portion of the proceeds were donated to the Miss Pink Organization to help support and fund resources for local pink warriors battling breast cancer.

LINK TO FULL MAGAZINE https://madmagz.com/magazine/2099600

July 2023 Caribbean Catwalk Showed Bold and Bright - Scene&Style Magazine Issue #78

Boston Caribbean Fashion Week is preparing to celebrate its remarkable 10th anniversary with an engaging celebration of style, beauty, and cultural diversity. This year's preview event "Caribbean Catwalk" took place in Downtown Crossing, where the vibrant atmosphere and favorable weather added an extra touch of magic to the occasion. The show unfolded with designers stepping onto the stage to present their awe-inspiring creations, each inspired by its own unique meaning and significance.

The open-air fashion exhibition showcased a stunning array of designs that artfully represented a diverse range of cultures. From the eye-catching reversible jackets that effortlessly blended functionality and style to the intricate and ornate headdresses that paid homage to rich traditions, the show served as a visual ode for fashion enthusiasts and cultural appreciators. Attendees were treated to a captivating display of creativity and craftsmanship that transcended boundaries and celebrated the beauty of different heritages.

At the heart of the Caribbean Catwalk were the models who brought the designs to life. Positioned on the elevated catwalk, they glided with grace and confidence, showcasing the garments from every angle. Their presence was hypnotic, capturing the attention of both the audience members and the photographers.

The models exuded diversity, representing a wide range of ages, genders, and looks, which added a layer of relatability and inclusivity to the show. It was a celebration of individuality and self-expression, where everyone could find something that resonated with their own sense of style and identity. No matter your level of interest in fashion you found common ground in the ability to appreciate the talent showcased and the beauty behind the large celebration of culture.

Throughout the event, the air was filled with an eclectic mix of music that heightened the experience. The carefully curated playlist incorporated culturally rooted tunes that complimented the rich heritage behind the designs, as well as upbeat songs that inspired a spontaneous dance-along from the crowd. The rhythm and energy of the music created a vibrant ambiance, ensuring there was never a dull moment. It enhanced the atmosphere and added an extra layer of excitement to the show.

Beyond the visual and auditory components, the Caribbean Catwalk went beyond the surface of fashion. The event provided a platform for the designers to share their personal stories and the deeper meanings behind their collections. After each designer's showcase, they took a moment to engage with the audience, offering insights into their creative processes, inspirations, and the significance of their work. This personal connection provided a deeper appreciation for the artistry on display, allowing attendees to understand the emotional and cultural narratives woven into each garment.

As the show reached its grand finale, an interactive element was introduced to the audience. An audience-included catwalk-off was held, inviting volunteers to take to the runway and showcase their own personal walks. Accompanied by lively music, these participants strutted their stuff with confidence and enthusiasm, in hopes for the chance to secure access to the 10th anniversary celebration of the Caribbean Catwalk in October. It was a moment of pure joy and shared celebration, fostering a sense of community and inclusivity.

To conclude the event, all the models assembled for a gallery-like showcasing of the designs. This immersive experience allowed attendees to approach each look up close, examining the intricate details and appreciating the craftsmanship from every angle. It created an intimate connection between the audience and the creations, providing a deeper understanding and admiration for the artistic endeavors of the designers.

With such a mesmerizing teaser, the anticipation for Boston Caribbean Fashion Weeks' 10th anniversary celebration is palpable. From October 18 to 21, fashion, beauty, and culture will converge in an unforgettable extravaganza. Guests can expect to be captivated by an even more extraordinary and grandiose showcase of creativity, talent, and the vibrancy of diverse cultures that the Caribbean Catwalk has showcased. It is an event that promises to be a treat for the senses, leaving attendees with a profound appreciation for the transformative power of fashion and artistic expression.

LINK TO FULL MAGAZINE https://madmagz.com/magazine/2098979

June 2023 Fashion's Future Dashed the Open Runway - Scene&Style Magazine Issue #77

Recently Boston Fashion Week collaborated with Downtown Boston BID for the return of the OPEN RUNWAY in Downtown Crossing on "The Steps."

The showcase was the first since the pandemic and an opportunity for anyone to enter to make their mark. The city streets were packed with trend goers, lunch breaks associates all getting a glimpse of what Boston has to offer in the industry.

The powerhouse panel included style maven Evelyn Reyes, Designer Diana Jaye Coluntino, and model Sonia Garufi joining Boston Fashion Week founder Jay Calderin in celebrating regional fashion talent and giving feedback to the budding collections.

The first set of looks to hit the Boston Bid runway came from Boston Arts Academy. High schools' hottest trends came in a Ferrari red gown, street wear denim, velvet and fur, fun crop tops that were being sewn by budding students.

Next to hit the stage was a designer well known Mel the Clothing and continuing to pave her glistening path with sequins and sparkle. Her designs are worn by sports celebrities and represent Boston pride with custom made dresses meant to catch the eye of the crowd at any game.

A runway favorite came from Ethan Donaldson with a men's collection with perfection in the patchwork. It featured funk denim and strategic sewing that shows this designer is the real deal! Following was another men's assemblage focal on recycled fabrics in a stellar suit from a Mass Art Boston budding designer.

Closing out the Boston Bid runway was fashions future coming from Mass Art highlighting a collection of dresses ranging from a golden 70's stunner, a plush floral formal, traditional full length, urban wear and the showstopper of an elegant pearl draped gown with recycled detail.

The alfresco fashion show provided a platform to fashion designers at every stage of their careers, including student fashion designers. The presentation of unique designs and bold fashion statements were created right here in the Greater Boston area. The event closed with BFW Founder Jay Calderin announcing the official dates of Boston Fashion Week 2023 being September 30th through October 7th. See you all in the front row!

LINK TO FULL MAGAZINE https://madmagz.com/magazine/2098977

May 2023 Yolanda Cellucci The Glitz and Glam of Fashion - Scene&Style Magazine Issue #77

Fashion is an ever-changing element, one where the old can be recreated by anew and then there is a timeless entity, Yolanda Cellucci. Recently the Peabody Essex Museum in Salem held an evening of elegance to celebrate this iconic woman in the industry.

 A cocktail affair took place in the grand hall of the museum. Guests were welcomed in for music and dancing, chic hors d'oeuvres and rubbing elbows with fashions finest. The festivities were put on pause to welcome the legendary Cellucci to the stage for a heartfelt speech of gratitude for those that have been part of her journey. Yolanda is always an all-white sight to be seen, the silk gown detailed with silver jewels, matching earrings, and a head dress feathers feet high was nothing short of spectacular.

After attendees were welcome to continue the party in the main room and enter the exhibit in the museum dedicated to the celebrity of the evening. The display unveiled more than 100 fresh works from the museum' global fashion and textile collection, including nearly 40 recent acquisitions that spotlight the vibrant and fine tailored collection of Boston-based entrepreneur and glamour of fashion Yolanda Cellucci.

Fashion moguls sashayed around wearing pieces they have purchased from the designer while admiring the display of collaborations with Stephen Yearick and cocktail dresses from the 1990s. Pairings with Bob Mackie's evening gown and jacket from the mid-1980s. Crepe fabric, netting, glass beads and sequins were lined along as priceless works of art.

Although well known for wedding gowns the legendary Yolanda Cellucci has produced iconic ensembles fit for the red carpet and office looks beaming with sparkle on chic suits. The sustainable fabrics used and accessories of glass beads, silk, polyester, cellulose triacetate all donned into these amazing pieces worn by celebrities in the early 90's and 2000's.

Some of Cellucci's most memorable pieces were her magnificent show stopping crowns. Costume designer Carol Salem collaborated with Yolanda's on the creation of fantastical headpieces worn by models in the shop's fashion shows. She found inspiration for some of her headpieces from local and international landmarks and attractions like Boston's Swan Boats and the Eiffel Tower.

The evening was an elegant success. It was a time to slow down, have a cocktail, dance a dance, and honor an 86 year old fashion icon still hosting her own television show, the upcoming 4th annual Our Girl Linda Dance Party to benefit St. Jude in memory of her daughter on September 21st (www.ourgirllinda.com). As if still being in the spotlight wasn't enough to admire this amazing woman, seeing her spend hours strutting in high heels and a head dress gives faith that life is what you make of it. Yolanda Cellucci is a portrait representation of a vogue lifestyle, and her entourage was in full force to celebrate the queen of glitz and glamour.

LINK TO FULL MAGAZINE https://madmagz.com/magazine/2098550

April 2023 / December 2022 Show Date, Designer Joe Malaika Drops SS23 Collection - Scene&Style Magazine Issue #76

Fashion tells many stories, while its shows expose the whole truth. Seems are seen if misguided, tailoring talked about if unflattering to the model chosen for the piece. The only gossip that moves through out the room at a Joe Malaika show, praise to yet another outstanding collection.

Recently crowned Best Designer by Boston Magazine, Joe Malaika released his latest collection at his annual Excessive Fashion charity show benefiting The Jimmy Fund at the Westin in Waltham.

Local celebrities like Yolanda Cellucci and the Mayor of Waltham were sitting front and center, glitterati mingling in the chic hotel and guidance through the evening was given by Hosts Alfred and Keyla Williams Co-Owner of Bogosplit.

Opening the Excessive fashion runway charity show was wowqing with a line of transitional pieces all in a funk flair, focal on denim and patch patterns with hints of leather and lace. The strategic zippers completely transformed looks. Following was, AtCozy Boutique. The pieces were focal on high end European flair in full trenches, fur knits, glamour gowns, a fluorescent pant suit, all staples for the winter wardrobe. The line was shown in a collaborative manor with a soulful live performance from Shola Iyiola, an international award-winning saxophonist.

The third designer had a take on traditional African art emerged in modern style. The patterns strategically sewn into chic two-piece dresses and pant suits, seductive cuts off the shoulder, bright bold colors, even a button down look for men and the mini men. In all a collection that can be worn on a red carpet or to make a statement at the office.

Fringe, sequins, and silk were highlights in another collaborative collection shown paired with a live performance of stunning vocals from Ester and Ezekiel Mutesasira singing siblings and winner of East Africas got Talent. The looks that hit the runway were attention grabbers in bright pastel gowns, patch work, everyday outfits, and the use of layered pieces.

The last collection to hit the Excessive Fashion runway was the birthday boy, man of honor, Designer Joe Malaika opened his portion of the show with vibrant nylon, traditional Ugandan colors and his brand logo embedded in mini athleisure looks that would rock it on the playground.

Following were block shoulders and bold colors which highlighted Joes talent for high end couture cuts and classic solids letting the structure of the garment speak. The third set of pieces were focal on vibrant spring style, bright neon lime looks in a chic short suit, a silk jumper for women, a mini fashionista and powerful dresses that will catch all attention this spring season.

Another highlight from the SS23 Malaika Collection was Ugandan flavor for all ages with that smooth African style for the aspiring fashion forward kid. From a forest green, embroidered print suit with swagger for the young gentlemen to a silk short jumper with ruffle for that budding woman.

Back to business and seductive style were a set of suit jackets. A strategic sewn pattern of popping pastels with chic cuts and class to give an office look a new flavor.

The last set of looks from the SS23 collection to show was sea glass and sequins with a Mirano vibe. The impeccably sewn top and matching pant had perfectly picked colors, with couture detail and chic flash. The showstopper of the evening was a one piece with sexy shaping, and the bling baby! This selection was a perfect way to close the runway with a reminder of where to get your next red-carpet ensemble.

Designer Joe Malaika's fashion collections speak loudly with culture and his love for lifestyle traditions are no secret. The closing of his show Excessive Fashion charity show featured an R&B superstar Rotimi added to his set with some Fugees flavor with his 2020 hit song, "In my bed." He ignited the African beats by performing his newly released single "Make you say." With the presence of a master on the mic traveling to sold out shows around the world and to don the Westin Waltham in Boston to give love to his African people.

Once again Joe Malaika hit a home run at his annual Excessive Fashion charity show benefiting The Jimmy Fund at the Westin in Waltham. To purchase designs visit www.joemalaika.com

March 2023 A Fashionable Legend Honored - Scene&Style Magazine Issue #75

Boston is a city blessed with iconic sports teams, restaurants, art, and one beauty that has made an impact on the fashion industry for decades.

Yolanda Cellucci is a portrait representation of a vogue lifestyle. Her career notably began in 1968. Already being an established model, she began entrepreneurial journey with a boutique in Waltham focal on women's wear and dazzling head pieces fit to complete any rouge outfit. Her shop grew into a powerhouse for lavish evening and wedding ensembles, international designs, style consultations, a day spa, all under one roof.

At a vibrant 88 years of age Yolanda can still be seen in the front row of fashion shows, supporting budding student exhibits, and hosting her on-air tv talk show "Style and Glamour." With all her current contributions and past the time has come to honor this graceful icon in more ways than one!

On, Friday May 5th from 5:30-8:30pm the 10th Annual Boston Design Week Awards celebrate the diversity of the design community in greater Boston with a spirited gathering. Yolanda will be receiving the Mentor of the Year Award. The evening will be a catered reception held at the Boston Architectural College on Newbury Street.

Following on May 11th at the Peabody Essex Museum will be a grand celebration and cocktail affair held in an exhibit dedicated to this stylish and elegant legend. In March, PEM unveiled more than 100 fresh works from the museum' global fashion and textile collection, including nearly

40 recent acquisitions that spotlight the vibrant and fine tailored collection of Boston-based entrepreneur and glamour of fashion Yolanda Cellucci.

These honorable events are mire episodes to a lifestyle of glitz and glamour of a women who has worn her heart on her sleeve while making a statement in many aspects of business and lead the way for the path women can now walk on.

If you would like to attend May 5th event visit https://BDWAwardsTicket.eventbrite.com. If would like a ticket for the May 11th occasion visit www.pem.org.

LINK TO FULL MAGAZINE https://madmagz.com/magazine/2090458

February 2023 BogoSplit Showcasing Across Boston - Scene&Style Magazine Issue #74

The recently voted Boston's Best Boutique by Boston Magazine is taking charge with relocating to a revamped location in Assembly Row, opening in Copley Place and now part of a fashion movement known as BAM on Fridays and Saturdays at the renovated City Hall Plaza.

This family trio of two bold brothers and a savvy sister are backing Boston designers with giving them a space to present and purchase designs. BAM is being hosted in partnership with Bogosplit, a Black, woman-owned tech company committed to supporting and promoting all small businesses. "We at Bogosplit have a true commitment to community building. Our mission is to create a vibrant and inclusive shopping experience that celebrates and elevates the creativity and diversity of the Boston community," said Keyla Williams, Co-founder and CEO of Bogosplit."

The market will showcase local designers and vendors displaying their clothing lines, skincare products, jewelry, wearable art, and more. BAM will kick off the start of each weekend with "Fashion Fridays," which will include a fashion show highlighting local models, influencers, and DJs, including DJ Maverik through May 6th.

If you can't make it to City Hall Plaza pop into their Assembly Row store or Copley Place location. This past fall the trio partnered with KB Fashion Productions, a long-standing fashion work force of Copley Place to extend into the chic mall style setting with a grand opening, sip and shop also a chance to meet their creators and a red-carpet fashion show.

Designers on site were VAVA ZADI the dapper don himself with his custom suits. Mel the Clothing who is as much fun as a "waterburger" with her iconic sequins Celtics dresses, purchase asap ladies and make a statement for the playoffs. Wowqing with a line of transitional pieces all in a funk flair, focal on denim and patch patterns with hints of leather and lace. Their strategic zippers completely transform looks. Also, legendary DJ Money Mav was spinning and showing his urban street wear line Mav Life Clothing.

The event was a successful reminder that you can and will when you find the right people to back you! Bogosplit was founded by Kenelly Cineus, Adriano Pinto, and Keyla Williams, a team of passionate entrepreneurs with a deep commitment to technology, innovation, and community.

Bogosplit is a dynamic and forward-thinking tech company that is committed to supporting small businesses. By providing a range of cutting-edge online resources through our platform and automated storefronts, Bogosplit empowers small vendors to grow their business. Visit www.flow.page/bogosplit for more information.

LINK TO FULL MAGAZINE https://madmagz.com/magazine/2089735#/

The fashion industry is one of the most competitive markets to break into. There are millions of brands, retail shelf space is not only expensive yet with the online ere becoming a declining trend. Now what to do when you begin your artistic journey or continue to thrive when your age becomes more than just a number?

Boston fashion week took a focused direction last year with each day being dedicated to an important topic of how to flourish in the business.

A trio of talent Kristie Raymond from Human Kind Casting, Kathy Benharris of KB Fashion Productions molded an educational event while Fashion Week Founder Jay Calderin moderated a panel discussion on ageism in the industry. The panel was made up of Boston iconic designers, models, makeup creators, photographers, and a shoe god!

Legendary fashion designer Yolanda Cellucci wowed the crowd when revealing she would be celebrating her upcoming 88th birthday. A women poised, classy and in high heels who is still seen at the front frow of fashion shows. Yolanda has been in the business for decades, notably for her stunning glamour designs and head pieces. Her advice to all was no matter what get up and start your day right. Make that bed, get out of your pajamas and even if you aren't leaving the house put on makeup. Her message was to make yourself feel fabulous!

Shoe Designer Chris Donovan spoke from a different aspect of Agism. Chris has only begun his career in the fashion industry. He had spent most of his life being a telephone wire repair man. As all greats do, he had his aha moment and transitioned to studying fashion in Italia. Once completed, it was suggested for him to join fashion competitions to become "seen." As he pursued the process he was continually rejected based on his age. He then decided to pivot from aspiring to work for a shoe design company to creating his own line. Chris Donovan has been recently recognized by the worldly Fashion Group International with the "Rising Star" award.

Each of the panelists spoke about their experiences, from making sure you feel good at any age to tricks of the trade. Right down to when being given an age restriction to enter a fashion contest; step on them, over them and create your own brand. The evening was beyond a blessing of ideas, information, and heartwarming inspiration to make any aspiring fashion professional motivated to keep on moving!

Recently the Peabody Essex Museum (PEM) unveiled more than 100 fresh works from the museum' global fashion and textile collection, including nearly 40 recent acquisitions that spotlight the vibrant and flamboyant collection of Boston-based entrepreneur and glamour goddess of fashion Yolanda Cellucci. On Thursday May 11th the Peabody Essex Museum will be holding a cocktail celebration in the exhibit for tickets visit www.pem.org.

LINK TO FULL MAGAZINE https://madmagz.com/magazine/2088629

Chapter Three – 2022

"Give a girl the right kind of shoes and she can rule the world." — Marilyn Monroe

December 2022 Slope Style Revealed Fashionably Late at the Liberty - Scene&Style Magazine Issue #72

The Liberty Hotel's Fashionably Late series can be counted on to deliver high end clientele, a DJ that strikes the mood and craft cocktails. On this occasion it was once again KB Fashion Productions making a statement on the old jailhouse runway showing the season's sexiest ski and snow looks.

The first set of looks to hit Fashionably Late runway were bright pinks from SKEA in psychedelic prints and pastels to catch all eyes down the slopes. Following were bright and bold snow puffers. Pants in soft pastels or striking blues and reds. Each look was paired to perfection with must have ski essentials by stylist Kathy Benharris and team.

Rocking the runway in the second set was casual ski lodge looks. Grabbing all the attention was, classic couples' outfits of denim and block colors, popping purple suits, and a stunning all white faux fur outfit. Most certainly the must have pieces for the night out in the lodge cocktail hour or that cabin by the fire vibe.

The last set of winter threads to hit the Fashionably Late runway featured on and off the slopes style. A standard flannel button up and tee look from CASANOVA men's boutique. The showstopper of the evening was a Brazilian flag inspired suit for female flair, chic moonboots to trench through the snow and a matching male jacket and pant outfit for her beau by her side.

The snow style show styled by Kathy Benharris had it all; full ski suits, fur trim, by the fire fashion was all a sleek peek into the hot trends for the winter weather. The evening was more than the event not to miss but a charity mixer to benefit YES!

YES's mission is to inspire youth through outdoor experiences and leadership opportunities that build confidence and prepare them to summit life's challenges. Give Youth a Chance. Inspired by Dr. Martin Luther King Jr. and his call to dream of possibilities, Richard Williams took his passion for skiing to Boston and founded YES, which was originally called the Youth Activities Commission. Donate at www.yesforkids.org

November 2022 bosFW Hajjar's Preview to Fashion Week Set a Standard - Scene&Style Magazine Issue #71

Fashion Week always brings excitement in a transition of looks and pulling those seasonal accessories. The pre-kickoff was host to iconic designer Denise Hajjar. This legend has dawned decades of runway shows and made her mark as a producer when the morning required a pivot in location.

The New England wind whipped along the Marina Bay Boardwalk which made it undesirable for guests to lounge and admire lavish looks. Hajjar managed to alert the media, make the move indoors and lined up over two hundred seats in the Victory Point entrance for a chic style runway. Her master DJ Denise LaCarubba charmed the crowd as backstage prep concluded and out came the models who were dressed for the occasion of the frigid waterfront weather.

The first set of looks from the Denise Hajjar Boutique featured; golden tones scarves, soft grey stocking hats, bold reds in wraps and fur head bands were features in the first set of looks from the fall/winter collection.

Following were faint greys and snowy white shades in head-to-toe outfits that were perfect for a casual Sunday afternoon. Next up were models strutting sweater weather, a line of hand-woven tops with bold swag prints and always paired with fine faux fur accessories.

After plaids prints and street sway trailed along the perfectly played out runway. A fall/winter collection that featured full length jackets for a hint of style heading into the office or an embroidered button up for a warm layer at an outdoor lunch.

The final set of looks showed everyday leggings in every color to pair perfectly with a long sleeve and scarf. Each outfit also highlighted handbags for the office to a night out in the North End. Following was a pop of color in the seasonal muted trend when a blonde bombshell hit the runway in a lemon and amber layered and ended with business attire of a classic black top to a charcoal pleated skirt reminiscent of look seen in Paris streets.

As always Hajjar hits every aspect of the seasonal trends from classic tops to stylish accessories. Shop her boutique on the Marina Bay boardwalk or visit www.denisehajjar.com.

October 2022 Deep Camel Leather Stuns at Boston Caribbean Fashion Week - Scene&Style Magazine Issue #70

Boston Caribbean Fashion Week has become a staple in the city and a highly anticipated calendar event full of seminars, panel discussions, interactive mix and mingles and much more. In their nineth year of celebration, the week ended with its annual fashion show being held at the chic new space of WarehouseXI.

The evening opened with a warm welcome from Althea Blackford, Creator of BCFW and VStyle Productions. After some heritage acknowledgement the runway opened vibrant and full of color with traditional dance and carnival costumes from Wendy Matthews.

The collection fashion began with Eden Natural Lifestyle Boutique. Featured dresses showed, an everyday look for the bold women in the board room in a classy long cut dress with that taste of flavor in an emerald leopard print, a hot pink with strategic ruffles, popping florals mixed with block bold stripes, a take on a chic Channel baby blue skirt suit with a painted canvas top, and a sheer peek a boo cut lace and mesh showstopper reminiscent of ruby red island night.

Following was a smooth flow with an Afropunk feel from Just Tahanee presented by Bogo Split. The line had it all; crochet knit vest, denim dresses, a deep burgundy and cream crop top and skirt paired with a velvet pullover, right down to the outfit of the evening a deep camel leather crop top with a soaring long sleeve and matching bell bottom pant fit to perfection.

Closing the Caribbean runway was Urban Pigeons a bold speaking collection; donning bright African inspired colors and patterns the pieces were shown in everyday jackets, pants, and handbags to spice up any outfit.

Boston Caribbean Fashion Week is a 7 day stretch of diverse festive fashion events. The focus is to celebrate and promote beauty, Caribbean culture, fashion, and style. To learn more or catch their upcoming events visit www.bostoncfw.com

September 2022 Our Girl Linda's Runway Charity Show Lit Up the Dance Floor - Scene&Style Magazine Issue #69

When fashion season in Boston rolls around many glamours memories of "Our Girl Linda" lighting up the runway come to mind followed by the warmth that only her smile could bring.

Recently the charity geared around Linda Cole Petrosian brought the cities top fashion designers and glitterati out to support St Jude's Children Hospital. The evening opened with Hostess legendary fashion icon and mother to Linda, Yolanda Cellucci welcoming guests and honoring the memory of Linda.

Cellucci kept the event rolling right into the fashion portion where Designer David showed a colling of flowing beauty in long length gowns and a blue dress with a slit up the middle and sparkle that caught everyone's eye.

Following was the timeless and elegant Designer Denise Hajjar. Showing pinks, hand beaded skirts, everyday dress for the office with pattern flare, and an iconic honeycomb piece worn by Linda in print publications.

Up next was a unisex styled jacket set of looks from men's designer and custom tailor Alan Rouleau Couture. He featured outer wear that can suit up a man or a women's taste for fine apparel. Right behind was Frugal Fannies Boutique, a shop well known to lady Linda. Her line was focal on a deep plum velvet shown in a dress and pant suit and a stunning red embroidered dress.

Gliding in next was the stunning Suphi Furs that had a whimsical in white fairytale theme with authentic one-of-a-kind furs. Bella Sera a boutique close to the Cellucci family followed with a collection of dazzling ball room dresses.

Debonair dress Designer Daniel Faucher was next to hit the runway with beautiful beading, a soft color scheme and an olive green, lace trimmed ensemble with couture cuts that had the feel of a royal event awaited.

Closing out the fashion portion of the fundraiser was Sondra Celli is a gem herself in a family of runway royalty. A sister to Our Girl Linda and daughter to the legendary Yolanda Cellucci, Sondra has left her own legacy of glitz and glamour. The collection she showed had a look for everyone from dresses, jackets, ball room right down to a evening out with each piece donning diamonds as bright as Linda's smile.

The night ended with a raffle drawing from the amazing gifts donated brining a total of over $50,000 raised for the St. Jude's Charity. The evening was a class act success highlighting the legend Linda was and closing out the only was she would have; the floor was open for guests to dance the night away.

August 2022 - Shades and Sex Appeal Hit the Swim Boston Runway
Scene&Style Magazine Issue #68

New England is known for its seasonal beauty, one of its most memorizing aspects are the sandy summers on the beaches. As a high-class society a chic sex appeal in swim wear is a must. Recently Performer Media LLC and The Boston Fashion Awards showcased the latest looks on the Swim Boston runway in the grand ball room at the Liberty Hotel.

As guests packed in the vibe was set from Jammin Wizard and live music from the local smooth sounds of Amandi Music. Once the VIPs were seated the MCs of the evening Night Moves Host Joshua Paul and bombshell also former Miss New Hampshire USA Lexi Chin opened the evening.

The first set of fashion to hit the runway came from a respected local designer that knows where to place that alluring tan line, Annmarie LaFauci. The first set of looks from LaFauci to hit the Swim Boston runway featured full piece suits with gold shimmer, tiger print and a stunning pearl toned top paired perfectly with a mini for a poolside outfit. Following featured basic blacks, gold glitter, blue polka dots in two-piece bikinis that flaunted the shape of all women and the beauty in a confident body. The showstopper of the evening came early with shades and sex appeal on a model so fierce head will turn at the roof top pool party on the criss cross marble pattern with chic nude tones.

Bogo Split Boutique was next to show highlighting greens, pinks, beige shades also floral, tropical, and a basic black pattern in the first collection. The second set of looks from the stylish store to hit the Swim Boston runway featured suits for a chic pool party to the bonfire on the beach. Bogo Split also sent men's looks down the Swim Boston runway with fluorescent flair.

During intermission a few of Boston's best were called to the stage to receive their trophies from this past Decembers Boston Fashion Awards 2021. Honored were Chris Donovan Fashion Accessories, Sharon Cox-Cole

Swimwear/Intimate Sarah Rochdi Female Print Model, Angela Cornachio – Scene&Style Publication.

Closing out the catwalk was a collection from designer Shekini. Their first set of looks featured pops of summer solid colors perfectly paired with Jewelinga accessories. Following were looks for the fellas in a bold blue baller short and a more casual outfit in an orange drawstring bottom and throw back high-top shoe. Looping back to the ladies, a hint of floral also a little bit of leopard was the focal point of fabric used in the last set of looks to hit the Swim Boston runway from Shekini that were matched up with the eye-catching pieces from Jewelinga accessories.

The event was a trend setting evening with live entertainment and first-class production. Performer Media is iconic for their premier presentations and VIP red carpets. This years Boston Fashion Awards a Performer product will take place during Boston Fashion Week following the daytime Denise Hajjar show on Sunday October 9th at 7pm in the Liberty Hotel.

July 2022 Hajjar Whirled SS22 Fashion Down the Marina Bay Boardwalk - Scene&Style Magazine

Issue #67

Recently Designer Denise Hajjar showed the season's must haves by her waterfront boutique and brought top entertainment to the Marina Bay Boardwalk at Eat. Drink. Model. It was the second annual fashion show fundraiser to benefit the Saint Mary's Center for Women and Children.

The evening began with guest strolling into the sounds from DJ Denise LaCarubba and taking a seat at their VIP table where over four hundred seats were lined along the bay promenade. There was a sectioned off silent raffle with prizes ranging from a night out at a local restaurant, red sox swag right down to elegant jewelry. All items were donated by Boston's top business and ticket sale proceeds went to giving the women of Saint Mary's Center the help they need.

Denise has always been a well-respected designer with timeless and elegant looks however has a reputation for more than just fashion coming down the runway at her shows. An unexpected break out of dancing opened the night with Kemar Bennett and Essy Sosa from the Fred Astaire gliding down the boardwalk.

Then on perfect cue the fashion began to flow; stripes, floral and psychedelic patterns in full length dresses were a few the first SS22 looks to hit the runway. Ladies say hello to the weekend! The second set of looks featured button-down pinstripes in an array of colors and accessories with flare and a tote that alerted with "hello to the weekend." The outfits showed causal looks, must have hats and handbags for the perfect Sunday stroll down the board walk.

The third set of looks were ones that have a fit for all. The Denise Hajjar Boutique and Marina Bay Living also carry unisex cloths for the mini me. The children's collection had an adorable summer bay style theme. A full line of patriotic toned stars and stripes followed in transition sweaters from the fourth to the fall.

The final set of looks from the Denise Hajjar Boutique SS22 collection to hit the Marina Bay runway featured soft shades in floral, funk and tied died prints perfect for a Friday ensemble into the office or a Saturday afternoon cocktail affair. The last lap of looks is always a party filled with glamour, gorgeous models and family that have been with Denise for decades and are a staple in the city of Boston.

At the conclusion of the runway portion of the Denise Hajjar charity fashion show to benefit Saint Mary's Center for Women, the organization honored a fashionable legend Yolanda Cellucci with the first ever Saint Mary's Women and Children Inspiring Women Award. Yolanda is a woman that have given so much to many, led young women into careers and brought beautiful children into the world that are following in her inspirational footsteps.

Following the Inspiration Award given to the legendary Cellucci, Hajjar herself was honored and given a plethora of gratitude from the Saint Mary's Center for Women with all she has done for the organization in her second fashion show to benefit the center.

The showstopper on the charity runway was designer Denise Hajjar herself grabbing her heels and closing the evening showcasing one of her talents by pairing up with Kemar Bennett and whirled down the runway in an extravagant ball room tango.

Designer Denise Hajjar is iconic for more than just her creations and charity runway shows. Her models are the best in the business, the crème de la creme guests and invites to the top media outlets. Always a chic and classy affair with plenty of party shenanigans! The evening was one to remember and a charitable success.

June 2022 The Ellie Fund Returned to the Runway with a Survivor Strut - Scene&Style Magazine

Issue #66

The night began with a VIP cocktail hour with live piano music, hors d'oeuvres, round tables for mixing and mingling, and auction tables for prizes ranging from; Round trip airfare for two, deluxe accommodations, professional travel specialist to book your trip, and amazing products from shops all over the city of Boston.

When guests were asked to take their seats for the runway portion of the evening it began with WCVB News Center 5 Anchor Maria Stephanos taking stage as the host of the event. She made her way down the catwalk in a stunning black and crystal dress that kept attention on her sparkle outside the newsroom.

The fashion began to flow in gorgeous gowns from Bloomingdales, heels from Boston's Best accessory designer Chris Donovan all featured on the ladies from WCVB and professional models well known here in the hub. The strut down the runway was synced with music from DJ Denise LaCarubba, with hair and makeup on the glamor goddesses provided by, goMLR, Noel McKinnon and Salon Capri. All were gathered and directed by 20202's Boston's Best Stylist Kathy Benharris Owner of KBFashion Productions.

In the second set of looks were perfect short suits for the office or a night out of dining worn by Ellie Fund recipients. The crowed roared as these strong survivors strutted their way down the runway owning their moment to shine. The last set of summer must haves from Bloomingdales collection came down center stage in duo form with current breast cancer patients and their doctors.

The evening ended there and in heart warming form to see bold and beautiful women continue their fight and sashay with a smile showing that the fight is just that, not a defeat a win from within.

The Ellie Fund was founded in memory Eleanor "Ellie" Popkin, who passed away in 1987 at the age of 49 after a courageous 15+ year battle with breast cancer. The Ellie Fund is a continuation of the charitable spirit embodied during her life and provides a way to give back to families who are going through the challenges.

Their mission is to provide essential support services for breast cancer patients to ease the stresses of everyday life, allowing the focus to be on family, recovery, and healing. Providing transportation to medical appointments, light housekeeping, nutritional and grocery assistance, childcare reimbursement, nutritious prepared/delivered meals, and integrative therapy services free of charge through our Healing Together Patient and Family Care Program and Metastatic Breast Cancer Support Program help to relieve a patient's burden while in treatment. The Ellie Fund is honored to provide assistance to breast cancer patients residing in and/or receiving treatment in Massachusetts. To make a donation or learn more about the organization visit www.elliefund.org

May 2022 Powerful Mentors Design for Little Sister Support - Scene&Style Magazine Issue #65

Recently Big Sisters of Boston hit the Copley Plaza Hotel runway in a charitable fashion show to bring together love, support, and donations to the organization that has been severing the city for decades.

Host and Emcee Lisa Hughes from WBZ-TV CBS/Boston opened the evening with heartwarming videos from the little sisters expressing how life changing it is to have a big sister. After guests wiped away the tears of love and gratitude it was time to get the party started.

Stepping up for the girls was Board Member Max Bardeen who got the bidding going in auction off fashion where attendees helped raised over $60,000 in donations at the event.

From there it was time to get the fashion flowing! DJ Maverik set the mood for the Little sisters, big sisters, Role Models, Board Members, and designers to sashay down the runway.

The designers chosen to represent the little sisters, models, and role models were a selection of Boston's best, strong women, and motivators. Kicking off the catwalk was Designer Angelica Timas with a pressed pattern into a deep leather with a lace collar and a stunning sparkle jumper that struck every time a sister moved.

Following were pastel vintage inspired dresses from the IAMKreyol brand. They took to the Big Sisters Boston stage for a fashionable mentorship focused on florals and block custom pieces. Up next was a take on a floral family collection. Showing silk textiles, a superior cerulean pattern paired with bright pops from brand LaLa Bee that strutted down the runway. Designer Melina Cortes-Nmili was arm and arm with a set of sisters from the organization at the charity fundraiser.

Making another loop around was IAMKreyol with off the shoulder courage. Little Sister Jalaya took the Big Sisters Boston stage in a block pattern paired with ruffles look and rocked every step. She showed not only a fashionable stride yet one with strength and pride for her big sister that was under the weather and unable to walk with her. She confessed to some fear yet contested she had come this far and would not turn back!

Closing out the collections was Salmagundi a Hats shop based in the heart of the North End, Boston. Some gentleman support was topped off with classic men's accessories. It's not just the ladies that keep Big Sisters Boston operating yet CEOs, Councilmen, and a collective group of proud men.

Big Sister Association of Greater Boston was founded in 1951 by the Reverend Harold Taylor, Assistant Rector at Christ Church in Cambridge. Their mission is to ignite girls' passion and power to succeed through positive mentoring relationships with women and enrichment programs that support girls' healthy development. To become a Big Sister please visit www.bigsister.org/get-started-on-your-big-sister-journey/

April 2022 Bianchi Brought Boston Couture to the Big Apple - Scene&Style Magazine Issue #64

This past NYFW 2022 showed collections from all over the world and one very particular creator of couture and bridal design, Boston's own Alexandrea Renee Bianchi.

EPN Fashion Week took place this past February in New York City, a power player in the world of fashion. Bianchi was one of many to take the runway and Scene&Style was able to catch up with the creative mind for a little insight into her sewing style.

Ali, what made you chose or were you chosen for NYFW this past spring? Bianchi replied in true artist flow of a pencil and notepad form, "I was given the opportunity to show at NYFW only a month before the show. Although I felt I wasn't fully prepared to show my full potential, I knew this was an opportunity that I couldn't pass up. With that being said, I told the producers I was nervous. I knew I didn't have thew time to come up with a full new collection. They sold me with saying, "This is a new audience, they haven't seen your work yet. I decided to show past pieces I was most proud of and a few new ones as well."

What was the inspiration behind the collection for the show? Ali exclaimed, "The ideas I came up with under pressure and time constraints are some of the best pieces I have ever created. Sleepless nights are where I made some of my favorite pieces for this show. I am an artist. I don't always have a direction when I create, I just follow my heart and trust my eyes. I made three pieces the day before I left for New York. They were my new favorites. Sometimes I don't know the direction I'm going while I create, but there is always one constant. My designs come straight from my heart, emotionally driven, each piece I create has a story behind it. Sometimes driven by pressure, sometimes driven by enlightenment, or just by a beautiful piece of fabric I find. The day of a show, the chaos in my creative soul comes to life. On that day, every single time I feel fulfillment. I am doing what I am supposed to do.

Are you still working in sewing rooms on Newbury? Bianchi was humble in saying, "Currently I am working at L elite Bridal in Boston as a bridal consultant, tailor, and seamstress. I work on high end designer gowns such as Oscar De La Renta, Monique Chuillier, Caroline Herrera, Amsaie, Ines di Santo, Berta, and Vera Wang."

This Boston starlit may spend her days buried in fabric tailoring that one of a kind fit yet keep her on your style radar. Those sleepless nights have taken her from a School of Fashion Design graduate to 2021 Boston Fashion Awards winner in the Best Designer Couture/Formal category.

With classic silhouettes, her designs are edgy, fun, unique and flirty, while remaining timeless, elegant, and feminine. Her pieces are all handmade, custom to the client. With each she focuses on creating a perfectly tailored and constructed garment.

Her collections are a combination of elegance from an era of ladylike class and a modern touch of dark punk with sexy seems. Bianchi is most certainly the future of Boston Fashion and will be showing at StyleWeek on June 16th at the Capital Grill in Providence. Visit AlexandreaReneeCouture.com for more on this lavish designer or follow @alexandrareneefashion

March 2022 Gucci & Adidas Collaborate on the Milan Runway - Scene&Style Magazine

Issue #63

Each time fashion week is on the rise, a vibe of intensity begins to stir of when secrets will be revealed. I am always amazed that classic designers find a way to reinvent themselves. This one happens to hit Scene&Style in a personal way.

I generally write a review from an onsite show I cover yet it's been a bit quite here in Boston. However, the buzz of worldly fashion had a huge headline taking all the attention, "Gucci and Adidas Collaborate for a Fall 2022 Collection." With the most recent shock in news, I thought I would hook up a personal piece.

I must admit when I read about the alliance I immediately rented "House of Gucci" curled up and shut the rest of anything out. I had been dying to watch it anyways and intimately engaged in every minute. The scenery, the pristine vintage fashion, the dark side of glamour, the acting. Lady Gaga, Pacino, well played on the genuine Italian.

The counterpart, Adidas. A strong piece of fabric that has been a part of my life right down to the cleats I scored my first goal in. It was in 2015 that I officially tattooed the brand upon my body. Days after completing the Boston Marathon I bailed on a slow lunch shift at Tia's Waterfront and went to permanently commit to "Impossible is Nothing" and the three stripes.

My heart belongs to the Azzuri and I bleed black and red for AC Milan. Football and fashion, that's me! My two passions are meeting up in Milan to make a cameo. Bellissimo! Taking place in a room of magical mirrors at the Gucci Hub in Milan, the space is the metaphor of #ExquisiteGucci. As Creative Director for Gucci Alessandro Michele writes in his notes on the show, "The clothes, in fact, are capable of reflecting our image in an expanded and transfigured dimension... Wearing them, means to cross a transformative threshold where we become something else."

The line between streetwear and luxury fashion has become so blurred, it's downright disappeared. Now, one of the top Italian fashion houses and leading athleisure legends come together to creative and combine. Gucci's Michele has spent the last few years reimagining the classic cuts and styles with the signature prints. He's done it again, combining Gucci with iconic German sportswear brand Adidas' iconic trefoil and three stripes.

Suits, jackets, dresses, and knitwear were just some pieces sent down the runway with a mixture of textures, layering and vibrant colors that accentuated. The classic three stripes were sewn down the seams of vibrant purple, green, red, and blue suits, as well as the tops of matching headwear pieces from baseball caps to berets.

Metallics and studs exploded on the runway, along with the use of furs and leathers which created electric and elegant looks. Draping oversized coats on top of mixed pattern ensembles contrasted well with the sheer and intricate lace work in geometric lines.

The Gucci x Adidas collection reimagines what the classic Adidas tracksuit could be, turning it into a hybrid formal tracksuit with the Adidas trefoil and Gucci underneath it. Accessorized head scarves, gloves and handbags also got some Adidas love.

The stitching, the placement of the three strips on the blue valor suit, solid tones, bold patterns all had me sold. The price tag is a bit out of my budget yet, as I imbedded in myself and the brand says, "Impossible is Nothing."

February 2022 Seductive Swim and Bedroom Lingerie hit the Runway - Scene&Style Magazine

Issue #62

Recently cupids arrow struck at the historic Liberty Hotel when Dynasty models and their shapely curves hit the runway rocking designer AnnMarie LaFauci's latest lingerie and swim wear collection in a Fashionably Late presentation.

The house was jam packed with vibes off the turn tables from DJ Frank White to set the mood. The red carpet for InBoston Magazine was laid out for guests, local celebrities, sponsors to mingle until the heads began to turn and all attention on the divas strutting in an exclusive sexy collection.

The first set of looks to hit the Liberty Hotel runway from designer AnnMarie LaFauci featured seduction in glitter and gold. Pieces of, a beige tone, strategic lay of glitter, ravish cuts of the stitch, and dynasty dolls left the guests drooling for more from the swim and lingerie line.

The focal piece in the second set was a classic Marilyn lingerie costume after was a black bikini with fish net wrap for the summer. A stunning leopard print swimsuit that highlights the beach body. Followed by dark and metallic paired with feathers, chic leathers, and strategic cuts for alluring style in the bedroom.

Closing out the collection was a sequence and sparkle theme; paired with winter furs, seductive burgundy velvet, daunting dynasty stares and a classic fashionably late runway piece of a 70's swim style from designer Ann Marie LaFauci.

The evening was desirable event filled with delectable cocktails from the hotel bar, music, mingling and a fashion show featuring a line of inviting attire that any lady would love to dawn, and any man would enjoy the view. AnnMarie LaFauci's collection can be viewed and purchased off her Instagram page @annmarielafaucidesigns.

January 2022 Boston Fashion Celebrates as a Community - Scene&Style Magazine Issue #61

2021 was a year we all found thanks and gratitude for the simplicities in life as they returned to our social schedules. Coming back in true professional form was the 10th annual Boston Fashion Awards presented by Performer.com. The event took place at the Liberty Hotel Boston this past December to honor the cities talent and celebrate face to face with family that supports and helps one another grow in our community.

In the grand ball room of the historic hotel was a magnificent setup from the red carpet, perfectly placed runway, and lighting to highlight the high-end production put on by Performer.com. The evening got under way with Host Alberto Vasallo from NBC10 Boston/ El Mundo Boston and Co-Host Gabriela Taveras 2018 Miss Massachusetts / Entrepreneur warming up the room with the duos class and humor while welcoming in the VIP guests to their seats.

The fashion began to emerge with iconic wedding dress diva Candice Wu Couture. A full collection of a white beaded fairytale flowed down the runway. Following was the first award of the event, "2021 Best Beauty Salon" went to Salon Monet and Owner Shelly Mendes. They are the official salon for NECN and have been giving Boston stylish locks for 14 years solid on Newbury Street.

Up next was the announcement for the "2021 Best Male Model/Actor" going to Lord Fenestor whom at the moment was hiding somewhere in the hotel. To accept his award was debonair designer Gnazo Zadi who took to the stage as Lord is often seen donning his custom-made suits. Continuing with the presentation was "2021 Best Makeup Artist" going to Owner of Haus of Beauty Heather Schofield for her continued contributions to the beauty behind the brush.

Next was a special gift, the "2021 Boston Fashion Awards Lifetime Achievement" given to the one and only Jay Calderin our leader and founder of Boston Fashion Week. A man that is innovative, a creator, a teacher at the School of Fashion Design, book author and icon to us all.

After was a category full of contributors who make our city fashionable, "2021 Best Fashion Stylist" given to a man that gives his heart to us all, industry leader and Saks 5th Avenue Guru, MC, Award Winning Journalist Gustavo Leon. Leon rushed past accepting his award to grab fellow nominee Bryan X Miguel to join him on stage. Giving a heartfelt speech how this fashion community builds each other to greatness. A personality never to be replicated Gustavo of course basked in his moment by sashaying down the runway for the press pit and giving host Gabby a little salsa dance.

Continuing was "2021 Designer Evening/Club Wear" went to Samuel Vartan who has been making his mark in the Boston industry for ten plus years with his European vibe. Vartan recently held a lavish show debuting his fall/winter collection that had a dark night feel of stunning sequence, silver seduction, and chic business attire.

Up next was, "2021 Best Designer Couture/Formal" a category packed full of pure talent. The winner went to Ali Bianchi, with Alexandra Renee Fashion. A diva dress designer who spends her free time sewing for worldly brands when away from her own collection. This Massachusetts native, School of Fashion Designer graduate has only begun. This talented lady has more up her sleeve to be seemed and contributions to the industry that have yet to be seen! The "2021 Best Photographer" award went to Mo Mendes shooting still fashion and art in Boston for 11 years with Granimo Studios.

Wrapping up the awards portion of the evening was the category for "2021 Best Runway Model" was a gem to our city. A woman with brains being a Suffolk Science contributor, beauty as a former Miss Bulgaria USA, Dynasty Model Elena Kollarova. A true professional in our industry as she was unable to accept her award, she was backstage being dolled up to walk for the final collection.

Closing out the production was a designer who needs no introduction with her worldly reputation and celebrity red carpet gowns, Isabel Lopez. The "Goddess of Glamour" showed a line of dresses with hand sewn beaded detail dripping from each piece. The culture, the vibrant colors, mesmerized from a gifted designer who owned the evening and the runway.

The 2021 Boston Fashion Awards was a victor all on its own. The night was full of top shelf entertainment, local celebrities, and class production from Performer.com. The evening is one that takes months of preparation from the crew and contributions from the city. The focus of the event is to put spotlight on the diverse talent located within the Boston fashion community. It was a blessing to gather as a family and celebrate one another. Visit www.bostonfashionawards.com to see what is in store for 2022.

**"One is never over-dressed or under-dressed with a Little Black Dress."
—Karl Lagerfeld**

December 2021 Malaika Dons Excessive Fashion - Scene&Style Magazine Issue #54

Recently the Hilton Boston, Woburn was host to "Excessive Fashion" featuring Joe Malaika and plenty of high-class entertainment from celebrity guests to local style.

The second you stepped off the elevator the show had already begun. The red carpet was crawling with famous faces, artists, stylist all dressed to impress. Local creator Jewlinga had set up shop front and center showing off her precious stones and accessories that were also donned on the runway.

The guest list was all it was expected to be with every seat filled, special celebrity guest rapper King Combs the one and only P Diddys son along with royalty, Her Highness Queen Dr. Best Kemigsia. The press pit was full of the city's top media outlets, photographers with Hill Zu as the featured. The evening opened with tribute to Joe's nation of Uganda and the traditional Tooro Anthem followed by the United States National Anthem.

Firing off the flair for the event was MC Gustavo Leon (crowned Boston's Best Stylist the following week) draped in a custom-tailored Joe Malaika suit. He welcomed to the stage a vibrant tribal dance with Ugandan inspiration, which Malaika originates from the African Islands and his designs show detail in the texture of his culture.

From there the fashion made way with At Cozy opening the glowing vintage New York style runway. Style such as a funk zebra with a taxi cap, power heels and a chunky chain from Jewlinga was one of many power looks. Glamour gowns, a glitter and gold cocktail dress paired with a custom NB Design feather mask perfect for a cocktail affair, and every day attire were highlighted from the trio of ladies. Which all can be purchased at her boutique in the Chestnut Hill Mall.

Following was star lit performance from singer Amanda Mena who put truth behind "sing your heart out." The local American Idol contestant amongst her long list of credentials put some power behind it when a mic malfunction left her with no music and riding solo with her beautiful voice and beat from the crowd clap.

Starting back up the style was designer Solome Katongole showing bright African colors, bold patterns in dresses, rompers, crop tops and pant suits. Hair and makeup of the evening from Salon Eva Michelle make an extra statement paired with the striking color tones of the collection.

After a final intermission it was time for the dapper don himself to give the guests what they came for. Malaika opened with an athleisure stride. Custom street wear suited up for yourself was the first set of looks from the SS22 Collection. Following was a women's line of sequins and silk. An assembly of a floral and Ugandan inspired color tone owned the runway.

A classic black and white men's suit was one to remember as Malaika took it to another level or creative cuts with the sequins detail and pattern placement. Popping out right after was a solid neon green women's pant suit with a sleeveless top.

Demanding attention was a collection of baby doll pink and polka dot suits for men and women, Malaika took it to another level of creative cuts with the sequins detail and pattern placement. The crowed got their price of admission when during a fitting King Combs mix playing an appealing male model lost the jacket at the end of the runway to reveal his toned skin. However, the King of the night was mini model Lawrence donning a red suit, with sequins MJ inspiration who owned the evening.

Closing out the Malaika SS22 Collection was a line of suits for men and women in peacock blue and strategic belts, featuring a feathered pattern with chic black focus and bold tone outlines.

Malaika made his mark in the Excessive Fashion evening full of live entertainment, superb style, and high-end design. The event was also a celebration of Joe's birthday and after his final walkthrough thanked guests, sponsors, and staff as a production that large takes a full team. His collection can be purchased at www.joemalaika.com

**November 2021 Vartan W21 Collection Debuted at Henderson House
Scene&Style Magazine Issue #53**

Post fashion week Designer Samuel Vartan revealed deep bold expressions in his winter collection known as "Dark City." The event took place at the historical Henderson House in Weston, Ma. Vartan and company welcomed in fall with the unveiling of a long-awaited collection with a party that was put on pause from March of 2020.

The evening began with hors d'oeuvres and champagne rounding the room. With brand Financial Advisor Semi Spahillari greeting guests and honoring CEO John Randall of "Amigo" a service provider over the last 50 years for children and adults with autism. Amigo was the charitable partner of the event receiving a portion of proceeds from the silent auction.

The venue was absolutely breath taking, the fashion was set up to flow down a grand staircase and models to mingle through out the rooms to orchestrated audio.

Opening was a stunning chic businesswomen look, a classic black pant suit with strategic cuts fit for the board room to transitions into martini meeting. Silver seduction followed, a classic black sleeveless with a striking streak of metallic made its way down the runway.

A dark night in Armenia was portrayed with a stunning sequence of classic black in a line of chic and edgy dresses. Showed pieces were Sparkle and mesh, a simple peek a boo with leather pockets, a long full-length button down. Continuing with; leather trim to a skirt suit, a zip up with imbraided texture, a hallowed dark hooded look, cropped velvet, pinstripes, and leather details.

As the collection continued, shimmer tones fit for office and feminine attire sashayed. Dangerous dresses alongside chic business looks of took to the catwalk. The showstopper of the evening was a backless golden sex appeal silhouette. Followed was a silver suit set, aurum metal colored button down, an eye demanding black cocktail, a printed leather gown with a deep cross statement, a full-length velvet with pop up cuts.

Then a staircase closing piece, a dark side of an all-black old-world robe with laced wings worn the graceful actress Naira Zakaryan. The final walkthrough glided in grand fashion around the spectacular venue from the Samuel Vartan Collection with the designer himself taking center stage to show his gratitude to his team, guests, son, and amazing wife.

The evening did not end there, Vartan guided all into a room set for the showing of the tailor to Naira Zakaryan's movie "Gate to Heaven" in which Samuel dressed her for the premier. From there all were invited to another round of appetizers, drinks, and dancing in the main hall late into the night.

Vartan's Winter collection, known as "dark city," is about being a musician, growing up in the 1980's, living and breathing rock and roll and city night life. It is as gothic and cool as Paris, Prague, Berlin, and London after dark. Nestled into his choices of leather, suede, cashmere, tweed, satin, and velvet are whispers of the art deco movement, film noir and the classic architecture of Europe's oldest cities. You can learn more about Vartan on his website or shop his latest collection at
www.SamuelVartan.com

October 2021 bosFW Bianchi Showed an Essence of Spray Style - Scene&Style Magazine

Scene&Style officially closed out Boston Fashion Week with taking on the night life. Star seamstress Alexandra Renee Bianchi brought together a crew for a one of a kind, must see show. A collaboration of Boston's best! The evening was hosted at Hava, MC Jason from Night Moves, DJ Big Tunez, Party Boston and the 617 Productions team set the scene for a night to remember.

Commanding attention from the first set of looks was French flair, a classic black mini meshed with horse feather detail. Following was a line of sheer elegance, pieces of bold blues for a rooftop cocktail affair, chic silvers, and creative cuts, with a tie died mini meant to make a statement.

Along came classics paired perfectly; a chic red velvet pant and black bustier cut top, bold pastel pops, all with fashionable flow. An essence of spray style showed; A tie died mini, off the shoulder with deep paint and prints, black splatter style mini meant for a Hava night, and a hot pink hoedown sort of sway with horse detail ravaged the runway from the SS22 Collection from Alexandra Renee Bianchi.

Making the backstage magic happen and the flawless faces of top models were perfected by Jacquelyn Vokey whose mission is to make every person she meets, happier and a more beautiful. Jacquelyn Started at Christian Dior many years ago as a Beauty Consultant and Makeup Artist and has now started her own business. With awards such as Saks Fifth Avenue 2009, Betsey Johnson 2010 Vokey has the right look for you. Contact her at jvokey12@gmail.com or follow @jacquelynvokeymua

The stellar hair styles were provided by Charles Maksou the Dry Cut Craftsman. An Eight time "Boston's Best", Charles continues the legacy of the Dry Cut from the legendary John Sahag. The method was founded in Paris, and Charles brought it to Boston in 1998, and was awarded "Boston's Best Dry Cut" after opening his first studio. With over 30 years of experience, what he enjoys most is being a sculptor. He loves creating the perfect shape for a client to enhance their natural features. To book an appointment call 617.797.4141 or visit drycutboston.com.

Coming from behind the curtain to the press pit was Robert Paris with MonsterJazz Photography grabbing the eye-catching angle. Also, iconic photographer Richard Bertone. Vokey and Bertone have been working together for years on projects such as BETSEY JOHNSON NEWBURY ST. with SHAG Hair Salon, Nicole Romano, & Project Runway Designer Kelly Dempsey, and much more.

Richard has been doing photography for over 35 years in Boston, Rhode Island, New York, and surrounding areas. Richard works with ideal clients such as Neiman Marcus, Saks Fifth Avenue Nicole Romano, Donna Karen New York, and works several well know celebrities. The best part about Richard is his work is privy to high end clients. You can follow Richard on Instagram or contact him at RICHARDBERTONE photography 617-733-6056.

The star of the evening is a Boston School of Fashion Design graduate from 2015 that has made a name for herself. Alexandra Renee Bianchi who was born and raised in the Boston area. While studying at SDF she fell in love with the couture, custom, bridal and eveningwear realm of the fashion world. As she creates her garments, she strives for quality and sustainability. With classic silhouettes, her designs are edgy, fun, unique and flirty, while remaining timeless, elegant, and feminine. Her designs are all handmade, custom to the client. With each client she focuses on creating a perfectly tailored and constructed garment.

October 2021 bosFW Hajjar Hosts First Ever Boston Fashion Week Show on the Bay Scene&Style Magazine Issue #52

Officially opening Boston Fashion Week, October 3rd on a gorgeous Sunday afternoon at the Marina Bay boardwalk was legendary Denise Hajjar with a 260-seat sold out show. With sponsors, Siros, Boardwalk

Pizza, Beauty Boston, Donato's Gelato, Port 305, Blue, Victory Point adding the gift bags and treats served.

Kicking off the event was Lady DJ, Denise LaCarubba Boston's sexiest me and spinning music to suit the style. The first looks to hit the runway were classic back and white, a chic and fun take on a night out or a Sunday stroll on the docks. Followed was, plaids and earmuffs, knits and furs, the layers that are always a must for the New England foliage season. In the next section was a showstopper! A leather look of chic meets Alexander Wang punk style for a board meeting that can transform into cocktail hour.

After were, winter mini's, cute cover ups and Hajjar staple head wraps and all seasonal accessories. Who said black and white is boring? Hajjar put together a full walk through of style with patterned skirts, pom hats, chic jackets, comfy sweaters all that can transition from day wear at the office to casual style. Pairing up with painter turned legging designer, Irina Gorbman Hajjar closed the show with athleisure looks. A sweater with swag, a pom hat, and cute boots, to custom artwork pants, for the perfect Sunday style!

In each mini collection showed were men's looks from head to toe that can be found at Marina Bay Living, a spin off and just a few doors down for the Denise Hajjar boutique. The event ended with a heartfelt thank you from Designer Denise Hajjar for all those that have supported her through her career and being a apart of the first ever Boston Fashion Week Show on the Marina Bay Boardwalk.

Boston born and raised, Denise Hajjar inherited her design interest and talent from her grandmother who was also a designer in Damascus, Syria. Denise decided after graduating from The School of Fashion Design, would stay close to her roots and start a business in Boston. With over 35 years in her own design business, Denise has established herself as a top designer. Hajjar having sold her creations nationally to department stores, specialty boutiques and individual clients worldwide.

Now blissfully married Denise has settled on the Marina Bay Boardwalk in Quincy where the Denise Hajjar Boutique has transitioned into catering to her local clients.

September 2021 bosFW THE CUE Opens Fashionably Late - Scene&Style Magazine

A much-needed cure for the fashion itch in the city of Boston came from Lindsay Tia and her boutique, "THE CUE." Tia being a preview to Boston Fashion Week and the long-awaited opening of the season "Fashionably Late" at the Liberty Hotel.

KB Fashion Productions and Tia are no stranger to the catwalk of the historic old jailhouse. The team wasted no time heating up the packed three floors with gorgeous Dynasty Models and the fall must have trends.

A taupe leather pant, top and jacket look appeared first and made a statement for the theme to follow. Next was a simple little black dress paired with a snakeskin green jacket for a perfect Friday night out. From there a classic black leather pant and beige top, closing the first sequence was a tawny toned tight leather top and pant look.

Second on stage was a flow of autumn orange and standard blacks. A spaghetti strap dress with daunting cuts and a foliage pattern made it's way down the runway. Followed by; a chic caramel skirt and a copper velvet button down made for a cute fall outfit. Last was a tan business pant paired with a black leather crop top, slap on a suit jacket and a great look for the office.

Closing out the event was a line of dresses. A cerulean colored layered off the shoulder, vintage lace style showed "THE CUE" has those sweet Sundays looks as well. Then came a patterned Channel brocade mini and the showstopper of the evening was a nude wrap showing all the right curves.

The final walk through for Tia and her fall collection carried at THE CUE received a rave review from the packed hotel. The looks paused for pictures and the dynasty divas draped in this season must haves brought back live fashion to Boston.

The Cue is a style lounge carefully curated for the trendy professional. Whether you're going from the boardroom to the bar, from day to night, or from busy weekdays to lazy Sundays, we all want to look our best. The Cue has everything you need to feel confident in our look - anytime, anywhere.

Lindsay Tia Reilly is the Founder and Owner of THE CUE, as well as the creator of the popular Lindsay Tia brand. Originally from Quincy, MA, Lindsay has a degree in Fashion Merchandising from Laselle College, with a certification from the London College of Fashion where she learned from several iconic fashion designers.

Upon returning home, Lindsay took her experiences from abroad and launched Lindsay Tia, a lifestyle brand focusing on luxury handbags sourced and sewn in the USA. Her signature line, the Bravery Bag, which spotlights the everyday courage shown by women across the country, defied the odds of making it in the handbag business and continues to be a beacon of support for many brave women who overcome their troubles daily.

Through THE CUE, Lindsay combines her heritage of working with high quality goods, her keen eye for style, and her desire to empower women through fashion. THE CUE serves as a local establishment for those looking for day-to-night style, "confidence through clothing," and a powerhouse women crew.

Located in Milton, right outside Boston, this 2nd floor style loft is unlike any other boutique. Shop online at www.shopthecue.com , shop in store, hire a stylist, or even host your event in their trendy NYC style space.

September 2021 Vartan Reveals Deep Bold Expression in his Latest Collection - Scene&Style Magazine

This coming Saturday at the historical Henderson House in Weston, Ma. Samuel Vartan Collections will welcome in fall with unveiling a long-awaited collection and host a party put on pause from March of 2020.

Scene&Style was able to sit down with the mastermind behind the sewing machine, Samuel Vartan. We got an opportunity to catch up and chat about the upcoming show and designs to hit the runway. Samuel, what was the inspiration behind the collection? He replied with enthusiasm, "The inspiration for our Autumn/Winter collections comes from a confident woman who is strong willed, smart, and most likely a leader in her work field. She is well versed worldly matters, works hard but definitely finds time to play and pamper herself. She does not chase trends but rather sets them. She definitely marches to the beat of her own drum, and she's gently opinionated on subjects that are close to her heart and mind. The clothes themselves are designed from several themes and topics close to my heart. They have a lot to do with my state of mind during these dramatic season." Vartan continued, "Black becomes the dominating color sprinkled with a few metallic colors as well as grays and the occasional wine/burgundy colors. I love fall foliage, so a lot of these clothes look amazing against this landscape riddled with all these colorful leaves. The collection is also somewhat on the bold side; definitely edgier than our Spring/Summer looks. At one point we had nicknamed the collection Dark City for my love of cities with an edge, skyscrapers, the asphalt jungle is the ultimate playground for this woman and collection. My personal influences come from my love places like Montreal, New York, Los Angeles, Berlin, London and Paris. Other influences are architecture, travel, industrial design, film, and music."

Samuel, how did you get to choosing a venue with such history? Vartan replied, "We came upon the venue The Henderson House through mutual friends, and we chose it for its opulent setting and the mood it created for this time of the year."

Moving past the show, what is next for Samuel Vartan Collection in the coming months? Samuel said, "Our goals going forward for the Samuel Vartan Collections brand is to continue pushing our online sales found at www.samuelvartan.com and to concentrate on building up on our e-Commerce site. We would like to start revisiting our wholesale business with specialty boutiques which has always been our specialty from the beginning. We are also working with films, actors, and directors such as in the recent case of our dear lead model/actress Naira Zakaryan who recently wore one of our gowns at the Boston premiere of Jivan Avetisyan's Gate to Heaven in which she starred in. We are getting more and more requests from local celebrities who want to be dressed by Samuel Vartan! Very exciting"!

Finally, Samuel You have quite a team behind you, elaborate on who handles what part of the business for you. Vartan boasted, "Our team derives of only a small handful of personalities who have always had a desire to be a part of this brand. Semi Spahillari is our advisor in all things related to financials; he's our numbers man. Eddie Vo handles all things related to media, visuals and most importantly he is the man behind the creation of the website. Also photo shoots, video and drone shoots as well as other surprises you will see at our event this Saturday the 23rd of October"!

With a prideful smile Vartan closed, "Finally my lovely life partner and wife Kiky Papadopoulos handles all the "little things" and basically wherever there are loose ends… For example, she's in charge of decorations (flowers, balloons, gift bags, etc.) also the organization of the silent auction items."

Samuel Vartan didn't look for fashion, Fashion found him. Vartan was born in Athens, Greece. A few years later, his family moved to Beirut, Lebanon and finally to Montreal, Canada where he has lived for most of his life before coming to the United States in 2003. Having studied illustration and communications in college, Vartan did not set his sights on fashion at first.

As a teenager, Vartan already had a strong sense of style and spent most of his money on clothing—pushing the closet space in his family home to the limits. Always playing music as part of a band and passionate about illustration and film, the idea of fashion design did not begin to creep into Vartan's consciousness until his first job working on window displays at a retail-clothing store. Putting things together and experimenting with different combinations became his favorite responsibility.

Around the same time, Vartan made the connection between music and fashion when he tagged along with a musician friend who was being fitted for stage clothes. Vartan became enraptured by what the designer was doing and tried sketching his own designs.

He smoothly translated his skills as an illustrator into fashion design and quickly began running a business out of his parent's home: working on sketches in his bedroom and bringing designs to reality at his mother's kitchen table. Friends, musicians and even the model/waitresses from his favorite café were soon wearing his designs. By 1998 Vartan had earned tremendous accolades and won the support of the fashion community at his first official show.

Vartan's designs are highly personal. His history as a musician, illustrator, animator, film lover, and world traveler culminate in each and every piece he creates. He debuts his collections twice a year as Fall/Winter and Spring/Summer.

Spring/Summer shows us the lighter side of the designer. Nicknamed "Mediterraneo," this collection is a nod to his birthplace in Greece, but also travels to places like North Africa, Turkey, Italy, Spain and the South of France. Soft hues of blue, white, and gray are punctuated by rich orange and red, reflecting the rustic beauty of the culture, architecture, music, and food of a coastal vacation. The smell of salty air mingles with swirling chiffon and relaxed linen, taking the wearer on a journey to the place of Vartan's birth and beyond.

No matter where Vartan chooses to travel in his designs, he remains true to his sense of style. Heavily influenced by the refined, well-tailored, classic styles of the early 1960's, Vartan's collections are not influenced so much by current trends as they are by the designer's sense of style. Looking back to timeless female icons like Sophia Lauren, Vartan cuts his clothes with a kind of elegance and minimalism that simply enhance the wearer rather than stealing attention from her.

Vartan works from the philosophy that "fashion is here today, gone tomorrow, but style lasts forever" and he believes that his designs can be worn for a lifetime. He is involved in every step of the design process so that his standards for quality are always perfectly maintained.

Vartan's Winter collection, known as "dark city," is about being a musician, growing up in the 1980's, living and breathing rock and roll and city night life. It's as gothic and cool as Paris, Prague, Berlin, and London after dark. Nestled into his choices of leather, suede, cashmere, tweed, satin and velvet are whispers of the art deco movement, film noir and the classic architecture of Europe's oldest cities.

Guests have been on hold since March of 2020 ready to redeem their purchase. This Saturday Samuel Vartan Collections will debut new elegant, dark, and sophisticated pieces. The evening will be class as always with music, food, fashionable faces and more. An event not to be missed, dress to impress. Grab your tickets to the Henderson House this Saturday.

September 2021 New England Fashion Week - Scene&Style Magazine Issue #51

When September rolls around you savor those last few beach days while getting that wardrobe read for fall fashion. You mark your calendar for the runway events that will showcase your must have looks and grab tickets to a can't miss occasion like New England Fashion Week.

With Rhode Island Fashion Week just passing, Boston Fashion Week set for October, NEFW was Sept 18th-19th, an event all its own focusing on the entire region and what talent they have to offer.

The 6th Annual New England Fashion Week that featured 16 designers and 60 models was held at W hotel in Boston and Hosted by: Shawn Pereira with performances by Nora StOnge, Katrina Crim, Sierra Reinitizer and Armaya Doremi.

The opening designer for NEFW was a local dapper whom dons his own collection. Gnazo Zadi told a darks nights tale with a seductive line of sheer pieces. VaVa Designs was followed by; The R Gene, Renu Gupta, Mariana, Lidiya Romanchuk, Erika Sky, Qlynton.

Jack Attack Clothing sent out sequins and lace looks that rocked down the runway. The collection from gave off a classic dress mixed with a funk vibe. Followed was, Tailor Fit a gentleman's customs tailor service, and closing the evening was Bel Ti Boutique who is committed to promoting confidence by providing a wide range of apparel to fit any women's unique sense of style.

Sunday's runways started off with designer Marcia, an Emerson College Alum with a collection focused for the mature women to feel empowered and confident. Closing the week was Gradon a SDF Boston graduate who found passion for design at an early age through construction with Legos.

Cynthia Hudson – Director, produced the fashionable event, with right hand board members Photographer Michael Rose, Jessica Leigh Pederson – Asst Director and Kayla Cinus – Asst. Director. The affair was a collaboration from many; Toni and Guy, Wonder Events, Bogo Split, Craig Sutton, Ultimate Salon Professionals, Enjoy Hair Care, School of Fashion Design Boston, W Hotel Boston, Shea Models rocked the runway, special guests such as Miss Massachusetts was seen sashaying around, food, a VIP cocktail hour, special swag bags that made each night one to remember.

August 2021 Shaco Couture Collection Highlights Wilderness Looks Scene&Style Magazine Issue #50

Sharon Cox-Cole, the CEO of Shaco Couture Designs, is an award-winning designer who hails over 30 years of experience in the fashion industry, combining original designs and haute couture skills with a keen sense of how to enhance each woman's fashion profile, style and fit. Scene&Style was able to catch up with the decorated designer for a little Q&A!

It has been confirmed there will be live shows this fall at Boston Fashion Week 2021; will you be participating in any? "Yes, I will be doing one just not sure which yet. I am excited to get back out on the runway." You have branched out into producing a men's collection. What has inspired that? Sharon Replied, "I have always wanted to do one. In the mid 80's I designed a lot of mend apparel. Plus many folks have been requesting it.I also did it to show my diversity in fashion with my theme being all people inclusive. In other words, I am an overall fashion artist. No genre is off limits. Be it; day, street wear, evening, business, active, weddings or whatever the occasion." Are you currently working on a line, or have you recently released one? Cox-Cole closed out the interview with; "I am! Currently the collection "It's the art in me" part 2" of SS2022. I released part 1 earlier this year".

Sharen has been in the business for some time, In 2018, Shaco went to another level when her fashions were published by two prestigious international fashion magazines: She was profiled three times in both the British Vogue Magazine and Vanity Fair, that highlighted the top emerging designers on the international stage.

Cole participated in the highly acclaimed Boston Fashion Awards and is a two-time winner of the coveted award for Boston's Top Couture/Formal Designer 2017 and 2018. She also participated in the famous Paris Fashion Week 2016 and received 3rd place recognition for Outstanding International Couture Collection. She displayed Shaco's innovative fashions at New York Fashion Week, 2016. At the 2014 and 2015 Atlantic City Fashion Week at Caesar's Palace, her fashions were displayed to a sold-out auditorium. In Spring, 2015 Cole was honored to be one of the five designers chosen to showcase at the Minnesota Historical Society of Minneapolis, MN, celebrating 50 years of Ebony Fashion Fair. In December 2015, Cole was the featured designer at a successful show fundraiser, benefitting Habitat for Humanity at the prestigious Westin Copley Plaza in downtown Boston.

In 2013, Cole received a prestigious award from KaribNation.Inc: Recognizing Remarkable Contribution to Caribbean Fashion in Washington DC. In 2012, Cole participated in Caribbean Fashion Week in Kingston, Jamaica that draws well-known international designers. As a result, she was recognized with as one of the three nominees for the Emerging Fashion Designers award.

Cole is described as ahead of her time and culturally diverse in her fashion genius, with fashions that are flawless, showing great attention to detail. Cole has undoubtedly established herself as a designer with designs for real women yet elegant enough for the supermodel. To purchase or view Shaco Collections visit www.shacocouture.com .

July 2021 DreamRose - New England Runways Have Re-Opened

Fashion is a physical form of expression for the consumer, a creative contribution for the designer. With the pandemic taking so much from 2020, quarantine became a way of life that forced runways around the world to press pause. Life has a way of recreating itself, the design industry took to virtual paths, innovative ways to present new collections. Fashion always finds a way and now it is back to front row seats, models strutting seasonal styles as the runways of New England have reopened.

First to hit the scene was the acclaimed Style Week Northeast on June 10th where they transformed the Capitol Grill patio of Providence to a pristine catwalk. It was the twentieth season for the Rhode Island-based fashion event that was labeled as a "micro-fashion week."

The evening featured three runway shows, including the SEED Student Design Challenge showing seven designs made by students from the Lincoln School in Providence as well as presentations by two local veteran designers Lalla bee and Jess Abernethy. There was an all-new SEED Student Design Art Challenge involving self-portraits made with various materials done by students at the Grace School.

The SEED Student Design Challenge was hosted by executive producer of "The Rhode Show," Ashley Erling and Coast 93.3's Morning Show personality, Doug Palmieri. Each piece was critiqued by a panel of eight judges, including handbag designer Kent Stetson; philanthropist Ting Barnard; real estate entrepreneur Christina Rosciti; LEIGH CEO Tracey Cugno, Rhode Island Monthly senior editor Jamie Coelho; OPTX CEO Lynne Diamante; Meeting Street School COO Susan Keller and real estate entrepreneur Michael Sweeney. The winning garment came from Isabel Gorbea representing the Lincoln School winning a $500 scholarship donated by the Friendship Foundation.

After the SEED presentation, Lalla bee sent her sexy floral based collection down the runway. It featured form fitting cocktail dresses, pops of hot pink and pastels. Designer, Jess Abernethy closed the show by debuting a brand-new collection. The pieces brought in an earthy tone of subtle greens in her iconic funk style.

On June 18th, the I AM KREYOL Collection came back roaring with a live presentation in downtown Boston in support of the Juneteenth celebration. The event was the first time the brand had made a public appearance and hosting an event since the pandemic. Designer Fontaine, stomped right back into the spotlight with a powerful installation.

The evening kicked off with vibrant Host; Bernaldine "Truth" educating and the history behind the Freedom Event "Standing on Legacy," giving, love, respect to the city of Boston in a Juneteenth experience.

Following was a Boston version of Badou. Local Miranda Rae gave her soulful version on a classic, shared original work from herself and grabbing full attention with her magnetic voice. Following and flowing through the entire evening was DJ Slick Vik with funk, hip hop, and top jams.

The Iam Kreyol Collection came charging out onto the flight of stairs towering over the city subway station. Slick Vik threw out a chilling mix as, the stunning style displayed many messages of "I Am Free." Making it clear that the power of freedom had arrived. After Vibrant Host, Bernaldine brought Designer Joelle on stage to give her passionate story to the celebration and brand awareness.

Kréyol is a woman's high fashion brand that aims to impact the world, one garment at a time. Their "for women, by women" initiative allows for your purchase to directly affect the livelihood of a woman artisan or entrepreneur. They believe in economic development and sustainability through artistry.

Being a family affair with Fontaine's brother Stanly expanding in his own men's wear "Paul Rameau." Mother, Yolette Fontaine has been Joelle's inspiration through her own sewing story. The eldest girl of five children she was given a passport and $500 as a gift from her older brother. She turned that into a business and began traveling to the United States & Panama, purchasing goods to re-sell in Haiti. This endeavor afforded her the opportunity and means to thrive successfully in a space where poverty was the norm. By 1980, she had put herself through engineering school, was a teacher and seamstress. Still making her mark, Yolette sews pieces for the brand.

As a young woman Joelle, aspired to be an architect. After many life journeys at such a young age come 23, was invited by a friend to a fashion conference at NYFW decided to submit the only three garments she had ever created to be considered as a potential designer. At that time Fontaine was an artist not a designer. She had absolutely no idea, but had passion, grit, talent, the audacity to believe she belonged there. She was immediately accepted, with only seven days to showtime. She created her first collection of 12 full looks, entitled "Kaleidoscope". Then moved to New York a year later, the rest is history.

Creator Fontaine has brought the Boston's fashion standards to a height. Her powerful looks that continue to come through were bold and speaking for themselves. Pieces were made specifically for the show and can be purchased at www.iamkreyol.com

The event was and opportunity for Fontaine to announce, post pandemic, KREYOL is in full production and "FREEDOM" has arrived.

Shortly after on June 23rd was "Eat. Drink. Model." Presented by the legendary designer Denise Hajjar once again leaving her mark on the Marina Bay Boardwalk, she herself created. Hajjar whipped up another sell-out fashion show of 400 plus of the city's glitterati seated at 42 tables along the chic docks of Marina Bay. The event was to benefit Saint Mary's Center for Women and Children in Dorchester.

It was a sit-down dinner event with local restaurants; Siros, Victory Point, Marina Bay Market, Port 305, Montilio's Bakery and Reel House serving their tastiest treats with the proceeds going to Saint Mary's. The evening also featured a silent auction with business such as ALBA, Granite Links golf course, Coach, Dorchester Florist/Coleen's Flowers, Cedar Grove Gardens, Abby Park, the Frugal Fixer, Top it Off, and Indie Salon and Skincare adding to the pot of money raised for the local savior to women and children.

After dinner, the runway began to rock from music by Denise LaCarubba and the Denise Hajjar styles from her Boutique, vintage pieces, and newly opened Marina Bay Living.

Summer looks fit for the boat and dinner on the boardwalk began to take center stage. Men's looks made their way as well as kids novelty anchor tees and crafted bucket hats for fishing showed from her newest fashion venture at Marina Bay Living. Always expected from Hajjar looks featuring pops of hot pink, trending tied dyed dresses, flowing pant suits, iconic wrap dresses in multiple patterns, fluorescent scarves for that hint of color, jackets with creative stitching, animal prints and more! The presentation featured over 80 looks to all be seen in her boutiques on Marina Bay or by visiting www.DeniseHajjar.com or www.MarinaBayLiving.com

That coming Sunday the 27th was Performer.com "SWIM". Held on the chic rooftop of ALBA restaurant in downtown Boston and hosted by the one and only EMCEE Gustavo Leon.

Sexy poolside style from designers Sharon Cox-Cole and Silvia Via were featured at the event making way for the must have summer style. The event was a mix and mingle long overdue for Boston fashion goers. It was also an opportunity for 2020 Boston Fashion Award Winners to pick up that hard earned trophy. In attendance to accept were David Josef, Gosia Krzyszkowiak, Donna Sousa, and Candice Wu.

As for now, that is where live fashion in Boston stands! It has been amazing to welcome back the backstage preparation of models from top hair and makeup artists, seeing designs hit the runway and the press pits filled. The runways of New England have reopened, keep your eye on www.BostonFashionWeek.com for the 2021 schedule where Scene&Style will "See You in the Front Row."

July 2021 Hajjar's SS21 Collection Hits the Boardwalk Scene&Style Magazine Issue #49

This past June legendary designer Denise Hajjar once again left her mark on the Marina Bay Boardwalk. Reinventing a runway, she herself created for the summer series of " EAT DRINK MODEL."

Hajjar whipped up another sell-out fashion show of 400 plus of the city's glitterati seated at 42 tables along the chic docks of Marina Bay. The event was to benefit Saint Mary's Center for Women and Children in Dorchester.

It was a sit-down dinner event with local restaurants; Siros, Victory Point, Marina Bay Market, Port 305, Montillos Bakery and Reel House serving their tastiest treats with the proceeds going to Saint Mary's.

The evening also featured a silent auction with business such as ALBA, Granite Links golf course, Coach, Dorchester Florist/Coleen's Flowers, Cedar Grove Gardens, Abby Park, the Frugal Fixer, Top it Off, and Indie Salon and Skincare adding to the pot of money raised for the local savior to women and children.

After dinner, the runway began to rock from music by Denise LaCarubba and the Denise Hajjar styles from her Boutique, vintage pieces, and newly opened Marina Bay Living.

Summer looks fit for the boat and dinner on the boardwalk began to take center stage. Men's looks made their way as well as kids novelty anchor tees and crafted bucket hats for fishing showed from her newest fashion venture at Marina Bay Living.

Always expected from Hajjar looks featuring pops of hot pink, trending tied dyed dresses, flowing pant suits, iconic wrap dresses in multiple patterns, fluorescent scarves for that hint of color, jackets with creative stitching, animal prints and more! The presentation featured over 80 looks to all be seen in Hajjar's boutiques on Marina Bay. You can make a day of it with dining al fresco or shop on-line by visiting www.DeniseHajjar.com or www.MarinaBayLiving.com

June 2021 Kreyol Presents "Freedom : Standing on Legacy Scene&Style Magazine Issue #48

Recently, the I AM KREYOL Collection came back roaring with a live presentation in downtown Boston in support of the Juneteenth celebration. The event was the first time the brand had made a public appearance and hosting an event since the pandemic. Designer Fontaine, stomped right back into the spotlight with a powerful installation.

The evening kicked off with vibrant Host; Bernaldine "Truth" educating and the history behind the Freedom Event "Standing on Legacy," giving, love, respect to the city of Boston in a Juneteenth experience.

Following was a, Boston version of Badou. Local Miranda Rae gave her soulful version on a classic, shared original work from herself and grabbing full attention with her magnetic voice. Following and flowing through the entire evening was DJ Slick Vik with funk, hip hop, and top jams.

The Iam Kreyol Collection came charging out onto the flight of stairs towering over the city subway station. Slick Vik threw out a chilling mix as, the stunning style displayed many messages of "I Am Free." Making it clear that the power of freedom had arrived. After Vibrant Host; Bernaldine brought Designer Joelle on stage to give her passionate story to the celebration and brand awareness.

Kréyol is a woman's high fashion brand that aims to impact the world, one garment at a time. Their "for women, by women" initiative allows for your purchase to directly affect the livelihood of a woman artisan or entrepreneur. They believe in economic development and sustainability through artistry.

Being a family affair with Fontaine's brother Stanly expanding in his own men's wear "Paul Rameau." Mother, Yolette Fontaine has been Joelle's inspiration through her own sewing story. The eldest girl of five children she was given a passport and $500 as a gift from her older brother. She turned that into a business and began traveling to the United States & Panama, purchasing goods to re-sell in Haiti. This endeavor afforded her the opportunity and means to thrive successfully in a space where poverty was the norm. By 1980, she had put herself through engineering school, was a teacher and seamstress. Still making her mark, Yolette sews pieces for the brand.

As a young woman Joelle, aspired to be an architect. After many life journeys at such a young age come 23, was invited by a friend to a fashion conference at NYFW decided to submit the only three garments she had ever created to be considered as a potential designer. At that time Fontaine was an artist not a designer. She had absolutely no idea, but had passion, grit, talent, the audacity to believe she belonged there. She was immediately accepted, with only seven days to showtime. She created her first collection of 12 full looks, entitled "Kaleidoscope". Then moved to New York a year later, the rest is history.

Creator Fontaine has brought the Boston's fashion standards to a height. Her powerful looks that continue to come through were bold and speaking for themselves. Pieces were made specifically for the show and can be purchased at www.iamkreyol.com

The event was and opportunity for Fontaine to announce, post pandemic, KREYOL is in full production and "FREEDOM" has arrived.

February 2021 Gucci Shows Logo Canvas with Retro 70s looks
Scene&Style Magazine Issue #44

Alessandro Michele's Gucci Spring 2021 Collection shown at Milan Fashion Week was a welcomed throwback. His clothes were shot as a look book, worn by his design team.

Michele showed his collection in a 15-minute video but over a 12-hour livestream during which the advertising campaign was shot. The focus was structural printed coats, of florid 7os-style floral dresses and shirts, and plenty of Gucci-logo canvas on hats, bags and shoes displayed up on screen in retro-seeming Windows 95-ish frames.

Faced with the impossibility of a runway show amidst the COVID-19 pandemic, the Gucci creative director organized a collaboration with Van Sant, a filmmaker whose circuitous, oblique storytelling he's long admired. "I could see through his eyes," Michele said at a joint press conference earlier this month. In a season of experimentation both analog and digital, Gucci's project- 90 edited minutes shot in Rome over a period of - 20 days ranks amongst the most ambitious esoteric.

Gucci and its fashion company peers are no longer just product makers, they are also content providers. Collina Strada's Hillary Taymour, one of the designers Michele selected for Gucci Fest, crystalized the change that is now in motion: "We're still artists and people are still looking at what we're going to do next," Taymour told Vogue Runway colleague Brooke Bobb. "But... there's a way to create a more educational model or expressive model, rather than a product model." In a campaign, Florence Welch gliding through a vintage store slipping handwritten notes into the pockets of jeans or the purse of a passerby...Billie Eilish frolicking with her pet robot dogs in what looks like the exurbs of L.A... the miniseries' star Silvia Calderoni's tour through Rome's empty ancient streets by scooter at night... Each of those vignettes charmed and in every scene the characters were wearing head-to-toe Gucci.

January 2021 Spring Fashion in Store from Versace Scene&Style Magazine Issue #43

The legendary Donatella Versace, the woman who brought Jennifer Lopez back onto the runway donning a replica of that famous jungle-print dress, is showcasing pastels and animal prints this SS2021 season.

Milan, the cathedral of creation, The Godfather of fashion. A city the world looks to for answers, inspiration. Life as we know it has taken a sharp left turn and has almost every industry frantic on how to conform to "The New Normal." As restrictions continually increase and the traditional runway restricted, Milan gave Society what it was looking for.

The Camera Nazionale Della Moda Italian presented, Milan digital fashion week this past July. The global showcase was for the menswear Spring/Summer 2021 collections and the men's and womenswear SS 2021 pre-collections. The Week was a continuation of the "China Project , We are with You." Inaugurated in February 2020 that enabled over 25 million people to remotely access all the Milano Moda Donna Autumn/Winter 2021 shows, hence for fronting the first digitalized fashion week.

Some designers decided not to launch their latest collection, yet as powerhouse in the industry took the opportunity to unveil a new creative side. Versace secured a worldwide exclusive with British rapper Aj Tracey perform an unreleased track, "Step On." Filmed in a warehouse during the campaign shoot, the video served as a teaser for the brand's Flash Collection that debuted later this past summer.

For Milan Digital Fashion Week, 40 fashion houses presented previews of menswear looks for next spring and summer and pre-collections for women.

Most of those collections were small being the time was limited. The factories were closed for an exceedingly long time. It was also an opportunity for designers to break away from the customary and create in an innovative way. Each designer was given a window of one to 15 minutes to produce their piece with free reign of expression.

The collections are out on the floor now the questions is when is the next live runway show from Versace to don them at?

Chapter Five – 2020

"Don't be into trends. Don't make fashion own you, but you decide what you are, what you want to express by the way you dress and the way to live." —Gianni Versace

December 2020 Support Local this Holiday Season with our Gift Guide Scene&Style Magazine

Issue #42

Designer Stanley Rameau is expanding the family business and bringing a solid men's collection to the city of Boston.

Paul Rameau is a social awareness brand founded in Boston that combines an ensemble of styles that represents the late creative: Paul Rameau. Founded by his son Stanley Rameau, the brand embodies classic influence and wardrobe essentials with modern, functional, & streetwear expressions.

"Paul Rameau represents the rebirth of my father's creative spirit that now lives in me and the concept of our clothes. After he passed, I knew my father would have wanted me to honor his life by doing my best to reach my full potential and Live My Renaissance. So, at Paul Rameau, our goal is to encourage you to take risks, neglect fear, and tap into your full potential where you will meet the best version of yourself."

Stanley continues, "Paul Rameau is named after my father and originates from the memories I have of him as I consistently reflect on the joy he found in his creative aspirations. His life embodied a unique style of artistry, originality, and spirituality that was showcased through his enjoyment of painting, carpentry, and music. I remember him as the man who always wore a pair of trousers and a button up as if he were ready for a day out in the town. In reality, he was always well dressed whether he was spending quality time playing our piano or building a bench just for the fun of it. My father, Paul Rameau, was my definition of a renaissance man."

Stanley's sister Joelle Fontaine is creator of the "I am Kreyol" brand a strong and successful women's line that has recently taken space in the Bloomingdale's Boston location. This family is on fire and on trend to make a loud statement in the fashion industry. Shop them both this holiday season at www.paulrameau.com and www.iamkreyol.com .

Other amazing local Bostonians to support this season are men's tailors like Alan Rouleau Couture, Denise Hajjar Collections for those stylish must have gloves, scarves, and hats. David Josef is bringing fun to his mask game, perfect stocking stuffers. Give the gift of fine Italian wine from V. Cirace & Son's. Or Guglielmo espresso you can pick up at Caffe Dello Sport in the North End. There you can grab your pastries from Modern, a must during the holidays! Treat your loved ones to a gift card for a night out on a DePasquale Venture at Bricco, Quattro, Mare, Trattoria Il Panino or Assagio's. Maybe it is some home décor you are looking for. Give a hand-crafted wine glass of sunflowers, snowflakes from "Painted by Peggy." She can create almost any design and can be found at Peggy Cornacchio on Facebook, message for details. Shop around the at brand new Marina Bay Living right on the Quincy boardwalk. They have adorable children's gifts, kitchen items, local treats, and novelty items for your favorite sailor. SHOP LOCAL BOSTON!

10-4-2020 "A Night Reminiscent of Paris" Denise Hajjar Scene&Style Magazine Issue #41

Fashion has fallen on hard times recently yet when you are one of the greats, you find a social distancing solution. Recently Denise Hajjar gave the Boston fashion community a breath of fresh air by organizing a live outdoor event, "EAT · DRINK · MODEL." A fashion show fundraiser on the boardwalk at Marina Bay, Quincy to benefit local first responders.

Hajjar had moved her boutique from Boston to the waterfront docks of the Marina Bay about a year ago. Countless plans of a grand opening continued to pass and then this past September, there was a solution. Denise approached local business on the boardwalk about interest in contributing to a fashion show. Everything began to piece together; tables, chefs-d'oeuvre's, wine were all donated by neighboring restaurants Victory Point, Siros, Port 305, and the Reel House. Goodie bags created with famous Ginger Betty cookies, a patriotic face mask, hand sanitizer and more. All fell into place with six feet of social distancing for 44 plus tables to line the boardwalk roped off for the sold-out event that included a place of peace, a press pit.

The evening began by honoring George Rollins, a retired Army colonel who went for his own strut down the runway. Guests invited to sit at some of the pre-sold tables lining the boardwalk included Quincy police officers, firefighters, nurses, a World War II fighter pilot all who were the inspiration behind the charity event.

In attendance were; local celebrities like Yolanda Cellucci, Bill Brett from the Boston Globe, Performer.com filming, Brian Pitcher, Robert Paris, Dan Minicucci, DJ Denise LaCarubba creating the vibe, the classic lineup of Boston's top models and so many more at a six feet social distancing manor.

The fashion portion began with a commanding message of, united we stand. The first looks to hit the runway were patriotic red, white, and blue cable knitted sweaters, t-shirts shedding light on sharing the peace, all paired with masks made by local middle schooler Jofin making his statement of "believe."

Following were looks of funk and flair. Wool plaid ponchos, off the shoulder pullovers, long trenches, and leather. Sexy scarfs matched up with faux alligator skin handbags. Then came the classic powerful woman details you expect from Denise. Stunning Chanel patterned coats, every perfect fall colored wrap, classy animal leopard print dresses, block sweaters, those clutch turtlenecks, and furs for when the weather is right.

Finishing out the fashion were pieces Hajjar will never part with, designs meant for her shows and shoots. Ball gowns with beaded detail, a full-length silver dress fit for a red carpet and the showstopper time and again of a black honeycomb cocktail dress that had the audience thinking it was Marilyn Monroe on the runway.

The show had it all; with over 50 plus looks, 44 plus tables and God had graced the evening with that last hint of sun and summer nights. Denise Hajjar-Casamassima took an idea for the Marina Bay boardwalk and created a runway reminiscent of Paris.

Issue #40

Italy is a mentor in the world of fashion; handbags, shoes, designer dresses right down to a simple yet everyday accessory like sunglasses. In 2020 the spring trend projects strong geometric frames and vibrant colored lenses inspired by styles of the late 90s.

Top of the list for the ladies is the throwback of the "small skinny sunglasses." A staple back in the '50s, then again in the 90s, slim and tiny frames came back with a vengeance last year and rapidly gained a following that swear to this style. The must have this season for men is the mirrored lens. Most certainly flashy and somewhat intimidating when you talk with somebody while staring at your own reflection. The reflective look can be both classy and stylish. On the opposite end of the spectrum are clear and translucent sunglasses . Or rock retro-vintage glasses with square and rectangular frames inspired by grandad's eyewear

A timeless and flattering to both men and women, aviator sunglasses are a popular choice for spring/summer eyewear. Even oversized cat eye sunglasses are the rave this season as well. Reserved only for women, this feminine silhouette is perfect for elongating the face and emphasizing the cheekbones. Fresh flat top sunglasses are one of the most recent designs to take over the 2020 sunglasses trends. Even keep it classic with the retro "Don Draper" metal

frames reminiscent of John Lennon's iconic round eyeglasses and the hippie era.

Regardless of what style best suits you if you research who is always on point with the season's trends, top designers in the world your #1 hit will be an Italian look. Heavy hitters like; Prada, Versace, Bulgari, Gucci, Valentino, Dolce & Gabbana year after year continue to create the must have looks of the season. Yet there is still a long list of Italian sunglasses designers raising the bar.

Italy has long been at the forefront of fashion, and eyewear is no exception. In addition to their renowned artistry and sophistication, Italian eyewear designers also infuse their frames with impeccable craftsmanship.

Sunglasses may just be the most important accessory you can own as they complete almost every outfit. Whether you're after a unique standby piece or a trendy retro design, there is a frame for every face. As far fashionable eyewear goes Italian designs are always placed on the top shelf.

June 2020 Italian Time Pieces Lead the Way *SCENE Magazine* / Scene&Style Magazine Issue #39

Italy is iconic for some of the world's favorite past times: pizzas, spaghetti, Nutella, opera, design, film and so much more. It is also where famous luxury brands started; Ferrari, Lamborghini, Ducati, Fiat, Gucci, Prada, Armani, Versace, among others. A fashion capital in the world and leader in watchmaking.

When it comes to production, Italy also has deep-rooted traditions. Several rich and high-quality watch brands have originated in Italy. Some of which have gained a high global reputation that attracted investors from large Swiss watch companies. Reports have indicated that the first mechanical watch originated from the Mediterranean country.

It was in the late 19th century, when watch production was ramping up around the globe Sotirio Voulgari and Senatore Borletti blitzed into the retail of timekeepers in Rome (1884) and Milan (1896) which was the beginning of the countries venture into the business.

Voulgari, who "Italianized" his last name to Bvlgari, would follow the philosophy of exclusivity his watches were to be made in a "bottega," an artistic workshop, and remain limited in production. In the 1950s / 1960s, dubbed Italy's "La Dolce Vita" era after Fellini's 1960 masterpiece film, Bvlgari's popularity skyrocketed.

The "La Dolce Vita" goddess herself, Anita Ekberg, proudly donned Bvlgari jewels. Consequently, many other glamorous leading ladies of the era also loved Bvlgari: Elizabeth Taylor, Monica Vitti, Sofia Loren, Gina Lollobrigida, and Audrey Hepburn.

Soon, the brand was embraced by Italian nobility, prominent businessmen, and politicians. This period of tremendous success provided Bvlgari with the influence and capital to further expand and diversify its product lines.

In recent decades, Bvlgari has broken world records with its ultra-thin watches featuring in-house movements and cutting-edge complications. High in demand are; the lady's pieces bursting with color and shimmer. To the men's that exude bold masculinity and timeless elegance.

Many of Bvlgari's most impressive pieces are featured in its "Haute Horlogerie" collection of high-end designer watches. The models in this contemporary collection truly push the limits of watchmaking excellence: Octo Finissimo Tourbillon Squelette, OF Automatique, OF Répétition Minutes, Grande Sonnerie Magsonic, Il Giocatore Veneziano and the Papillon to name a few.

Officine Panerai is undoubtedly the second brand that comes to mind when considering Italian timepieces. In the "Pre-Vendome" era, Officine Panerai was producing popular watches inspired by their military icons. They introduced re-editions of their historic Radiomir, Luminor, and Mare Nostre watches in the early 90s.

In recent years, Panerai has demonstrated their horological expertise with the release of their own manufacture movements. They've been known to push the limits on case materials, introducing innovations such as Carbotech and ceramic. These Pre-Vendome, or "Pre-V," Panerai watches are extremely collectible in the modern day. The PVD versions even more so.

As we move away from the typical picks of Gucci, Prada, Armani, Versaci. In 1942 Ilvo Fontana designed a watch to meet the newest requirements of the Italian Royal Navy. Though his designs were not produced, they survived until Ilvo's grandson, Italo, brought them to life almost 20 years ago.

Since then, the U-Boat watch brand has been producing oversized timepieces easily recognized for their canteen-style crown cover and varied material options. From PVD to forged carbon and bronze, U-boat exhibits the bold attitude that has garnered them a loyal following.

Founded in Florence, Anonimo was the brainchild of Federico Massacesi of Ferragamo and Dr. Dino Zeo, an ex-CEO of Panerai.

Anonimo would release the Polluce Bronze, the first bronze diving watch, in 2006. Considered an innovator at release, the true impact of the Polluce would not be felt until later, when the likes of Panerai and Tudor followed suit with their own PAM 382 "Bronzo" and Black Bay Bronze 79250BM.

Today, Anonimo has pared down their offerings to just 4 lines: Sport, Militare, Professional, and Dino Zei. All of these embody the brand's compromise with functionality, appealing designs, and robust quality.

Visconti is another Florence-based watch brand more commonly known for their writing instruments. Newest in the business they stepped into the watch space in 2013.

Although Visconti Watches are powered by Swiss movements, their cases are a product of their extensive research into cutting-edge materials. Previously employed in their luxury pen lines, the Florentine watchmakers have been able to translate this expertise into watches. Markedly, their current Opera watch exemplifies this commitment to craftsmanship and sophistication.

Giuliano Mazzuoli timepieces, as many of the other brands originate from Florence. Giuliano, the brand's founder, and designer had previous success in designed pens, agendas, and notebooks.

Mazzuoli drew inspiration from his clockmaker DNA and stepped into the watchmaking space. Aiming to create a watch like none other before, Mazzuoli searched through books and articles on watches looking for inspiration.

In the end, inspiration found him. An air pressure gauge in his shop would serve as the foundation for his first watch, the Manometro. From there, he would expand on the round case theme, as well as the automotive look, to create the Transmissione Meccanica and the Contagiri model lines.

Giuliano Mazzuoli's watches are true eye-catchers and may take a couple of looks before being truly appreciated. Nevertheless, the designs are spotless, as well as truly functional.

The list of designers can go on for hours yet the Spring seasons top pick for men are a Brega E600 SEA-AMALFI, Movado, Forzier, or MeccanicheVeloci. As for the ladies; a Ferragamo Gancino stainless steel with black leather strap and gold face, Emporio Armani, MVMT or Versace. So, the next time you're in Milan, Rome or Florence make sure to pop into the authentic watch retailers and grab yourself an accessory that could perfect every outfit through the test of time.

May 2020 Fashions Front Line Hero's *Aspiring Magazine* Scene&Style Magazine Issue #38

In a world where most of us are at a standstill, Boston's finest fashion designers are on the front line and putting in overtime making masks.

As we devise "the plan" to return to the new normal, the only solid answer we all seem to have is, you must wear a mask. They are no longer just for the essential works, nurses, doctors, and care takers yet for all to add an as accessory to the outfit.

Since the beginning of this worldly pandemic Boston's fashion community has taken a stand and not a dime only donations to properly cloth our community. Who knew the talent of sewing would become the most essential position? Designers immediately transitioned from working on the release of their Spring 2020 collection to producing protective gear. The mode of sleepless nights thinking about that perfect cut or sought out seem turned into a blur of factory production on how fast and how many masks can be made today.

Local Designers taking on the trend are David Josef, Denise Hajjar, Kinda Tuma, Kelly Dempsey, Angelica Timas, Ashley Rose, Thread Tech Corporation, Joe Malaika, EJ Battle with Battle Designs, Sondra Celli and more. Josef is keeping our cities celebrities safe and stylish with his contributions, Dempsey is bringing that funk fabulous vibe so not to lose ourselves behind the unwanted accessory.

Scene&Style was able to catch up with the timeless and elegant diva, Denise Hajjar. When I asked how she has been spending her days, Hajjar replied, "I get into my store about 4:30am every morning and crawl into bed about 8:30pm each night. By about 9:30am I have around 40 masks made, I average about 100 per day and have maxed out at 135 in a day. I inquired about where all these fantastic patterned pieces were headed? Hajjar explained, "Everywhere! Anywhere from 100 to a health clinic in Montana, 150 for an elderly home on West Roxbury, 5 went straight to Italy, 1,000 to a local golf course for employees and members, right on to 70 masks for my dearest friends and longtime model Jane Conway Caspe's mothers nursing home. I get orders all day long and would be lost without my essential employee Charlotte and my man Mario here with me everyday to filter orders and prep the masks." I must admit I was envious of not only the time spent being productive yet touched by her care for each mask made.

All our designers are heroes right here in the hub, selfless super stars. Donating their time taking to the front line to fight a battle we have all asked to stay inside for. They are our angels keeping us safe using their sewing machine as their sword. This is a very confusing and uncertain world we are all living in and now more than ever is the time to appreciate the little things. A mask that saves lives and makes a fashion statement, I am all in.

THANK YOU!

April 2020 Thog Street Style is the Supreme Brand of OKC Scene&Style Magazine Issue #37

Oklahoma City's "Two Heads on Gold" is making a fashionable statement by bringing two great minds together with the ambition of completing a goal for the culmination to be gold.

Thog is a funk brand focused on the fellas with a mainstream of t-shirts and hoodies with hard emblems and slogans. The looks are fitted with a slight swag of baggy to keep it street. The shirt line features photos of hip hop greats, athletes, simplistic brand representation and incorporating that solid OKC look or deep purple and orange that run deeps in the city.

This thread of life is not just for the gents yet also for the ladies. Past collections have featured crop tops, fitted shorts with that comfort feel of fabric choice, fly draw strings perfect to pair with a body suit, backpacks and more.

The key to his must have flavor is that when he drops a shirt that's it. If you don't grab it right away, you won't his collections are there until their gone. This supreme brand of OKC is worn by the city's top rappers and DJ's. One of OKC's hottest artists, Grand X National was spotted sporting the "aimer la vie" t-shirt in the streets of the city.

Ghana native Graham' Anang is the mastermind behind the creations. Moving to OKC when he was 12 years old found his way into the fashion game there yet expressing his roots in each piece. Scene&Style

was able to snag some one on one time with the designer. When asking Graham, "What is the inspiration behind your work?" He replied "To get people to learn to work together and achieve something. To inspire someone that's stuck in life with something and that thing just might be someone coming in to share their ideas. Also, to give OKC something really special as well. Make people talk about the city not just the Thunder or Sooners but fashion, street fashion, Thog." Asking, "Who is your target audience?" Anang confidently said, "Everyone." Closing out, "What is coming up for your brand; events, collections?" Graham' replied, "I do have a pop-up shop coming after the pandemic is over and will be sharing the location and date via my Instagram. As for a new collection, there is always one in the works."

Two Heads on Gold, "Thog" is a creating a fashion culture all its own in the heart of Oklahoma City. A lifestyle brand that is exclusive to each release. To see more of what they have to offer visit them on Instagram at "twoheadsongold" where you can DM them to grab your gear.

February 2020 A Fearless Leader in Boston Fashion Scene&Style Magazine Issue #36

The iconic Kathy B. has been making moves in the cities style scene for years now and the hard time put in is paying off! Kathy Benharris has made herself well known as the stylist to book for that fancy photo shoot or runway mad. Kathy is a widely recognized as one of New England's leading fashion experts. She is the Regional Director of Fashion Group International also leads the 1.5k member strong Boston Fashion Meetup Group. Her clients include individual brands, designers, international charities, private clients, retail entities, and publications. She and her team have developed, styled, and produced events during New York Fashion Week, Boston Fashion Week and takes over nationwide ski style in the winters.

Benharris and her amazing production crew stunned the city by bringing the "B" puck to Copley Place for a power hitter fashion show in February of 2015. The Bruins wives, girlfriends, Maggie Inc and Dynasty models took center ice for a Neiman Marcus styled fashion show to benefit the Bruins Foundation and Dana Farber.

The evening was a hit from cocktail hour to final struts down the runway. The 100-foot runway was an expansion from the previous year and was a must for the sold-out show. The second floor was blocked off for a VIP cocktail reception with donated treats from the city's tastiest restaurants. The night welcomed host Jenny Johnson, the Bruins sitting front line on the runway, NESN, Channel 7, The Boston Breakers Rachel Wood, and their Olympic Gold Medalist Cat Whitehill along with owners/staff and the Hubs finest faces were all in attendance.

The runway doesn't stop there! Benharris and her Rockstar crew have a plethora of clients that rave about them. Listing a few are The Liberty Hotel, L.K. Bennett, MLR Artist Management, David Josef, Denise Hajiar, Angelica Timas, Neiman Marcus, Reebok, Salvatore Ferragamo and more.

Her team's top two superstars are Grace Goodearl a social media expert, content specialist and social media strategist in the fashion industry. Another vital piece in the business is Billie Gage a top tier stylist in the New England area.

KB Fashion Productions only goal is to exceed their client's expectations by delivering excellence in all aspects of styling, fashion event production, and content creation. From conception to completion, they use their well-honed skills as stylists and producers to tell their clients unique fashion story in Boston, on the mountain and beyond. If you're looking to be seen by the city visit www.kbfashionproductions.com and book your next event.

January 2020 Snow Style from the Lodge to the Mountain – Scene&Style Magazine Issue #35

Recently KB Fashion Productions took over the mesmerizing Liberty Hotel catwalk and main floor for a rendition of a Fashionably Late showcasing the season's hottest snow style.

Some of the first pieces to hit the runway were lodge looks; the iconic pom hat with a long sleeve Fera top and Skea mini 3D hologram skirt, paired with Pajar fur boots for the ladies. For the gents; a casual Ralph Lauren camouflage outer wear jacket over a Patagonia fleece and Pit Viper glasses. Also was an on point themed rock retro trend of a power blue Til I Die hoodie, jeans and biker boots.

Following was a feminine flair of underlining base layers from High Pine styled with fur hats, essential slope goggles worn well by the gorgeous Dynasty Models & Talent gals. As for the men; a camel Burton brand pant, a stitched pattern half zip Patagonia and eye wear to steer off the snow.

The last round of looks featured the down and dirty part of the ski trip, rocking the slopes and surfing through the powder. Glamour girl Tina Makuch complimented a cutesy yet effective outfit of Obermeyer zebra ski pant and a fur trim Parka. Obermeyer ran this portion of the runway as for the men a Ferrari red jacket paired with a solid black pant made a bold statement.

Benharris alongside her team Grace Goodearl and Billie Gage always give you a show of class, sex appeal and the "it" way to be styled. They hit the mark on each look from sipping hot toddy's in the lodge to rushing down the mountain when style must mesh with dependability in the product.

From conception to execution, KB Fashion Productions team handles all aspects of runway and event production. They have produced hundreds of fashion events, from fundraisers to runway shows, and are thrilled to work with designers, creatives, models, agencies and brands to produce an unforgettable fashion experience that exceeds their client's goals. If your looking to vamp up your next event and impress your guests visit KBFashionProductions.com and book the best!

Chapter Six – 2019

"Style is something each of us already has, all we need to do is find it."
—Diane von Furstenberg

November 2019 / December SCENE Winter Issue How Italy has Influenced the World of Fashion – Scene&Style Magazine Issue #34

Fashion is a form of expression, a statement letting the world know exactly who you are without speaking a single word. Italia has been a chapel, a beacon from the beginning when it comes to influencing the manner in which the world dresses.

Milan itself has created a vogue lifestyle within its city's walls that millions from around the globe flock to each year even if only to sneak a peek. Italy takes the trophy in most all categories of wearable design; watches, shoes, dresses, sunglasses, handbags even right down to the leading hair stylist.

Cashmere; that warm silky fabric that makes an impression on sweater season with an exclusive tag labeled, "made in Italy." Or as a Bostonian that must have by mid-November is the latest release in Moncler jackets.

One of the most impactful moments in modern music was 20 years ago at the Grammy Awards when Jennifer Lopez stunned in that iconic, green Versace dress. The piece was gushed about for decades so much so that Donatella Versace in honor of her brother Gianni redevised the ensemble. This past fall, Lopez closed the Milan Fashion Week runway for the 2020 Spring/Summer jungle themed collection.

The city of Milan is recognized internationally as one of the world's most important fashion capitals, along with Paris, New York, and London. Milan's fashion history has evolved greatly throughout the years. Milan began as a center of fashion in the Middle Ages and Renaissance, as in Venice and Florence, the making of luxury goods was an industry of such importance that in the 16th century the city gave its name to the English word "milaner" or "millaner", meaning fine wares like jewelry, cloth, hats and luxury apparel. By the 19th century, a later variant, "millinery", had come to mean one who made or sold hats.

In the mid-19th century cheaper silk began to be imported from Asia and the pest phylloxera damaged silk and wine production. More land was subsequently given over to industrialization. Textile production was followed by metal and mechanical and furniture manufacture. In 1865, the first major department store in the country opened in Milan by the Bocconi brothers (which was called Alle Città d'Italia and later in 1921 became La Rinascente). This was a novelty at the time with regards to retailing in Italy. Though, traditionally, artisans would sell the items they made directly or to small stores, the opening of these new department stores modernized the distributions of clothes in the city.

Italy's fashion houses are legendary, from Dolce Vita to Prada, Versace to Valentino. The country has always been known for its meticulous craftsmanship and luxury materials, but it was only after World War II that Italy emerged as a fashion destination.

"Before the war, Italian fashion was always following the direction of French fashion, just like everyone else was. It wasn't until after the war that Italy's fashion industry got the confidence and the economic support to come into its own," says Stefano Tonchi, one of the curators of the exhibition Bellissima: Italy and High Fashion 1945 – 1968. During the '50s and '60s, while French labels like Christian Dior and Jacques Fath turned their focus fully on couture, only Italian fashion designers truly understood the need for women to have comfortable, versatile clothing that was also tailored and refined.

Italian day wear took off in America and paved the way for the ready-to-wear collections coming out of fashion houses today. In an effort to restore and stabilize the Italian economy after World War II, the Marshall Plan provided American aid for Italy's textile businesses, which were mostly small, family-owned operations. This investment spurred the production of the leather, fur, silk, and wool–still the country's most prized luxury materials to this day.

Part of the reason Italy was the first market for day wear was a coterie of women designers who understood the needs of women. Germana Marucelli, Mila Schön, Simonetta, and Galitzine: "this group of ladies were all coming from Italian aristocracy, and they found themselves without a job and without any money after the war," says Tonchi. "What they knew was clothes, they loved clothes, and they had the technical know-how to create these collections."

Who are these influential designers? The ones that have molded fashion, create the collections the world is eagerly awaiting each spring and fall.

A few that have paved the way and passed on are; Elsa Schiaparelli of Rome, Italy. Along with Coco Chanel, her greatest rival, she is regarded as one of the most prominent figures in fashion between the two World Wars. Starting with knitwear, Schiaparelli's designs were heavily influenced by Surrealists like her collaborators Salvador Dalí and Jean Cocteau.

Emilio Pucci, Marchese di Barsento born in Naples, Italy. Pucci was a Florentine Italian fashion designer and politician. He and his eponymous company are synonymous with geometric prints in a kaleidoscope of colors.

The beacon of designer shoes; Salvatore Ferragamo birthed in Bonito, Campania, Italy. He worked with many Hollywood stars in the 1920s, before returning to Italy to start the eponymous company making unique handmade footwear. His scientific and creative approach to shoes spawned many innovations such as the wedge heel and cage heel. Film stars and celebrities continue to patronize his company, which has evolved into a luxury goods empire spanning the world.

A man whom needs no introduction, the late and dearly respected Gianni Versace of Reggio Calabria, Italy. Still listed as #3 on the most influential fashion designers of all times Versace continues to impact todays trends. Gianni was the designer and founder of Versace, an international fashion house, which produces accessories, fragrances, make-up, and home furnishings as well as clothes. He also designed costumes for the theatre and films. As a friend of Eric Clapton; Diana, Princess of Wales; Madonna; Elton John; Cher; Sting and many other celebrities. He was the first designer to link fashion to the music world.

Still with us continuing to create are designers like; Donatella Francesca Versace born in Reggio Calabria, Italy. She is the current Chief Creative Officer of Versace, a division of Capri Holdings. Versace was founded by her brother, Gianni Versace, and upon his death in 1997, Donatella inherited 20% of the company and became its chief executive officer.

Valentino Clemente Ludovico Garavani born in Voghera; Italy best known as Valentino resides at #8 on the list of influential designers. Founder of the Valentino SpA brand and company. His main lines include Valentino, Valentino Garavani, Valentino Roma, and R.E.D. Valentino.

Listed #9 of the most influential fashion designers of all time; Giorgio Armani of Piacenza, Italy. Armani is an Italian fashion designer, particularly noted for his menswear. He is known today for his clean, tailored lines. He formed his company, Armani, in 1975, and by 2001 was acclaimed as the most successful designer that Italy had produced, with an annual turnover of $1.6 billion and a personal fortune of $8.5 billion as of 2013.

The list of greatness continues, as #14 of the most influential fashion designers of all time is held by, Miuccia Prada of Milan, Italy. Miuccia is the designer and entrepreneur behind Prada and Miu Miu. The youngest granddaughter of Mario Prada, she took over the family-owned luxury goods manufacturer in 1978. In March 2013, she was one of the fifty best-dressed over 50s by the Guardian. As of 2014, she is listed as the 75th most powerful woman in the world by Forbes.

Rolling in at #23 on that same list of all-time influencers is; Roberto Cavalli born in Florence, Italy. He is known for exotic prints and for creating the sand-blasted look for jeans. He is the father of fashion designer Daniele Cavalli who is following in his footsteps.

Roberto Capucci, Nino Cerruti, Fendi, Gucci, Alessandra Facchinetti, Bottega Veneta, Dolce, the list of legendary designers to shape the designer world continues. The future of fashion hides within the youth strolling the streets of Milan looking for their unique voice that will impact the world. Currently the #1 fashion designer in Italy is Giorgio Armani. A staple of truth that Italian fashion will continue to reinvent itself. It will break the mold time and again while the rest of the world drapes themselves in our style.

October 2019 "A Fashion Finale Like No Other – Denise Hajjar"
Scene&Style Magazine Issue# 33

The Boston fashion community is one of loyalty and genuine gratitude for the contributions many make that create something so special. The fashion forward and timeless elegance designer Denise Hajjar had an intimate gathering to showcase her fall collection for Boston Fashion Week 2019.

The host of the evening was Hajjar's current residence inside Setting the Space, a chic home décor and staging company. The evening began with a

VIP cocktail hour welcoming the city's finest fashionistas like Yolanda Cellucci, Designer David Josef, Photographer Kris Nordstrom, DJ Denise LaCarubba and more.

Once the place was packed Hajjar's famed models began to strut through in staple jackets for that funk fall fashion. It was a line of long trenches with cherry blossom patterns, golden orange shades and a classic leopard print that sold out stock at the end of the evening. Following was a string of cocktail dresses, off the shoulder, deep greens, comfort fabrics with playful prints. With any season Hajjar can be relied upon to put out pieces that are suitable for daywear to evening events. Looks of cashmere sweaters paired with a simple black pants hit the runway. Also, those in demand wraps, cover ups and cardigans came storing through in emerald, beige, grey, soft pink, and plaid. No collection is complete for Hajjar without her hand stitched and custom design dresses that closed the show with high hip cuts and painted patterns.

After the final walk through Hajjar took center attention to give a heartfelt thank you to her team, the venue and then... bells began to ring! Music came back into focus while models and guests sang along, "We going to the chapel and we're gonna get married." Designer and longtime friend David Josef groomed Denise with a vail, champagne and invited her man Mario to join them. The family Denise had known for so many years had asked Josef to speak for them. Josef painted the picture of Hajjar's career and that she had been married to her business all this time. He boasted that he was beyond happy to hear the latest news that Denise had recently been proposed to by a man that brought a smile to face that was new and full of life. Josef also let the cat out of the bag that Hajjar had asked himself and the third of the Boston fashion legends Daniel Faucher to help design her wedding dress.

The evening ended in love, laughter, and plenty of champagne. Denise Hajjar has contributed so much to the fashion world and for her event to close with a finale for the bride to be was deserved. The Roots of a timeless fashion family gathered to celebrate on of their own and always in our hearts and never forgotten Linda Cole Petrosian. Boston is a city like no other and so is their community.

October 2019 bosFW "Boston Fashion Week Opening Celebrating 25 Years" Scene&Style Magazine

Boston Fashion Week kicked off their 2019 edition by celebrating 25 years running. The invite only ceremony took place this past Sunday, hosted by the Mandarin Hotel.

From the moment you walked in it was a VIP experience. The chic interior design of the hotel to being greeted with a glass of crisp rose. Local celebrities sashaying around the room to catch up with one another and grab that red carpet pose for the creme de la creme photographers on site.

Lining the walls was a digital photo installation from the legendry Tracy Aiguier and stylist Terri Mahn presenting 100+ images featuring 55 local designers. In real time, a live fashion presentation featuring 20 local fashion designers such as Shaunt Sarian, La la Bee, Denise Hajjar, David Josef and more.

While mingling delicious Asian infused passed apps made their way around and self-serve plated dishes were on each side on the room. A perfect lead up for Founder Jay Calderín to toast and give the sincerest thank you to the city's finest of fashion and industry professionals. Calderín set the stage for the future and School of Fashion Design Boston graduate AK Liesenfeld. The budding designer gave a presentation on "Fashion in VR" an innovative side to a show room. It was a virtual reality world where her personal creation was shown followed by Calderín throwing on the goggles and creating his own 3D space right in front of guests.

From there the evening was the city celebrating themselves by hugging those they haven't seen, sharing laughs, swapping photo's, talking collections, making new contacts, and enjoying the creative company in the jam-packed room.

When Calderín spoke on stage he boasted that, "Boston Fashion Week puts on a celebration like no other city. We pride ourselves on civic innovative, bringing the community together and having leaders' step to the plate and deliver." Calderín also summed up the city in the classiest way on the bostonfashionweek.com website; "Never doubt that a small group of thoughtful, committed citizens can change the world. Indeed, that is the only thing that ever has." – Margaret Mead

September 2019 bosFW 9-24-2019 "Boston Fashion Week Opening Celebrating 25 Years" Scene&Style Magazine Issue #32

Boston Fashion Week kicked off their 2019 edition by celebrating 25 years running. The invite only ceremony took place this past Sunday, hosted by the Mandarin Hotel.

From the moment you walked in it was a VIP experience. The chic interior design of the hotel to being greeted with a glass of crisp rose. Local celebrities sashaying around the room to catch up with one another and grab that red carpet pose for the creme de la creme photographers on site.

Lining the walls was a digital photo installation from the legendry Tracy Aiguier and stylist Terri Mahn presenting 100+ images featuring 55 local designers. In real time, a live fashion presentation featuring 20 local fashion designers such as Shaunt Sarian, La la Bee, Denise Hajjar, David Josef and more.

While mingling delicious Asian infused passed apps made their way around and self-serve plated dishes were on each side on the room. A perfect lead up for Founder Jay Calderín to toast and give the sincerest thank you to the city's finest of fashion and industry professionals. Calderín set the stage for the future and School of Fashion Design Boston graduate AK Liesenfeld. The budding designer gave a presentation on "Fashion in VR" an innovative side to a show room. It was a virtual reality world where her personal creation was shown followed by Calderín throwing on the goggles and creating his own 3D space right in front of guests.

From there the evening was the city celebrating themselves by hugging those they haven't seen, sharing laughs, swapping photo's, talking collections, making new contacts, and enjoying the creative company in the jam-packed room.

When Calderín spoke on stage he boasted that, "Boston Fashion Week puts on a celebration like no other city. We pride ourselves on civic innovative, bringing the community together and having leaders' step to the plate and deliver." Calderín also summed up the city in the classiest way on the bostonfashionweek.com website; "Never doubt that a small group of thoughtful, committed citizens can change the world. Indeed, that is the only thing that ever has." – Margaret Mead

August 2019 Rooftop Fashion Rocks the Revere Scene&Style Magazine Issue #31

Recently Boston's most fashionable from entrainment to beauty banded together to bring the city a chic jam-packed show at the Revere Hotel Rooftop.

The evening was organized by KAModeling in their 4th annual Networking Group yet their first time including a fashion show. The night jumped off with suave radio DJ Sterling Golden hosting the event and welcoming in guests. Famed MC Gustavo Leon guided the event along with his demanding presence between designers yet stealing the spotlight was his gorgeous counterpart and pageant queen Iva Nicole.

With the seasonal fashion trends about to shift the showcased designers set off what is in store for Boston. Opening was Lyrical-Apparel by Duane Grant with a vintage take on athleisure. Following was Maria Lucce Designs with elegant gowns. The Lucky Onez from Marviel Builou presented a casual and comfort look for the ladies. VaVa by Gnazo Zadi gave the crowed flavor with their funk street looks and sex appeal. FashWand by Azi brought a bold turquoise piece that stunned, and the line was highlighted by statement shoulders and lace. Closing the runway was, Ali Bianchi with her industrial meet's couture collection. She experimented with unique lines and fabric layering. Unconventionally incorporating seatbelt buckles, with beautiful silks and brocades.

Complimenting the fashion was Charles Maksou from Dry Cut on Newbury Street with the master stylist making the hair pop and Bonnie Gagnon MUA giving the models that glow. Owner of KAModeling Kassandra & Lorraine Muñoz brought in a powerhouse production team of Andrew Powers and Robert Parris also head photographer with MonsterJazz Photography. The media in attendance was the creme del la cream; Michael Rose, Rubylens Media, Kenn Bennet, Hill Zhou CYI Studios, Jeff Moy, Michael Bausemer and its never a show without the personality of Brian Pitchner.

This year was the 4th year KAModeling hosted the event and their first highlighting fashion yet their mission is still the same. To bring as many opportunities as possible to all those who "Aspire beyond the 1st shot". If you would like to learn more about what they offer, or upcoming events visit them in Instagram at @KAModelingUS .

**July 2019 Angela Timas Heats Up Summer at Steeped in Style
Scene&Style Magazine Issue #30**

When the city heats up from summer waves finding the right outfit can be a force unless you have that go to designer like Angelica Timas. Her collections transition from spring to summer and day to night with a few cuts of the cloth and strategic stitching.

Recently the designer showed pieces at the Marilyn Riseman "Steeped in Style" Fashion Show Series held at the Boston Public Library. The afternoon teatime presentation was flooded with chic beauty and sex appeal. Silk and velvet floral patterned dresses, tops paired with solid white pants slid through the room. A classic sequence in a pastel pink spaghetti strap dress, yellow and orange blossoms, and petals in a pant suit, and a stunning all white crop top with a flowing pant glided throughout grabbing attention of each guest.

Angelica Timas was born in Cape Verde Island, her parents moved to Portugal when she was just months old. At age 15 her parents move yet again to Boston, MA, where she completed high school, undecided between voices of passion and a reason, a degree in fashion was not an option early on in life.

With no formal training in fashion Angelica has mastered her skills by self-taught knowledge and true passion for what she envisions in her work. The aesthetic of her collections is inspired by various passions: Her culture, her history, nature, her love for architecture and the simple things that life has to offer. Timas stands by, "I design primarily for the woman who shares the same traits as Chikke, the versatile woman who is also a trendsetter who is bold, simple, but very elegant and chic."

Timas now has settled into a beautiful new studio, which is a multi-purpose space. Timas commented, "It's our office, where we will continually work to provide the best service to our customers, through improvement of technology and platforms. It's our production studio, where new collections come to live from conception, to sampling, to runway and released for e-commerce. It's our creative meeting space, where we toss around ideas and concepts for our editorials."

Also, an event space where they throw occasional events for their friends, family, press and partners. Lastly, it's their showroom where they display their garments and meet with their clients to discuss choices and garment needs, custom choices, while showcasing their past and present collections.

Next up on deck for the designer will be showing her SS20 Collection at StyleWeek Northeast on September 20th. Angelica's studio is located at 516 E 2nd Street, Studio #312 in S. Boston. They are by appointment only and can be contacted at hello@angelicatimas.com, by calling 857.205.9381 or visit angelicatimas.com

May 2019 Get dolled up for Queer Me Out with Carmen Carrera Scene&Style Magazine Issue #27

Boston is known to be strong and brimming with pride! This year's celebratory week is host to a major event; QUEER ME OUT! Presented by FGI Boston, in partnership with W Boston on Monday June 3rd. Get up-close with the movers, shakers & boundary breakers who are pushing the LGBTQ+ movement forward.

Listen in on "Let's Talk Transgender Rights", An exclusive conversation with Carmen Carerra and James Lopata, Editor in Chief of Boston Spirit Magazine, Moderated by Lifestyle Editor of Boston Spirit, Scott Kearnan.

The event will begin with a Cocktail Hour on the Mezzanine Level of W Boston from 6:30pm to 7:30pm. Followed by the star-studded discussion from 7:30pm to 8:30pm. The floor will then be opened for a minute question and answer session with guests. The exclusive event will be taking place on Monday June 3rd from 6:30pm to 9pm at the W Boston 100 Stuart Street, Boston. There will be a cash bar available and after party at the W Hotel Lounge. With sponsors like; Boston Spirit Magazine, Boston Pride, BBsquared, MLR Artists, Massachusetts LGBT Chamber of Commerce and Massachusetts Transgender Political Coalition you know it is going to be one rocking party. Purchase tickets atittps://carmenxbospride.eventbrite.com

Vivacious and vibrant, Carmen Carrera is an American reality TV star, model, and burlesque dancer. She is more popular by her stage name Carmen Carrera. A New Jersey native, she began her career as a showgirl and rose to prominence as a contestant on the third season of Logo TV's 'RuPaul's Drag Race'. After the show's run, Carmen-who had originally been born as a male-immediately underwent gender reassignment surgery to transition into a woman. Despite her relatively short stint in the television, her personality and natural beauty shone through and she landed her first modelling job at 'W' fashion magazine. Later, she worked with RuPaul again as a drag professor in his spin-off show

'RuPaul's Drag U. In the following years, she modelled for some of the big names in the fashion industry, acted on the big screen and small, and also starred in music videos. Carrera is also an active contributor to various causes and charities related to AIDS and the LGBTO community.

Join FGI Boston, the W Hotel Boston and sponsors this Monday June 3rd for a celebration of equal rights and cocktails of course. Tickets can be pups:/ed menxbospride. eventbrite.com

May 2019 Scene&Style Magazine - FGI Boston Set Up Camp for the Annual MET Gala

Fashion can make a statement, create a trend, guide a lost soul into their destiny or just be a damn good time. The most recognized night in the industry is the annual MET Gala when celebrities from all over the globe stroll into New York City in their finest expressions. This year the Fashion Group International of Boston chapter held their first ever viewing party at The Ghost Walks in the cities Leather District.

The event is often referred to as the MET Gala, it's officially the Metropolitan Museum of Art Costume Institute benefit. Each year, there's a theme — this year, the exhibition is "Camp: Notes on Fashion," taken from Susan Sontag's essay "Notes on Camp." The theme for the 2019 gala gave guests an over the top opportunity to demonstrate their style.

Host of the local evening was Master of Ceremonies and avid fashion icon Gustavo Leon. As ticket holders arrived in their desired costumes, they were greeted by FGI Boston Board Members with refreshments and hors d'oeuvres.

The cocktails and conversation came to a cease when MC Leon grabbed the mic and began to bring full attention to the big screen televising the red-carpet arrivals. Hosts at the live event were; Anna Wintour, Alessandro Michele, creative director of Gucci, Harry Styles, entertainer, Lady Gaga and Serena Williams. Guests gathered around to gossip and gaze at looks ranging from; Kim Kardashian West's shocking silk organza and crystal Thierry Mular gown that had viewers around the world wondering if she had work done beyond being sewn into the dress. The always stunning Katie Perry showed up lit in a 40-pound chandelier by Moschino Designer Jeremy Scott and the lighter side with seeing the love and bashful smiles from Jennifer Lopez and soon to be hubby Alex Rodriquez.

As garb continued to glide down the red-carpet Leon introduced Stylist of the evening Taylor Greeley and model Cassidy Benson from Maggie Inc Agency. Greeley was given the opportunity to showcase her skills and create "camp". Some might ask, well what is camp? Camp is the embodiment of exaggeration and drama mixed with fashion — it's intentional and it's meant to turn heads. The art of being headass while also being haute couture. In past years of the Met Gala there have absolutely been on trend outfits with the theme; Rihanna dressed up as the pope, Sarah Jessica Parker with that strange nativity scene on her head basically anything Gaga wears is considered "camp". At the viewing party, model Benson was wore multiple looks one being by Lory Sun Artistry's headpiece and corset (pictured below) with makeup and hair by Paula Roderick Voisembert.

When the red carpet rolled up, and gala doors closed in NYC the party in Boston began. FGI Regional Director Kathy Benharris took a minute to thank guests for attending and give insight into what The Fashion Group International has to offer for aspiring and established trend setters. The night was a success for the group with a great turn out and many themed looks to let fashionistas know Boston can rock "camp" with the best of them.

The Fashion Group International is a global, non-profit, professional organization with 5000 members in the fashion industry including apparel, accessories, beauty, and home. The FGI mission is to be the pre-eminent authority on the business of fashion and design and to help its members become more effective in their careers. To do this, FGI provides insights on major trends in person, online and in print; access to business professionals and a gateway to the influence fashion plays in the marketplace.

The next event for the FGI Boston chapter is Monday June 3rd at The W Hotel with model and activist Carmen Carrera. For more details, benefits and how to become a member visit www.boston.fgi.org.

April 2019 The Dance Party of the Decade for "Our Girl Linda"
Scene&Style Magazine Issue #26

Boston's fashion industry has been hosted to many legends yet one will always stand out, hold a special place on the runway and in our hearts, "Our Girl Linda". Linda Cole Petrosian was more than just a famed runway model in our fair city. She was a warm smile, vibrant energy and brought laughter to each and every room she glided through. Linda was a special soul one that touched many lives and her family will be honoring her memory the only way they see fit, DANCE DANCE! On Friday May 17th at the American Legion Nonantum Post 440 the "Our Girl Linda Dance Party" will light up the floor. It will be held in memory of Linda Petrosian with proceeds to benefit the Saint Jude Children's Hospital that Linda was very dedicated to.

Linda Cole Petrosian, daughter, sister, wife, mother, friend, was also one of Boston's most in demand models to ever grace the runway. She had an ethereal beauty and effervescent personality, but it was her unpretentious authenticity, staunch loyalty, and unbridled zest for life that drew people to her. All these qualities earned Linda a huge fan base in the fashion industry and a large group of devoted friends. Linda lived life with boundless energy and passion, managing to fit a lot into her too-brief stay on this earth. She married the love of her life, raised two sons of whom she was very proud, built a successful modeling career, and donated her time to numerous charities. Linda was also known for her love for dancing.

Whenever the spirit moved her, Linda would spontaneously break into a dance and it didn't matter where - on the runway, at the beach, or while shopping. Linda died at the young age of 57 from esophageal cancer leaving behind a rich legacy of love, kindness, generosity, compassion, and contagious joie de vivre. In her memory, the first annual OUR GIRL LINDA

Dance Party will be held May 17th to raise funds for Saint Jude's Children Hospital which was one of Linda's favorite charities.

Her family hopes you will join them for a delightful evening of dancing in Linda's memory and to benefit a great cause. The event will be held at American Legion Nonantum Post 440 295 California Street Newton, MA from 7pm-11pm. For sponsorship forms, more information, or questions text/call 617-438-6682 or visit https://ourgirllinda.eventbrite.com.

Please consider joining Linda's posse of devoted friends by making a generous donation to the OUR GIRL LINDA Dance Party.

March 2019 The Space is Set for Designer Denise Hajjar at her new location Scene&Style Magazine

Issue #25

Spring is a time for new beginnings, brighter colors and recently Denise Hajjar brought both to her clients and friends.

Hajjar is constantly evolving and keeping current with her business and designs. This past January she packed up her boutique at the Intercontinental Boston Hotel and moved to the chic Assembly Row, sharing the floor with "Setting the Space". They are a home décor and staging company that ranks amongst the top in the country. Their vibrant colors, antique pieces yet modern look mold perfectly with the Denise Haiiar brand. Last week the two hosted an official welcoming party for Hajjar where Setting the Space was closed off to the public for the VIP private event. The evening started with prosecco and homemade Italian appetizers supplied by the Casamassima kitchen. The 100 plus RSVP's began to pour in and mingle with a big welcome from Denise Ramos Store Manager/Designer for Setting the Space.

Ramos rallied up guests and stunned wearing an original Denise Hajjar design to get the runway going with the 2019 Spring Collection.

The show featured vibrant Ferrari red button down tops. A line of gorgeous suede coats with a subtle floral pattern and soft blended colors. A classic beige dress with a pastel garden tone, paired with a line of tweed totes. Keeping it casual was a flowing peach long sleeve and satin white pant. As always, looks that could transform from the office to the cocktail hour in an all-black dress finished with a cream Chanel style of jacket. The presentation had everything from trend, silk dresses. pops of bold colors, retro leather jackets right to custom tailoring only Hajjar can provide.

The final walkthrough brought a twist when dance instructor Peter Walker grabbed Hajjar unexpectedly and gave the guests a peek at her ballroom moves. The evening ended with Denise thanking many and a special gift for local celebrity Yolanda Cellucci.

Photographer Kris Nordstrom had created a beautiful tribute picture of Denise and Yolanda's daughter the late Linda Cole Petrosian. Cellucci was moved to tears along with Hajjar for a perfect end to a perfect evening.

You can slip into her Spring 2019 collection and more at her new location 490 Assembly Row Somerville inside Setting the Space. You can shop online at her website www.denisehajjar.com. Or for any inquiries call 617-266-2296.

February 2019 Scene&Style Magazine - Denise Hajjar to Host Cocktail Celebration in New Location

Decade after decade Designer Denise Hajjar stays current with her collections and timeless style. 2019 has already shown accomplishments for the famed designer with showing at the most recent New York Fashion Week and print magazines showcasing her work.

The list continues next week with Thursday March 14th being the official celebration at her new location in the trendy Assembly Row located inside "Setting the Space". Which is a lifestyle brand of home furnishings, interiors, staging company / interior design firm with 6 retail stores. You can learn more about this fantastic setup at www.settingthespace.com .

The event will begin at 6:30 p.m. with light fare, desserts, prosecco and of course a fashion show set to display what is currently available from the designer. There will be a raffle drawing and 15% off anything purchased that night. What a steal, so invite your friends yet be sure to RSVP as space is limited. You can confirm by calling 617-266-2296 or email denise@denisehajjar.com . There is plenty of metered parking right out front along with indoor garage options available.

Boston born and raised, Denise Hajjar inherited her design interest and talent from her grandmother who was also a designer in Damascus, Syria. Her grandfather also in the industry, was a pattern maker and owned a dress factory from Beirut, Lebanon. Denise decided after graduating from The School of Fashion Design, would stay close to her roots and start a business in Boston. With over 35 years in her own design business, Denise has established herself as a top designer. Hajjar sold her creations nationally to department stores, specialty boutiques and individual clients worldwide.

Furthermore, Denise has designed costumes for many celebrities; television, theatre, commercials, and movies, such as "Johnny Slades Greatest Hits," starring John Fiori of the Sopranos. Also "Undercurrent" starring Lorenzo Lamas and Brenda Strong (who currently is the voice of Mary Alice Young on the television show "Desperate Housewives." The uniforms for the "Boston Children's Chorus" are stitched each season by Hajjar. She has received the Lifetime Achievement Award in Fashion, Vision Leader Award, Exceptional Women Award, The Distinguished Alumni Award and Rising Star of the Year Award, to name a few.

Denise's philosophy, "Giving back should be the rule, not the exception." are not just words to her. Local charities Hajjar has been involved with are

American Heart Association's, Go Red for Women in Boston, The ALS Association - Eleanor's Affair, Dress for Success – Boston, "Big Sister Association of Greater Boston", Catholic Charities, Boston Medical – Cancer Cares Cat Walk.

This decorated designer is still bringing Boston classic style year after year and excited to continue with being a part of an amazing brand, "Setting the Space." Mark your calendar and RSVP next Thursday March 14th for an evening of food, fashion, and networking. Denise Hajjar / Setting the Space is located at 490 Assembly Row – Somerville. Visit her website at www.denisehajjar.com or follow her on social media at; Facebook / Denise Hajjar Boston, Instagram / denisehajjarboston.

February 2019 Scene&Style Magazine - Hajjar Hits the NYC Fashion Week Runway

The divine dress Designer Denise Hajjar is kicking off 2019 with style. From moving into her new location at Setting the Space in the modern Assembly Row and now this Friday February 8th making her NYC Fashion Week debut at The Ballroom in the Watson Hotel Midtown New York City.

Entrepreneurs and Professionals Network better known as EPN will present "Style and Opulence Fashion for a Cause." The evening will comprise of: A red carpet photo shoot, runway fashion defile by six outstanding designers, live music performances, red carpet interviews, a live DJ and more. The red-carpet arrival time is 7:30 p.m. and show time being 8:00 p.m. with a strong suggestion to dress to impress. Part of the proceeds will help purchase a backpack for students as part of EPN's book back program giveaway to students.

The featured model will be Maxim Covergirl Actress/Model, Janel Tanna. Running the red carpet will be Victoria Henley from America's Next Top Model Association and host at iHeartRadio who will provide full media coverage. Showing Designers will include; Elizabeth Delgado featuring her "Passion" Collection, Daniel Chimowitz featuring his "Walking Canvas" Collection, Denise Hajjar featuring her incredible Ready to Wear and Evening Wear Collection, Daniel Alexander featuring his "DA of Oz" Collection and his new DA Heel Collection, Tiffany Aaron featuring her Couture Bride and Bridesmaids Collection, Martha Jackson featuring her "Boho Royale" Collection.

Entrepreneurs and Professionals Network "EPN" is a global organization headquartered in New York City. Their activities include regular networking events at sophisticated venues throughout the Tri-State area, marketing, personal and professional branding. Through our online media proprieties, EPN reaches an international community of small and large business owners, investors, thought leaders, industry executives and technologists. They empower, motivate, and inspire entrepreneurship and leadership worldwide using the most powerful forms of media.

Boston born and raised, Denise Hajjar inherited her design interest and talent from her grandmother who was also a designer in Damascus, Syria. Her grandfather also in the industry, was a pattern maker and owned a dress factory from Beirut, Lebanon. Denise decided after graduating from The School of Fashion Design, would stay close to her roots and start a business in Boston. With over 35 years in her own design business, Denise has established herself as a top designer. Hajjar sold her creations nationally to department stores, specialty boutiques and individual clients worldwide.

Furthermore, Denise has designed costumes for many celebrities; television, theatre, commercials, and movies, such as "Johnny Slades Greatest Hits," starring John Fiori of the Sopranos. Also "Undercurrent" starring Lorenzo Lamas and Brenda Strong (who currently is the voice of Mary Alice Young on the television show "Desperate Housewives." The uniforms for the "Boston Children's Chorus" are stitched each season by Hajjar. She has received the Lifetime Achievement Award in Fashion,

Vision Leader Award, Exceptional Women Award, The Distinguished Alumni Award and Rising Star of the Year Award, to name a few.

Denise's philosophy, "Giving back should be the rule, not the exception." are not just words to her. Local charities Hajjar has been involved with are American Heart Association's, Go Red for Women in Boston, The ALS Association - Eleanor's Affair, Dress for Success – Boston, "Big Sister Association of Greater Boston", Catholic Charities, Boston Medical – Cancer Cares Cat Walk.

It is hard to believe that a decorated diva like Denise Hajjar will be showing for the first time at New York Fashion Week, yet it is easy to understand when you see her loyalty to the list of clients in Boston. Don't miss the fifteen fabulous pieces hitting the runway this Friday February 8th held in The Ballroom at the Watson Hotel Midtown New York City. To see more on this timeless and elegant designer visit www.denisehajjar.com .

January 2019 Scene&Style Magazine Issue #24 - Boston Fashion Celebrates Their Finest

As the holidays near in, each year you can expect to mark your calendar for the annual Boston Fashion Awards. The cities finest come together for a night of live entertainment, fashion installations from nominees, and the praising of all that make our stylish community what it is.

This year the awards were held in the event space of the contemporary and upscale restaurant La Fabrica Central in Cambridge and hosted by

Jennifer Mariel Ruiz. The evening began with a cocktail hour for guests to mingle at the lavish long oak bar. The opening act of the night was Vincent King and band giving their soulful rendition of "The Shape of You." Following was the first runway presentation from Shaco Couture paired with Jewelinga Designs. The evening continued with more from designers such as The Lucky Onez, also Vava featuring a rocking street style and a Boston icon Angelica Timas with her sexy and sophisticated looks. In between there were performances from Simone Cardoso and Teddy Mathews. All while rotating the announcements of winners in categories like; Hair Salon, Female/Male Print Model, Designer Evening, Swimwear, Couture and more.

A highlight was the honoring of the 2018 Fashion Achievement Award presented by MC and manlicious Model Gustavo Leon. After a heartwarming speech and insight into the life lead, winner David Josef was welcomed to the stage to accept his award while giving thanks to all legends that have helped him grow all the way.

The 2018 ceremony was filled with festive moments, collections, musical performances, and respect for those that give their all on and off the runway. The Boston Fashion Awards focus is to build a positive image of the Boston fashion scene internationally and strengthen the fellowship within the local industry while raising funds and awareness for select local charitable organizations. For more information on the event, list of winners and nominees visit www.bostonfashionawards.com .

Chapter Seven – 2018

"Dress shabbily and they remember the dress; dress impeccably and they notice the woman." —Coco Chanel

November 2018 Scene&Style Magazine Issue #23- Slope Style in the She Shed

Once the leaves are no longer a crisp orange color New England knows its time for the annual Boston.com Ski and Snow Expo which returned for its 37th year in the cites Seaport World Trade Center.

The four days of slope style fun brings mountain representatives from all over the country, entertainment from the Skyriders, International Trampoline Champions and this year rocking live music from Shark Martin. The room is lined with booths of must have accessories from the newest and time-honored brands like Powe., Nordica, Inferno, SKEA, and plenty of beverages from beer to the tasty protein recovery drink Trimino.

In her 5th year local stylist Kathy Benharris has been making the expo a fashionable one. Benharris has presented runway shows with the current season's snow styles, rotating entertainment of local dance sensations and more. Every year its chic and fresh and in 2018 it was "Her Turn" in the "She Shed" sponsored by Sunday River Mountain. They teamed up with Benharris to show their commitment to supporting female winter athletes and have an entire month in January dedicated to it.

The She Shed was a replicated lodge where ladies gents and kids of course could come take a load off by the fire and relax. The Shed featured an outfit of day styled by the Benharris team, hair, and make-up tips on site from MLR Artists and sick braid twists to look sleek on the slope from Carbon Salon diva Lindsey Grenier. With all the fabulous fashion a girl could need right in the She Shed why not finish off your time with some Yoga! Guru Kristina Grinovich with Namasayido was there to educate on the importance of stretching, focus, and even demonstrate some techniques to take your snow game to the next level.

Scene&Style was able to catch up with the Queen of Snow Style Kathy Benharris for a little one on one chat by the fire. When asked if the She Shed is new to the expo this year, how did that come about? Benharris replied, "I am passionate about all winter sports with skiing being my obsession. I love sharing the joy of being on top of a mountain in the winter and am always looking to encourage other women to experience all that the alpine lifestyle offers. I envisioned a space that would look like an inviting ski lodge that would welcome skiers and snowboarders to connect with others that share their interests. Sunday River sponsored Her Turn at the She Shed and much of the decor came from the resort and our home there. Check out Sunday River's Holiday Hang Over Event for a female focused weekend of fun. The Shed also featured female specific skis and snowboards by Rossingnol, Volkl, K2 and Meier with fashion and accessories from Country Ski & Sport."

Looking for some backstage insight, what is the inspiration behind the She Shed? Kathy followed with, "Simply put - my love of playing on the snow and wanting to help others celebrate everything that the winter offers is what drove this creation. I was thrilled that so many influential skiers and female sports leaders spent time in the She Shed sharing their expertise and connecting with others. We also had yoga and beauty experts to give tips on how to maximize the upcoming season.

Closing out the conversation, I've heard that you have had some snow celebrities hang out in your She Shed this weekend, who were a few favorites? Benharris sighed, "It's so hard to pick "favorites" because every female that appeared in the Shed brought her own special magic and pedigree. Olympian Donna Weinbrecht was incredible to feature in the She Shed. Donna shares her gold medal with everyone and is so genuine and giving of her time. It was also great to host Wendy Clinch of The Ski Diva Forum who drew a large crowd and brought with her a message of confidence."

The Boston.com Ski and Snow Expo is an event New England looks forward to year after year. It gets slope junkies excited and with stylists like Benharris has them looking sharp when they get to the mountain. For more information on the event visit www.skisnowexpo.com.

November 2018 Scene&Style Issue #22 (10-6-2018) bosFW "The Real Oliver Thomas Shows Fashionably Late Styled by KB Fashion Productions Collaborating; Angelica Timas, Simone Simon, Irina Gorbman, Lindsay Tia, were Jevela Jewelry, T. Jazelle, Tracy Belben"

Fashion isn't all about overly expensive labels in a one size mini fit for all. For the modern women it is about functionality with a stylish look. Fashion Week 2018 brought the ladies of Boston exactly that and more featuring Oliver Thomas bags at the Liberty Hotel's Fashionably Late.

As guests poured into the lavish lobby of the hotel hot jams came from resident DJ Frank White while gals were able to grab a seat at the pop-up braid bar hosted by Carbon Salon who also provided the hair for the Dynasty models of the evening.

Right on queue the fashion began flowing up on the catwalk. A bright canary yellow duffle bag tagging along with a bedazzled "bonjour" black dress from William Edward Boutique and color wise perfectly paired opened toed stilettoes from Burju Shoes that were brought together by Stylist of the event Kathy Benharris. From there everything a girl could need from utility to get through the day to look stunning at night came down the runway.

Designers like Angelica Timas contributed to the looks with a playful dress and a new release from Oliver Thomas in a bold red cross body belt bag. Or a chic Simone Simon skintight cocktail one piece paired with an Oliver Thomas deep blue camo cross bag. Irina Gorbman brought in her painted pieces of a matching yoga pant and bra to show the versatility of what the black duffle from Oliver Thomas collection has to offer. Lindsay Tia The Cue showed a full white ballet skirt with a black T-shirt and the Oliver Thomas Ferrari red backpack for that laid-back look. Other designers to pair up were Jevela Jewelry, T. Jazelle and Tracy Belben with funky flow, sparkle, and shimmer and a not so granny fanny pack in the Oliver Thomas line. The final look to hit the runway came from Oliver Thomas himself rocking the newest launch from the brand, customizable dog coats.

Scene&Style was able to catch Designer Sue Fuller before the show who looked smoking in an all-black honeycomb sewn Angelica Timas off the shoulder dress. When asked what the inspiration behind the whole collection was, Fuller replied. "It was to solve the heavy multi bag syndrome that women have. Everything we produce is ultimate and light weight. We have a ton of secret stash compartments on the inside, so you can separate your dirty clothes from your clean. There is lots of organization and functionality to the designs with RFID blocking in all our bags."

Fuller continued with, "The name of the company is after my dog, "Oliver Thomas" and is meant to be a fun functional line that can go from day to night and week to weekend. Our product is vegan and fully machine washable. We don't want anyone to take themselves too seriously. If you look at our website, we have really fun headlines that say; "This bag will not make your legs nor your weekends longer" or "This bag won't make you fabulous if your miserable to begin with."

When asked to choose her favorite piece from the collection Fuller tensed up a bit with a reply of, "It's like having to choose your favorite child." Then moved into describing their latest piece "We are introducing the kitchen sink duffle it has a great organization on the outside for all of your shoes if you are going to the gym, it also has a secret stash bottom when you are trying to organize your day. You can fit about three pairs of shoes in the bottom. It has a great super sporty crossbody strap that is contrasting that looks truly relevant and fun. Then of course, you can customize any of our bags with one of our patches and just a hairdryer. You can pick your own badge." Fuller then showed her statement for the evening "Bullies need not apply." "We have over 50 badges that you can choose from".

What is the statement you want your collection to be making? Fuller expressed, "In total we talk about how important it is for people to not take themselves too seriously and just to have fun. We want them to collect the collection. That is why everything is all about easy care. You just put it in machine wash cold, hang dry. It's lightweight, we talk about if we haven't lightened your load today then we haven't done our job. We wanted to make it uniquely yours. That's why we want you to customize it with our badges. We're hoping that by putting badges on people will come up to you, connect with you and continue to form relationships."

Post show as the jam-packed jail house began to clear Scene&Style was able to snag the Producer Kathy Benharris. Kathy was enthusiastic when saying, "It was important to Oliver Thomas that the clothing, shoes, etc. be sourced from Boston area purveyors of fashion so everything that was in show came from local designers, brands, and boutiques. As the stylist, I wanted the looks to convey confidence, playfulness, and sass. Oliver Thomas bags are incredibly versatile so from athlesiure to dressy, I wanted to present a wide range of looks that were based on real life activities and saved an editorial statement to close the show. For the finale, I did go for it with an editorial look by using a tiara that matches the Oliver Thomas logo and a cape to showcase the Oliver Thomas badges because they are amazing, and I wanted to show as many badges as possible to close the show. I believe every female can be her own superhero and it was great to work with a brand whose product is truly fabulous."

The Oliver Thomas brand believes "Open-mindedness is the new black." Nobody needs another bag. Nobody really needs another anything. But you want stuff sometimes and there's nothing wrong with that. They just won't try to sell you that their bags will make neither your booty nor life story juicier. Their bags carry stuff. Not self-worth.

October 2018 bosFW Scene&Style Magazine - Roxbury Faith Restored Through Fashion

During hard times blessings come in many forms and beloved Boston designer David Josef gives his heart to others finding hope through "Faith in Fashion". The charity event took to the runway recently for its second annual show with returning co-hosts Marjorie Clappord, Chris Spinazzola, and Daniel James Forrester. The 2018 edition was held at the Newton American Legion Post with proceeds going to the "The Cory Johnson Program."

The evening began with light refreshments and brimming inspirational music from the Roxbury Presbyterian Church Choir accompanied by Willie Archibald, Issa Bibbins, and their Jazz tailored band. Their fun and uplifting vibe set the tone for celebrity signer Linda Gaines sister of Donna Summers, whose soulful voice was a perfect preview for who was next on stage. Deb Johnson's mother of Cory Johnson strongly sat and stole hearts with her touching story of how she lost her son and the strength Roxbury Presbyterian provided. Following, Reverend Liz Walker graced the guests with the beauty of her spiritual sermon. The room became lighter as she preached on love and how "this is a time for healing."

With all in a trance of tenderness and warmth it was time to let the bidding begin. Broadway's Mary Callannan opened the live auction and brought the entertainment with her vibrant personality. Items donated that were up for grabs ranged from a portrait painted of the Roxbury community featuring Rev Walker from Michael Guarino Fine Arts or a full suit from men's designer Allan Rouleau. Contributions also came from; St. John Kitts, MS Walker & The Smoke Shop, Nik Walker "Hamilton", Janine Mammano, Teatro Restaurant and Karen Ward Holmes WCVB-TV.

After all bidding wars were over it was onto the fashion! Opening was the man of the evening, David Josef showing his latest collection. Always with his glamorous touch looks of chic pant suits with beaded florals, form fitting velvet, sexy jumpers with sleek cuts, off the shoulder shine all began to flood the runway. Following was BlancoMaj was a flirty line of fall jackets. Then the men hit the stage wearing styles from Lord & Taylor. Nouveau Fashion Gallery made an appearance with an all-black line-up featuring dresses from deep desirable cuts to modern business like looks.

Marie Galvin brought stunning styles and a showstopper in a jacket with a peacock design and teal trim. Closing the fashion portion was Boston beauty Denise Hajjar. She pulled glimpses from her boutique of denim full length coats, fun and flowing dresses, multidimensional wraps, bold reds, feathers, and fur.

This wasn't your average fashion show of the dark or trendy music as the live church band continued on and revved up the runway with vocals and a jazz band funk feel. Celebrity models donated their flawless strut such as; Olga Konstanzia, Lucille Murray, Hollis Colby, Sonia Garufi, Jacquie Williams, Munjeet Geyer, Jane Conway, Christy Cashman & Susan Solomont and the one who gives us all Faith in Fashion, Yolanda Cellucci. Mixed in were those that represent the community as church models; Sherrice Grogan, Jana Mills, Kim Houston, Robin Lee, Mekah Mcintosh, Marcia Bibbins, Jamaya Mill, Shondell Davis, Gloria White Hammond, Louise Johnson, Marcia Fearon, Edward Lewis, Michael Austin, Douglas Lomax, Devon Thompson, Andre Donegan and Eugene Huffman. Bringing all the ladies to their luscious looks were Rebecca Alvarado B'GlamBoston, Stephanie Kim, Beckah Mua, Jessica Villegas-Montiero providing hair and make-up.

Scene&Style was able to chat with Founder David Josef post show who expressed, "The night was the definition of love. Everything you said on that stage was from the heart. Whether it be the amazing choirs, Donna summer's sister singing her music, to the incredible church ladies who were modeling, to the professional girls who donated their time. Every designer contributed their clothes because they believe in the cause. We all believe it's the time for healing, I can't thank everyone enough for being there." The evening was another charitable success for Josef raising around $200,000 for The Cory Johnson Program and benefiting Roxbury Presbyterian Church.

The Cory Johnson Program for post traumatic healing is a community-based approach to addressing the epidemic of PTSD in urban neighborhoods, fostering connection and empowering individuals to take an active role in helping themselves and others heal. All programming is free and takes place at 328 Warren Street, Roxbury. "CAN WE TALK?" is a Community Conversation on Trauma, 6 PM the final Thursday of every month. It is a safe, supportive space in which to share your story, or listen to others. The evening begins with dinner at 6 pm, then Rev. Liz Walker opens the time for sharing. Free childcare provided. If you are interested email colleensharka@rpcsic.org for more information or visit https://rpcsocialimpactctr.org/the-cory-johnson-program-for-post-traumatic-healing/

Nestled on one of the main veins in the community, Roxbury Presbyterian Church has stood on the corner of Warren and Woodbine Streets since 1865. At the beginning of the 1800's Roxbury was home almost exclusively to upper and middle-class Yankees. Beginning in the 1840's many Irish immigrants flooding to the Massachusetts to escape the potato famine. As immigration continued some Irish families settled directly in Roxbury, or second generations families moved from Boston to Mission Hill and later in the Dudley Street area.

Though their community is typically labeled as violent and marginalized, Roxbury is a vibrant, diverse, and eclectic group of people with tremendous assets and rich history. Though their challenges of violence and trauma are real, Roxbury Presbyterian Church stands to be a beacon of light and hope in response to the changing needs of their community that they are so proud to call home.

10-5-2018 bosFW Scene&Style Magazine "Reina Valentina Makes a Fashionable Debut."

The new and very formal fabulous online boutique Reina Valentina put the word out on the Boston Fashion Week calendar that they have a must-see product. They highlighted looks in a show at the sexy lounge area in the Seaport Residences.

There was a visual insight into the team behind the trending store in tiffany type photo frames of the girls placed upon the candy and cake filled tables. The roped off room for networking oozed elegance from the fresh flowers that were lining the space from wall to wall.

The second you stepped outside onto the roof deck you were memorized by the beautiful view of a skyline of Boston. Also greeted by sick beats from DJ Alcide who at one point was counterpart to the live entertainment from a magnificently talented electric violinist. As you made your way to the back with the wadding waterfall and full deck furniture there were Prickled flavored cocktails and freshly grilled treats.

Once the overflowing number of guests were spread into two sides the fashion hit the perfectly placed runway. The Rock Royalty stood true to its name being looks like deep navy-blue dresses with long flowing length and a deep V-neck cut or a knee length off the shoulders topped with beautiful, jeweled crowns began to flood the runway. Cutesy pants suit options with flashy jackets made their way, sexy leather and lace tops, simple silk camisoles, bold patterned pants, the collections had it all. Whatever the modern woman with a classic eye may be looking for from work to play can be found in the Rock Royalty shopping cart.

Reina Valentina is a women's modest chic fashion online boutique. They are committed to women being fully self-expressed by providing them a blend of modesty and contemporary style. They support the empowerment of women business owners and socially conscious brands by sourcing and sharing stories from these women. They aren't all about the dollar Reina Valentina believes in; Empower, Promote, Share & Give Back! They give a portion of proceeds to The Hunger Project.

Boston keep your eyes peeled for these beautiful business ladies who also run a marketing company. These ladies have impressive professional skills and a chic online boutique with a fresh approach to traditional designs.

**December 2018 Scene&Style Magazine Issue #21 (10-3-2018) bosFW
"Hajjar Ruled the Runway Once Again" – Denise Hajjar**

Fashion is an expression, a way to tell a story without speaking. Legendry Designer Denise Hajjar gave the city a novel from her timeless tale of style. Hajjar poured her heart into Boston Fashion Week with producing 54 looks including her fall collection.

The event was held at the Intercontinental Boston which is host to her boutique. The evening began with rows of guests streaming from the hotel entrance right down to the Rumba lounge getting into the mood with music from DJ Denise LaCarubba.

Hajjar is a solid professional and never keeps a crowd waiting as the show started right on time. Models began to command attention with their flawless walk and queued performance. As for the fashion, Hajjar's classic look of pattered wrap dress in multiple options flooded the scene. Ferrari red suit jackets, fur galore from head pieces to funky vests. Full length flowing dresses, chic everyday outfits making noise in the office, seasonal green snakeskin leather skirts, simple yet flattering white tops. Dozens of fall jackets from faux fur trims to multidimensional patterns, black cocktail numbers, bold jewelry paired from SharynAndCO also handbags from Andrea Valentini. Even comfortable evening wear, off the shoulder sweaters, baby pink power suits to straight up sexy beaded minis. With 54 looks hitting the runway Hajjar made a statement being her boutique has it all!

Hajjar is known for her celebrity line up of models and the evening ended with a special tribute to the glittering smile that had stunned her runway for decades, the late Linda Cole Petrosian. Following was a jammed packed after party held in her boutique with light bites and plenty of shopping.

Scene&Style was able to catch up with the famed designer who expressed her focus for the show. "This time I decided to show a collection of clothes and accessories based on how I would like to see women dress. I showed looks and trends full of color, texture, and details. Whether it's clothing or accessories. EVERYTHING will be put together so that the audience can also have it in their wardrobes."

Boston born and raised, Denise Hajjar inherited her design interest and talent from her grandmother, who was also a designer in Damascus, Syria. Her grandfather, who was from Beirut, was a patternmaker and owned a dress factory in Boston. After graduating from The School of Fashion Design, Denise decided to stay close to her roots and start her business in Boston. Now in her 30th year, Denise has established herself as a top designer, having sold her designs nationally to department stores, specialty boutiques and clients worldwide. She is immensely proud that all her clothes are cut and sewn in Massachusetts.

Denise is also the creator and founder of the "Big Dreams Start Small" event to benefit St. Jude Children's Research Hospital. She fervently supports the research, treatment, and commitment of the medical teams at the hospital, knowing that St. Jude is a "beacon of light in a parent's darkest night." Denise lives by her philosophy: "Giving back should be the rule, not the exception."

Denise's boutique currently resides in the Intercontinental Boston Hotel located at 510 Atlantic Ave Suite A, Boston and can be reached at (617) 266-2296. Hajjar has been dressing women for decades in her timeless designs and trendy styles. Hajjar offers personal tailoring, wedding dress creations and is now carrying skin care products and even grooming kits for men. Whether you are in search of a red carpet look or a pair of Sunday jeans Hajjar has it all. SHOP online at denisehajjarboutique.com or treat yourself to a trip to the store.

10-3-2018 bosFW Scene&Style Magazine "Lasell's Fashion Creativity was Put to the Test- Presented by KB Fashion Productions."

Boston Fashion Week isn't just a time for established designers to showcase their talents but an opportunity for the cities students to snag some exposure. Producer Kathy Benharris has extended ties to Lasell College and a fondness for their fashion program. Benharris took the outfits off the runway and created an exhibit in the Seaport District for 10 emerging designers to make a mark.

The pieces were inspired by Boston's newly renovated and trending section of the city, "The Seaport" with a non-textile construction restriction. Articles such as CDs, grommets, mirrors, duct tape, coffee filters, plastic wrap, and tarps were amongst the list of items used in the concept of creation.

Ensembles displayed were what appeared to be a purple velour suit, but the fun was the mystery to what the fabric could have been. A wedding white lace dress with colored coffee filter flowers, a grey high neck dress with a black vest that resembled leather yet was a tarp, a plain leather mini sleeveless dress with the drama being CDs glued on creating rotating color. Designers: Christa Augustus '20, Linda Avila '19, Eunice Bruno '19, Elizabeth Castaldi '19, Cailin Flannery '19, Panna Kiss '19, Marianna Lenskaya '19, Sabrina Michaud '20, Samantha Rego '20 and Elizabeth Witherell '20 were giving a Project Runway type of task and killed it with the creativity and imagination.

The Fashion Design and Production Major at Lasell has a professional focus, rooted in Connected Learning, which seeks to educate students by promoting self-expression, academic exploration, and critical thinking in academic, civic, and career-relevant areas.

The Fashion Design and Production degree program prepares students to navigate the fast-paced fashion industry by offering expertise in business, textiles, garment design, pattern making, buying, operations, and more.

The Lasell Fashion Collection contains over 2,000 items dating back to the 19th century, which helps support students in understanding historical style details, construction techniques, textile usage, and societal function. Lasell's School of Fashion has degree programs in Fashion Communication and Promotion, Fashion Design and Production, and Fashion and Retail Merchandising.

10-1-2018 bosfw Scene&Style Magazine "Boston Fashion Week Opening- The Power of Women, The Future of Boston Fashion Featuring; Gina deWolfe of deWolfe Leather Goods, Cecile Thieulin of Simone Simon, Meghan Doyle Tallulah and Poppy, Joelle Fontaine of I Am Kréyol, Graciela Rivas Leslin of Graciela Rivas Collection, Melina Cortes-Nmili of lalla bee."

Boston Fashion Week officially opened with a highly attended runway event in the newest space to the Financial District Exchange. The evening began with cocktails, light bites, mingling with the city's elite as every table and seat was taken by someone that a newcomer to the industry was waiting in line to meet.

The evening was themed, "The Power of Women, The Future of Boston Fashion." As Founder of Boston Fashion Week Jay Calderin took stage to thank all that had a hand in the production of the evening gave praise to the grandest of ladies in his life, an example of a powerful women, mom.

Calderin then brought attention to a beautiful slide show gracing the walls with still images flooding feet high yet still couldn't fully express the enormous impact she had on all. Linda Cole Petrosin; was a tribute to the power of women, a local legend on the catwalk and the 2018 season was dedicated to her memory as she recently lost her battle with cancer.

As Jay began to share fond memories there was only one that could get up there and exude the energy Linda did, her mother Yolanda Cellucci. Yolanda took center stage was a commanding grace, strength of our girl lost and a warming remembrance. Cellucci shared she lived a life of love, laughter and dancing, a fantastic woman. A wife, a mother of two and sister to designer Sandra and daughter. She made her thanks known to all the friends, flowers and cards over the past three years that gave Linda the spirit to survive. Cellucci smiled and said, "God above had decided he needed another angel and someone like Linda to get the dancing going." She then transitioned into that her family will be holding an honorary dance party for Linda, being Linda is still alive within us. When she passed, she raised over $35,000 dollars that went to Saint Jude's Hospital. Yolanda closed with a thanks to all and a reminder, "don't count Linda out, she's still here, she's alive and well within every one of us."

After the Queen had spoken and demanded the evening have a high volume of life the introduction to the future of fashion, the ones to continue on the power of women began in a flawless video production giving insight to each designer. Gina deWolfe of deWolfe Leather Goods; Strives to buy pieces within the food industry so that no part of the animal is wasted. With that makes her designs unique as they will have scars, brands of marks which brings a level of respect for the animal.

Cecile Thieulin of Simone Simon Collection; Inspires to incorporate elegance, technology, comfort stability as an architect she uses her background to create and connect the human body between the cloths and structure of the fabric. Meghan Doyle of Tallulah and Poppy; Doyle dished that in high school she would take apart designs, reconstruct them and receive a rave response. With that she began sewing lessons, playing with patterns, got herself a business degree then was off to the Boston School of Fashion Design. From there she chose the name Tallulah as it means to live a fulfilled life and Poppy because it means funky and fun. Her brand is bold, bright, and full of patterns.

Joelle Fontaine of I Am Kréyol; Finds her textures and fabrics first and from there works on the designs with her mother who creates the stitching. Her main goal is to be able to make an impact with recently raising money to work with artists in Hatti. Joelle makes every effort to be a good example for her son, to make sure he knows he can be whatever he wants. "If you have a goal and see that goal in the end you know you can win. Whatever failure you deal with along the way is just part of your process, this too shall pass."

Graciela Rivas Leslin of Graciela Rivas Collection; Graciela will start with the sketch of the idea and from there the pattern and production. Texture or shape is generally the focus and creates the drama of her collection. She has a high respect for women designers and those who have made their way to be globally recognized it doesn't happen overnight the passion for their craft inspires her.

Melina Cortes-Nmili of lalla bee As a fluent Spanish speaker is thankful for her cousin who runs the production end of the business in the Dominican Republic. Bee expressed its amazing to put her art out there yet if she didn't have the network, she does it would be impossible to make all that happen. "It's not just about a collection, it's not about a business it's a lifestyle." Lalla leaves the audience with this, "Fashion shows are awesome, creating is awesome but it costs money. We as women must be able to create a balance, be assertive in our negotiations, as much as we are designers if we expect to make money, we must also be entrepreneurs."

With that being said it was time for the fashion! Bold statements and playful patterns opened the runway from Iam Kréyol. Always bringing a fierceness to her designs, autumns tones of orange and soft browns were a highlight. Shown in dresses for a modern woman whose style speaks in a quiet room, everyday denim skirts and loud lace were fished with breathtaking decorative teal jackets.

Following was Simone who made a play on pastels and solid stripes. With the audience feeling like they had spent an afternoon in Paris from the feel of the collection. Simone's style is fit for the office or making an appearance at an after-work event.

Next was deWolfe showing well stitched wallets and handbags in simplistic denim outfits to keep the focus on the product. Trendy backpacks in a cherry red shade, even a little something for the men in a casual leather envelope look for those on the go meetings. Even an everyday over the shoulder multipurpose carrying case in a cool deep grey for the gents.

Brightening the runway was Tallulah & Poppy with turquoise tones paired with hard fall colors. A use of native patterns kept the eye on the details. Simple beiges with bold furs, silk skirts, metallic dresses kept coming down the runway with one in wonder where does the girl find the time?

Lalla Bee came with a cohesive collection in the colors and patterns that seemed to find their way into each piece. Sharp shapes and commanding greens brought a bold expression. Peek a boo pattern in the underlining, flowing floral dresses, even a sexy lace the lady brought it all including a neon tail to a red-carpet style.

Closing was Graciela Rivas expressing a European standard with her own details. Satin dresses with beaded trims. Pretty pink ruffles with deep cuts and high hems, a red cocktail dress that catches the eye yet fit for an evening at the opera. Cute all black club numbers, pure white pieces all made an impact as the final collection to show at the opening of Boston Fashion Week 2018.

With a sense of a major city fashion show, the evening was a hit and Boston making it known, fashion lives here. Downtown Boston BID/Platform Downtown hands a hand in the entertainment of; photographer Tracy Aiguier, and video production team Nicole O'Connor of Shanachie Studios and Eric Leone of Paul Horton Visuals together creating in-depth designer profiles and editorial imagery. Also featuring Ryan Edwards of Masary Studios and a special Sound Sculpture + DJ set.

9-31-2018 bosFW Scene&Style Magazine "MadeINcubator, Panelists; Gretta Monahan, Leah Gardner, Kathy Benharris, Elisha Daniels, David Josef, Anna Foster, Janet Howard"

Boston Fashion Week isn't all about the shows, it gives the city an opportunity to highlight their finest and newcomers to the community to grow from knowledge shared from experts in their specific fields. Boston's first fashion incubator, MadeINcubator hosted a panel discussion in a castle of royal fashion Bloomindale's Chestnut Hill.

Host of the event Lisa Pierpont Editor in Chief of the magazine got right to the business with the first panelist Gretta Monahan; Beauty, Fashion and Wellness Expert. Monahan begins by telling the tale of how she fell in love with fashion. At an early age she was graced by the glamour of a local legend Yolanda Cellucci by being able to assist in her boutique on weekend mornings. As she spoke on her current products, she attributed that her local spa G Spot is based on inspiration with what she learned from Cellucci. Monahan was passionate about saying, she loves having her stores here in Boston. There is no community like this community, fashion is fierce in Boston she proclaims on her journeys through Paris, Milan NYC that Boston fashion is smart.

The next up on the panel was Leah Gardner, a Blogger Expert and Designer. Gardner shared her story of having a Chemistry background with a well-off corporate position yet wasn't satisfied. She secretly a fondness for fashion and started a style tip blog that seemed to be taking on a life of its own. When Pierpont asked if blogging is a viable business Gardner replied, "It can be very competitive but if you do your research on how to market yourself it can be rewarding."

Following was a leading lady in the industry Kathy Benharris, Stylist and Event Producer. Benharris began by creating the picture of the magic behind a fashion show. She spoke on how her team gets to tell a fashion story from what you see, smell, taste and hear. They come up with creative ways to make each event its own. She praised the workout of day of by burning the most calories during a show and prides herself on that she is only as good as her team. When Pierpont asked her to boast a bit about who she has worked with, Benharris replied' "Size does matter"! She went on to the 110-foot runway show she produced at Copley place with the Boston Bruins and proceeds benefiting Dana Farber. She also bragged about styling Miss Monahan for an event and how it was an honor that lady love bloomed between the two. When asked how she found her way it was based on being an adrenaline junkie. The love for taking on a project as if she had been handed their baby and teaching it four languages, rocking every aspect, and watching a client leave ecstatic they had worked with her. Being a general in the industry as the Leader of the Boston Fashion Meetup and soon sliding into the Regional Director role of The Boston Fashion Group International she finds inspiration in networking and connecting people. She strongly believes in network and connecting. To find your people, your fellow creatives and go make magic together, keep focus on your clients.

From there moving on down the panel was Elisha Daniels, Stylist, Designer and Author. Daniels has had her hand in many aspects of the business. She has contributed to from retail, marketing to private clients. She glowed when saying styling is her niche. Still in Neiman Marcus, Saks Fifth Avenue, and a list of high-end clienteles, she spends 6 days a week focused on dressing each in their own unique way. When sharing she is a breast cancer survivor makes a clear statement that all projects, she signs onto gives 20% back to the Breast Cancer Research Foundation which Daniels is a Board Member of.

Next up was the one and only David Josef, Fashion Designer. Josef opened with a quick bio from his impressive resume of 45 years with highlights such as being 19 in 1977 thinking he could conquer the world saved money and bought a shop in Lexington when there was no social media and made his way becoming a tv sensation on local programming shows. From there, a show room in NYC on 7th Avenue where he sold to

Neiman's, Saks, high end retailers. In 2000 came home to build a space in the South End as a custom designer. When Lisa asked what are the worries of a fashion designer a specific story came to mind, "Neiman Marcus had a 100% sell through with two of my dresses and wanted a reorder in the next three weeks. Yet I was booked through the next season. Every day is a different worry the fashion design is easy, its everything else. It was that experience which brought the change to custom design and not wholesale work." Josef explained he wants to work when he wants to work and be his own boss. Which has created a problem, Josef expresses that because of people like Kathy Benharris believing in him he is busier than he's ever been in his life. Josef was asked to give his opion on what new designer need to do when building their brand. He gave a warming answer of, "You have to have the talent in which brand you plan to build." Then quickly claimed social media! "Right now, it's all about social media you can build an image that you aren't and create the persona you want."

David gave credit to knowing what he does of social media from the lady to his right, Anna Foster. He isn't trying to sell himself he now understands how to share his brand and talents. Josef has helped create charity events such as "Faith in Fashion" and "Runway to the Rescue" and says every ticket he sells is straight from Facebook.

Nearing the end was Anna Foster, Brand Strategist, Speaker, and Fashion Maven. After giving many thanks to those that were behind the event Foster expressed her many roles within the industry. Seven years ago, Foster started her business "A Mavens World" and explaining a maven is a Hebrew word for a person in the know. Foster felt strong that we as women we wear many hats and feel that society says we should only wear one. Anna expressed that is unrealistic in her opinion and she works with small businesses to find their niche, their happy place. Her brand connects people to help them wear those few hats and be successful with them. Over the last seven years she has produced an event for the opening night of Boston Fashion Week. She prides herself on helping open the doors in the city for women of color, creating a platform for them to connect and grow. Foster is currently focused on her global women's conference and to bring more energy to Boston. She touches on the subject point that it's a tuff time for entrepreneurs with the internet and social media as boutiques are going out of business and with A Mavens World really trying to find that space in between for business to survive. She tributes to using failure as a steppingstone to success and encourages to embrace it and be mindful to have strategy and sharpen your skills. Foster has always been a person that gave support to events and the community so she is quick to be honest when others get it wrong. "The early part of our generation is getting it backwards; they will direct message me and immediately ask for help. My answer is NO! I don't even know you; can we meet first.?" A Mavens World teaches the process to building solid relationships and a reputation that gets a yes answer. Ann ended with, "If there is anything you can take away from me being up here it's that the human connection is huge, networks and relationships are even huger."

The final seat on the panel was held by Janet Howard, CFDA Designer and Product Development Specialist. Also is a Co-Owner of The Martini Factory, a manufacturer for designers. Howard looks at her work as being a dream maker, designers can come to them and they create what they are looking for. They hope to take the aches and pains out of being a designer and let them enjoy the fun. Howard expressed that she felt like a little bit on an outsider as they are in SoHo, NYC. It was soon after her partner was called out of the audience as a well-known local, Kim Barbieri Co- Owner of the Martini Factory. Barbieri was a bit more comfortable on the panel with digging right into the business side of Boston fashion and where it needs to be. Barbieri soundly stated, "When you guys have Boston Fashion Week you must have the right people in the audience. You cannot just have your friends and family, yes, it's a nice thing but you have to make sure the event coordinators are inviting; press, fashion directors, managers of high end retail stores because they are the only people who are going to make you successful."

That may have closed out the scheduled discussion, yet the show went on. Honorary chair and Fashion Designer Joe Malaika stepped up to say a few words, a question portion took place with fellow Designer Samuel Vartan getting up with curiosity in the celebrity filled audience. Then it all came to a close with all taking their fantastic goodie bags and getting up for a mix, mingle and network at the knowledgeable event.

MadeINcubator is a Massachusetts-based nonprofit organization that is revolutionizing the way designers learn, build, and succeed in fashion. We use fashion as an anchor to build economic development in the greater Boston area, a region once revered for its rich textile industry. MadeINcubator is the City of Boston's first fashion incubator and its mission is to change the fashion world through innovation, by developing ecosystems that allow exceptional fashion entrepreneurs to create new products and companies better and faster. We are here to support the business of fashion in Boston through a 5-month intensive program, as well as free and low-cost public workshops and networking events. MadeINcubator will foster in a new meaningful and impactful economy in Boston by giving fashion designers the technical product development, business tools and training they need to create innovative products and competitive businesses based in Boston. Visit MadeINcBoston.com for more on the work they are doing.

9-30-2018 bosFW Scene&Style Magazine "Fashion on Fire Featuring; Madeline Ventresca, Lalla Bee, Jaclyn Robichaud Doyle, Em Watson, Yetta Procope, KHANGLE."

For the second year in a row a new charity gala made its way onto the Boston Fashion Week calendar. Producer Olga Kwasniewski put together a beautiful benefit for the 2017 season and this year she most certainly lit the "Fashion on Fire."

The word went out the night before the big show that all seats had sold out and became an exclusive evening. Again, hosted at the marvelous

Hilton, Woburn the space was lined with sponsors, light bites, auction tables, red carpets with plenty of high-end gowns worn by guests.

With a keen eye Kwasniewski changed the runway setup from the previous year in the elegant ballroom for fresh look. The entertainment began with the Blessed Sacrament Color Guard showing off their flash with the flag. Welcoming remarks came from host Antoinette Antonio, Anchor with News Channel 5 Boston.

Local rising star Madeline Ventresca opened the runway with looks from her latest collection featuring dresses with a leather bustier, a risky see through lace, pops of teal and silk beiges. Following was the first appearance of designer KHANGLE and his men's collection. Out after was the first live performance of the evening by vocalist Patrice Peris. Brining the style back out on the runway was a metallic look from the Lalla Bee Collection. Memorizing the attendees was Kristina Danga an electric violinist who brought a modern sound to a classical art while swaying to the sound in her sexy chic attire. A Midnight Glow of elegance and sparkled style from designer Jaclyn Robichaud Doyle brought the attention back to the trends. Just before intermission, The Ruchita Dagli Collection brought a Middle Eastern sashay with an edgy take on a traditional style.

As guests made way back to their seats the show reopened with an easing performance from the soul of mother nature by the Dance Artists Ballet Academy. Storming out next was designer Em Watson making an American statement with authentic African fabrics and a modern twist. Following was, the future of fashion Boston Arts Academy Fashion Design and Technology School with a robotic movement and collaboration from students to present "The After-Party Collection." Creator Yetta Procope showed a Caribbean flavored collection of neon tones, twisted head wraps and skin-tight highlights. Closing out the fashion portion of the evening was the return of famed designer KHANGLE with his women's collection giving a dark Vietnamese drape of golden shadows.

The evening was a solid success from the performances, fashion, and the passion behind it all, to benefit Project Smile.

Project Smile is federally tax-exempt non-profit organization which donates stuffed animals, coloring books/crayons, small toys and children's reading books to police and fire departments for police officers, fire fighters and paramedics to give to children involved in traumatic situations. Project Smile has recently launched the Operation Elder Care program which provides stuffed animals to elderly people who are making the difficult and frequently traumatic transition to life in a nursing home. Established in November 2003, Project Smile was founded by Catherine Pisacane.

October 2018 bosFW "Bianchi Gets Steeped in Style" Scene&Style Magazine Issue #21

Boston Fashion Week continued in a traditional style with the legendary "Marilyn Riseman's Steeped in Style" hosted by the beloved Jane Conway Caspe in the historic Boston Public Library Courtyard featuring designer Alexandra Bianchi.

Guests were seated at their high-toned tables and began by indulging in their sophisticated selection of tea and hors d'oeuvres. Handpicked models by Bianchi began to grace the room in beige tones with dripping pearls off the hip in a sexy wide leg pant suit. Also, in a blush baby pink simplistic satin dress with the drama in the back of a sash and pearl looped from shoulder to shoulder. Keeping it cohesive was an elegant rose colored one piece with stunning floral patterns and an attention commanding train. The design to steal the show was a silver shadow wedding gown with a cloud fabric trailing from the neckline. Bianchi continued to send out wedding themed must haves with the casual look of nudes and floral flows for that flapper lady sort of feel with the music paired perfectly set in the jazz club era.

The show was a collaboration team that has been popping up at Bianchi's presentations. The swinging hair styles were provided by Charles Maksou the Dry Cut Craftsman. An Eight time "Boston's Best" award winner in his newest location on Newbury Street Charles continues the legacy of the Dry Cut from the legendary John Sahag. The method was founded in Paris, and Charles brought it to Boston in 1998, and was awarded "Boston's Best Dry Cut" after opening his first studio. With over 30 years of experience, what he enjoys most is being a sculptor. He loves creating the perfect shape for a client to enhance their natural features.

No outfit is complete without a flawless face which was created by Jacquelyn Vokey whose mission is to make every person she comes in contact with, happier and a more beautiful. Jacquelyn Started at Christian Dior many years ago as a Beauty Consultant and Makeup Artist and has now started her own business. She currently resides in Central Mass and travels for her clients. With awards such as Saks Fifth Avenue 2009, Betsey Johnson 2010 Vokey has got the right look for you.

Alexandra Renee Bianchi, born and raised in the Boston area, graduated from The School of Fashion Design in 2015. While studying she fell in love with the couture, custom, bridal and eveningwear realm of the fashion world. As she creates her garments, she strives for quality and sustainability. With classic silhouettes, her designs are edgy, fun, unique and flirty, while remaining timeless, elegant, and feminine. Her designs are all handmade, customary to the client. With each client she focuses on creating a perfectly tailored and constructed garment.

With dresses made morning of Bianchi impressed with a royal fashion week show. Her collections are a combination of elegance from an era of ladylike class and a modern touch of dark punk with sexy seems. Keep your eye out from this emerging designer as she spends her off time in the sewing rooms of Yolanda Cellucci and Vera Wang! Bianchi is most certainly the future of Boston Fashion.

September 2018 bosFW Scene&Style Magazine TANGOELLA gets Steeped in Style

Recently the fashionable lunch hour event, Marilyn Riseman's "Steeped in Style" welcomed modern looks from Ella Tang and her most recent TANGOELLA Collection.

The afternoon is always a two-show spilt with down timed filled feeling like a pampered queen with the elegant tea and crust free finger food at the chic Café Courtyard restaurant in Boston's historic public library. Hostess and always flawless model Jane Conway Caspe welcome guests with that photographic smile and sets the stage for the show.

The fall focused pieces came out draped over the gorgeous models showing a more casual play of cashmere sweaters and fitted pants paired with jewelry to transition the look from day to night wear. The beige cashmere made multiple appearances from scarves, patterned capes and knitted tops played with skirts. There was a quick pop of two deep blue and gold sparkled gowns that were perfect for a red-carpet runway sort of affair.

When the show came to a close Scene&Style was able to catch up with designer Ella Tang and hear a little on her inspiration for this collection. Tang commented, "This is my first year using cashmere. I like the concept of day to dense transition. Also investing in your wardrobe, I enjoy creating pieces you can invest in, garments to wear all year round. I am really focused on being Eco friendly as well, yet upholding sustainability."

The TANGOELLA signature style is sensual meets edgy. Central to the TANGOELLA design are the elements of balance and proportion. Versatile timeless pieces introduce a rhythm that impacts the wardrobe. The philosophy of Tangoella is that clothing should make one feel effortlessly beautiful and empowered.

With close attention to real-life day-to-day needs, the masterfully constructed pieces from TANGOELLA are inspired by the casual and formal activities that define cosmopolitan life. The distinctive modern attitude transitions seamlessly from day to night.

Ella Tang established TANGOELLA's first complete collection in Spring 2015. Ella's artistic sensibility to designing collections that convey modern with an edge became a driving force in her creative life.

Although creative inspiration is elusive, Ella credits her love of design to early exposures to couture, mathematics, and dance. Gifted in spatial thinking, Ella swam against the tide and forged her own path. Traveling to America from Taiwan, she attended the University of Massachusetts where she was awarded a master's degree in computer science and mathematics. She immediately enrolled in the School of Fashion Design in Boston and graduated two years later with a degree in Fashion Design.

For more on this designer, current collection or to shop visit tangoella.com.

September 2018 Boston Fashion Week Honors Linda Cole - Petrosian Scene&Style Magazine Issue #20

Beach days are almost gone, trend reports are out which means Boston Fashion Week is on the horizon. This year is set to take place September 30th- October 6th. This edition is dedicated to the magnificent Linda Cole Petrosian who recently passed away. A legend, catwalk queen and a smile that could make you forget about anything but the beauty she brought into the room. Ladies and gents walk tall this #bosfw18 there is a graceful spirit amongst us. The pre-fashion begins Friday, September 28th at 7pm, Hilton Woburn. The beautiful Olga Konstanzia returns with "Fashion on Fire" Presented by Project Smile. A charity gala featuring Boston's top designers, talent, music, and dance with a cocktail party sponsored by Svedka.

Opening Night; "The Power of Women the Future of Boston Fashion" takes place September 30th for a 7pm show at Exchange 100 Federal Street Presented by BFW. The evening will focus on the power of women in fashion and features a group of six professional designers who represent the future of Boston fashion both creatively and in business.

Tuesday October 2nd the timeless legendary designer Denise Hajjar welcomes guests for a 6:30pm show at Denise Hajjar Boutique/InterContinental Hotel. The reception will follow the show at the boutique, with appetizers, refreshments, and shopping. 15% will be taken off any purchases that night!

Hajjar expressed. "This time I have decided to show a collection of clothes and accessories based on how I would like to see women dress. I will be showing looks and trends full of color, texture and details." Thursday October 4th 10 pm show Fashionably Late at the Liberty Hotel presents designer.

Oliver Thomas who believes in burning the fashion rulebook. Check out a new collection paired with looks from Boston based designers and brands with styling by Kathy Benharris and hair and makeup by Carbon Salon. Closing out the week on October 6th; Artist and designer Betsy Dolinko presenting a lavish collection incorporating lacework and tambour beading. Sarian Designs, Surell Accessories & D'Antonio Boston Platinum & Diamonds runway shows will follow with drinks and music provided at the location of Sariar Handbags and Accessories in Newton Center. Listed are only a few of the many events, presentations and lectures for more information and what #bosfw18 has to offer visit www.bostonfashionweek.com.

August 2018 Caribbean Fashion Week Lights up the Ink Block
Scene&Style Magazine Issue #19

August is host to Caribbean heritage and for the fifth year is a row V Style production brought an entire week of cultured fashion events to the city of Boston. They generally preview the week with an outdoor gathering at the ICA to showcase what's in store. This year's theme was "The Beauty of it ALL" and began with an opening reception at the artsy Piano Craft Gallery featuring a favorite I Am Krevol, among others. Following events were; a dance and music workshop presented by Racines Black Dance Festival, a sip and chat beauty talk series, pop up shops yet the highlight is always the runway presentation where Scene&Style was on site! The venue was the trendy outdoor space,

"Underground at Ink Block." The day was dreary yet interstate 93 provided shelter for models and guests. Before the style took to the runway hostess Marsha Monroe welcomed "Island Vybe Dance Fitness" and instructor Tae Johnson front and center for a taste of her workouts with beats by DJ Larry Jordan.

Once the crowd was warmed up the Fashion began with brand designed by K'Sean Burrell-Naton presenting carnival costume and swimwear pieces that literally rocked the runway with the gorgeous models that made you feel like you were on the island. Following was the latest in contemporary African flair of traditional attire from "Dress with Confidence" designed by Yolanda Sealy. Representing the United States was the always fashion forward "Sparkle T" who graduated from Lasell College showing her eye-catching corsets and bustiers. A Nigerian collection from Dami V. of expressive textiles through wearable artform came from yet another Lasell graduate, Damilola Gilbert. Coming from the Commonwealth of Dominica was, "The House of Nasset" in a chic and ever creative line of crochet creations that closed out the runway presentation. It was another successful event for V Style Productions and colorful of the Caribbean culture and art. To find out more visit BostonCFW.com

June 2018 Men's European Fashion Comes to Boston's Newbury Street Scene&Style Magazine

Issue #18

Recently Suitsupply the ranked "No. 1 suit" by the Wall Street Journal brought their chic European style to Boston's Newbury Street. They welcomed the cities crème de la crème of fashion in for a VIP private opening. Owner, Fokke de Jong was also in attendance assuring his new clients of their "open kitchen concept," being you can have a Heineken and wait while your tailored right in the comfort of the store.

Boston is a nearly 9,000-square-feet standalone shop where locals can have a giggle over the nights spent at the former industry hot spot, "Daisy Buchanan's". Spanning across four floors, the store offers a spacious, vibrant atmosphere where customers can shop full collections of seasonal suits, jackets, shoes, outerwear, accessories and attire alongside the brand's core Never-Out-Of-Stock collection and Custom Made to Measure department. For style-conscious locals looking to experience the brand to the fullest, Suitsupply's trained associates will combine product knowledge with personality to create an unmatched shopping experience that is tailored to each individual client.

Suitsupply's 100th location represents an exciting step forward in its destination retail strategy. In a first for the brand, Suitsupply Boston will feature a unique in-house café concept called Café Susu. Located on the ground floor, Café Susu will bring both customers and local passers-by a relaxing space offering beer and wine and a variety of coffee drinks, fresh-pressed juices, and light healthy fare to enjoy while waiting for alterations, or to grab on the go.

In an industry where fast fashion dominates, and craftsmanship is quickly disappearing, Suitsupply brings a new energy and elegant aesthetic to the world of men's fashion and tailoring. Using only the finest sustainable fabrics, no attention to detail is ever spared and tailoring is done on-site while you wait.

The evening was a hit; the overflow of cocktails and delicious apps from high end catering company "Eats Meets West" to the onsite dapper don's ready and waiting to get our cities men fitted and looking fine at the 240A Newbury Street location. Visit us.suitsupply.com for more on the brand.

May 2018 Peach and B/SPOKE Teamed Up for Fashionable Charity Ride Style Scene&Style Magazine Issue #18

Recently booming athletic brand Peach teamed up for a charity ride with local fitness studio B/SPOKE in the quaint Wellesley Center location of Massachusetts.

The night got spinning with a sweaty and enthusiastically lead charity ride raising funds for Dress for Success. Who are an international non-profit that helps women gain economic independence by providing a network of support, development tools, and professional attire.

After the class came to a close the fashion hit the runway. The show began with Founder and CEO of Peach Janet Kraus alongside Kate from Sloane Ivy, a local boutique. The two ladies gave a bit of background on each of the brands and how the combination of the two comes together for great chic and comfortable style.

Athleisure looks from the latest Peach collection "California Dreamin" rocked the runway with classic pastels in a sunset pant, block patterned recharge yoga bra paired with recharge legging. Classic pieces from the Dolce Vita collection were spiced up with heels, totes, and hints of street style from Sloane Ivy.

The evening came to a close with ladies mixing, mingling and sipping on some tasty sangria while shopping the seasons must have!

ELEVATE YOUR EVERYDAY is the mission behind the Peach brand. They design contemporary fashion for gym, work, and play. Their products are sold through an amazing network of stylists who create a fun, personal shopping experience. Peach was founded on the simple, yet big idea, that a lifestyle brand could help women "elevate their everyday." Their mission is to be a force for good for women by helping them to thrive personally and professionally.

Peach's most recent collection "California Dreaming" is an escape to the coast. Other lines offered are "Work Ethic" to climb the ladder with polished work staples. Another new edition is totes from "Christen Maxwell" where form meets function with a touch of shine. You can never go wrong with "Peach Classics" closet building blocks and essential pieces you'll use every day. SHOP at discoverpeach.com

Magazine Link https://madmagz.com/magazine/1363772

April 2018 Denise Hajjar Shows at Steeped in Style Scene&Style Magazine Issue #17

Timeless style and tea recently took place with the revamped version of the Marilyn Riseman fashion series and designer Denise Hajjar showing her spring 2018 collection. The setting of the event was perfectly suited to honor the memory of the late socialite Riseman. Held in the chic courtyard garden of the historic Boston Public Library, the fine white tablecloths, a full menu of assorted teas, delectable plates of horderves and desserts and of course the divine fashion.

Bold and bright colors in classic floral patterns were the highlight of Hajjar's collection. Always bringing a wide range of options from her boutique and colors ranging from a pop of teal, hot pinks, fresh greens, to calm beige's. The show featured pieces for head to toe looks fit for a cocktail occasion, off to the office or a silver sequenced number for a glitzy night out in the city. Her staple wrap dress that exudes class and a casual comfort was paired with a multi-purpose sash and must have accessories like local designer Andrea Valentini handbags.

Steeped in Style is a bi-weekly series of informal fashion shows in honor of Marilyn Riseman. The shows highlight Boston's best and brightest fashion designers and local boutiques. Each show is held during afternoon tea service at The Courtyard Restaurant, a stunning tearoom within the McKim Building of Boston's Central Library in Copley Square. Seating times are available at 12:00pm and 2:00pm. Seating is limited, and reservations are strongly recommended. Call (617) 859-2251 for more information or go to tcacourtyard.com to reserve your table!

The remaining Steeped in Style Fashion Show Schedule: April 17th- Gina DeWolfe, May 1st- Anna Nieman Couture, May 15th- School of Fashion Design Collection 2018 student show, May 29th- By Jeffrey Dickerson, June 12th- Mesese Designs by Diforo Designs by Diforio, June 26th- Nstilla, July 10th- Shaco Couture- Sharon Cox Sharon Cox-Cole, July 24th- Rimma Zaika-Veksler, August 7th- Samuel Vartan Collections, August 21st- Nathalia JM JMag, September 4th- TANGOELLA- Ella Tang, September 18th- Jewlinga- Inga Puzikov http://www.jewelinga.com/ and Maria Bablyak , October 2nd- Ali Bianchi, October 16th- Daniel Faucher Couture October 30th- Emily Mathes Kuvin and Deborah Harper, November 13th- Luxe Boutiques ,November 27th- Mehan Meghan Doyle Wilkinson, December 11th- AtCozy Boutique and Nina Bublik.

Cover: Model – Jane Conway Gaspe Denise Hajjar Deigns 510 Atlantic Ave Boston, 617-266-2296, denisehajjar.com

March 2018 LaFauci and Sarian Pair Up for a Seductive Fashionably Late Scene&Style Magazine

Issue #16

Love comes in many shapes and forms yet what better way to celebrate Saint Valentine then to see lovely Dynasty Models and their shapely curves hit the runway. Recently Annmarie LaFauci debuted her 2018 lingerie collection featuring Shaunt Sarian handbags in the chic Liberty Hotel for an edition of Fashionably Late.

The place was jam packed and jaws began to drop when the show started off with a rocking red fantasy worn by Dynasty Diva, Tina Makuch. It was a bold one piece, spaghetti strap with peacock fathered feel and highlighted with a mustard pocketbook from Shaunt Sarian. Following were looks like; a bikini style with a sequins pop and zigzag pattern and layered gold chain necklace that draped from the midsection strategically to the thigh finished with a classic red Shaunt Sarian purse. A jewel and pearl style filled out the top to a solid gold sparkle bottom on the darling beauty Angela Brathwaite. Daring outfits of ribbon, lace and furs continued out on the runway in all the fabrics and deviant cuts that any lady would love to take into the bedroom along with gorgeous locks styled by Salon Viari. The showstopper was the solid faith of the finale; a velvet and leather mixture with gold trim that featured a piercing statement piece of a cross closed the 2018 Annmarie LaFauci collection and was finished with a snakeskin clutch from Shaunt Sarian that brought the seductive evening to an end.

From swimsuits to seduction LaFauci is known for her bathing suit line and took a stab at lingerie and rocked the runway. Annmarie also ventured out during this past Boston Fashion Week 2017 by showing stunning night and club wear designs that kept it classy with a sex appeal. You can see more of Annmarie's work or contact her for your own special cut on Facebook at Annmarie LaFauci.

Shaunt Sarian is a native to Lebanon and growing up in his family's handbag workshop. Shaunt travels the world in search of inspiration and exotic materials for his handbag and accessory collections. Luxurious textures such as pythons, ostrich, sting ray, patent leather and calf skin are available in a variety of gorgeous colors to create a one-of-a-kind handbag for each client. Each handbag is a statement, a tribute to modern artisanship and design enticed by a European flair. You can purchase or take a peek at SARIAN HANDBAGS & ACCESSORIES located at 95 M Union Street, Newton, MA. Contact by email: shaunt@sariandesigns.com or call 617.431.7000.

February 2018 Love Fashion and Song in an Operatic Evening Scene&Style Magazine Issue #15

An evening of operatic love came together on Saint Valentine's Day in an evening at Café St. Petersburg in Newton Center. The chic café had a European feel with a tucked away back room setup for guests to enjoy a private performance accompanied by tea and traditional pastry.

The show began with Junhan Choi, a baritone from South Korea, winner of several international competitions opening the "La Ci Darem La Mano" piece with his lovely Ukrainian soprano, Olga Lisovskaya to join him for a stunning duet. Lisovskaya, who has performed at some of the most prestigious concert halls in the world, including Carnegie Hall, will sing love solos and duets from Opera, Operetta, Broadway, and song literature.

They were accompanied all evening by Levon Hovsepian, piano who is a Komitas Conservatory graduate performing throughout Armenia, Estonia, Moldova and has appeared as a soloist with the Yerevan Symphony Orchestra.

The musical presentation became enchanted with models gliding around Choi in a solo number where each lady's love was draped in a glamourous gown from At Cozy boutique and gems from Jewelinga designs. The show came to a close with a live auction of fantastic items up for bid and an invitation for light appetizers and wine to keep the night alive in their Russian tradition in At Cozy Boutique located just at the top of the stairs.

Magazine link: https://madmagz.com/magazine/1296761

January 2018 Consolidation is the New Black Scene&Style Magazine Issue #14

Recently Director of Women's Wholesale with Giorgio Armani, Julia Alarcon visited Saks Fifth Avenue Boston location. She introduced the Spring/Summer 2018 collection that hit the runways and educated on the restructuring of the companies many divisions.

Consolidation is the new black and Giorgio Armani is the latest designer to announce a new brand strategy, he revealed his decision to cease the Armani Collezioni and Armani Jeans brands and use only the Giorgio Armani, Emporio Armani and A|X Armani Exchange names. The new strategy will be effective starting with the spring 2018 season. Armani Collezioni and Armani Jeans will be blended into those three main lines. Armani is the latest in a string of designers and companies that have streamlined collections, including Ralph Lauren, Burberry, Marc Jacobs, Dolce & Gabbana, and Paul Smith.

The idea of these new changes is to represent the brand in a different way to the customer's benefit. The name Emporio Armani emphasizes an "emporium," Armani told WWD. In highlighting the brand's nature, bringing these two lines under it will only further give the label a more expansive reach. Overall, customers will be able to have a more one-stop-shop experience by seeing the Armani Collezioni and Armani Jeans incorporated into the main lines.

Armani said the goal was also to "serve a different public, showing different lines within one single space. Customers want to enjoy the shopping experience. Their request is to be entertained. We should keep in mind the meaning of the name Emporio," the designer said. "It should be an emporium." At the same time, he claimed this diversification would help wholesale accounts to sell and display the collections. "There will be advantages in carrying jeans under the Emporio label, for example. "There was too much confusion with so many collections," the designer continued. "Times have changed and we have to evolve." You can read more about the combining collections view and shop the current classic chic styles at Armani.com.

https://madmagz.com/magazine/1263695?

Chapter Eight – 2017

"My relationship with fashion has always been that each of us stars in our own movies and costumes ourselves to play the part we want. You take blouses and jeans and dresses, and you put them together, and they tell your story." - Marc Jacobs

December 2017 SKEA Hit the Fashionably Late Slopes with Ski Wear Scene&Style Magazine Issue #13

Warm winter fashions in New England are a must and the industries finest snuggled in for a year's end Fashionably Late at the Liberty Hotel featuring SKEA Limited 2017/2018 Collection.

The event was produced by Benharris Productions always brining the cities sexiest and being a festive time of year all were early sipping bubbly cocktails alongside ski sensation and SKEA front Lady Diane Boyer.

When fashion hit the chic old jailhouse runway one of the first styles was a seasonal must have in an haute hologram look. The matching jacket and pant were polyurethane warmth paired with a keychain pom and ski goggles to have you set for a sexy and funky look to hit the slopes. Following was for the competing fashionista, in an anthracite grey, waterproof and breathable suit and a shaded fur for glamour appeal straight down the slope. Another must have look was brightening up the scene in a metallic teal; with a white fur hooded trim, traditional SKEA knit hat to top off your ski style and attract attention to your skills down the slope.

For more of a sparkle off the slopes; a gold sequins vest, SKEA bunny pom hat and mini skirt perfect for an evening cocktail by the fire. Also hitting the runway with a tote and matching top look in a beige and brown faux fur cape and SKEA zip mini skirt, and a Shaunt Sarian Finnish Raccoon bag suitable for a cocktail date after a day on the slopes. Closing the show was a statement piece of; a full winter white finished with a fur hooded trim, a one of a kind top with more than one message in sequence and goggles to finish off your ski style. The show was a warm snowy themed success and ladies begging to be pointed in the direction to purchase!

Born and based in Colorado, SKEA 1s designed for women, who ski, by women who ski. As ski instructors, professional skiers, and US ski team members, SKEA knows what works and why. Since 1972, their passion for fashion, the mountains, and an active lifestyle have been evident in every thread of the SKEA line. Beautifully crafted style performance wear, for on slope and off. Share their passion for the mountains. Wear SKEA and SHOP at www.skealimited.com.

December 2017 Scene&Style Magazine Boston Fashion Awards 2017

Every year when the holidays roll around you can expect a highlight in Boston fashion to announce the party location and the nominees in each category for the Boston Fashion Awards. For 2017 the event was held in The Supper Club at Capo's with a local celebrity line up of hosts; emcee Maverik, daytime personality from Jam'n 94.5 who rocked with his Caribbean flavored tracks. Alongside Maverick was MTV reality show personality Nicole Spiller plus NESN TV hostesses Kylie McCoy and Bianca Reyes.

It wouldn't be a show without some exclusive designers showcasing and a cocktail dress focus from SooDee Boutique featuring bold Inga Jewelry Designs was first to hit the Boston Fashion Awards runway. Others featured were Manny Sorto, VaVa who showed a collection of Roman reds, leather, and gold also Early Birds with a sexy and seductive line of custom leather jackets.

In a traditional awards fashion in between the announcements of category winners were live performances. Who knew Maverik wasn't just a DJ. He performed a few of his singles and left the stage stunned from his hidden talent. The alluring female trio Eclypse gave us their rendition of Christmas favorites and Devin Ferreira with his vocals and saxophone. Rocking the stage for the evening was front runners The Natalie Joly band.

The night's attendance featured top industry professionals like nominated photographer Dan Minicucci, Denise Hajjar nominee for couture wear and Gustavo Leon recipient of the Fashion Achievement Award were just a few of many out at the annual event.

It wouldn't be a show without some exclusive designers showcasing and a cocktail dress focus from SooDee Boutique featuring bold Inga Jewelry Designs was first to hit the Boston Fashion Awards runway. Others featured were Manny Sorto, VaVa who showed a collection of Roman reds, leather, and gold also Early Birds with a sexy and seductive line of custom leather jackets.

In a traditional awards fashion in between the announcements of category winners were live performances. Who knew Maverik wasn't just a DJ. He performed a few of his singles and left the stage stunned from his hidden talent. The alluring female trio Eclypse gave us their rendition of Christmas favorites and Devin Ferreira with his vocals and saxophone. Rocking the stage for the evening was front runners The Natalie Joly band.

The night's attendance featured top industry professionals like nominated photographer Dan Minicucci, Denise Hajjar nominee for couture wear and Gustavo Leon recipient of the Fashion Achievement Award were just a few of many out at the annual event.

The evening ended with an elegant lace runway presentation from the Isabel Lopez Spring/Fall Collection that had guests wondering what's next for 2018 fashion in the Hub. The Boston Fashion Awards carefully selects its nominees each year and leaves the voting up to the public. They express that it is always such a tuff battle to bring each category to only a few with so much established and budding talent in the city. Here are the listed winners for the 2017 year; FEMALE: PRINT MODEL Vanessa Grisales, FEMALE: RUNWAY MODEL Danielle Ringler, MALE: MODEL/ACTOR Wesley Scales, DESIGNER: COUTURE/FORMAL Sharon Cox-Cole, DESIGNER: EVENING/CLUB/ECLECTIC Angelica Timas, DESIGNER: CASUAL/SPORTSWEAR, Melissa Thyden (Cosmic Unicornz) DESIGNER: SWIMWEAR/INTIMATE Molly Curley DESIGNER: ACCESSORIES Jaye Carrero, PHOTOGRAPHER Eric Levin RETAILER LIT Boutique, MAKEUP ARTIST (TIE) Donna Sousa (co-winner) Phiphi Liang (co-winner) WARDROBE STYLIST Natalie Mason, HAIR SALON Eva Michelle. Visit www.BostonFashionAwards.com for more information.

The 80's. Everyone remembers the 80's. Maybe not everything, but at least the shoulder pads, leg warmers, and crimped hair. That was the decade that David Josef, an extremely successful fashion designer based in Boston, climbed his way to the top. As a young entrepreneur, Josef opened his first store, The David Josef Fashion Studio, in Lexington in 1976. After Bonwit Teller fell in love with his designs soon thereafter, huge department stores like Neiman Marcus and Bloomingdales were carrying his masterpieces.

Business was booming as stars like Cher and Cyndi Lauper sported his label at different events. However, the economic crash in 2000 and the loss of his mother proved to be very detrimental to both Josef and his business. Losing both the store in Boston and his motivation to keep working left the once highly publicized designer looking for a new start. When the opportunity presented itself, Josef took it. He had found himself a new clientele, women seeking conservative yet attractive clothing suitable for

formal occasions. He opened his current store located in Waltham and began serving the public once again. Since his re-entry into the fashion world, Josef has become even more involved in giving back to the community. For the past four years since it began, he has participated in Fashion to the Rescue, a fundraiser to raise money for Aimee Takaha's Farm Animal Sanctuary in Arizona. Takaha works to save and rehabilitate animals that have been abused, couldn't be cared for, or were in line to be put down. She works tirelessly to make sure they are cared for and adopted by a good family. People with autism, Down syndrome, blindness, and PTSD are often able to visit the location to interact with the animals, an activity proven to be very calming and beneficial to these groups. Because the sanctuary is a non-profit, it relies heavily on donations, one of the main reasons why Josef's help is greatly appreciated. This year the event began with drag diva, the one and only Verna Turbulence with a Beyoncé dance number. During the live auction, surprise guests New England Patriots players Eric Rowe and DJ Foster brought a gift to add to the "We are the Champions" package, a Tom Brady signed football that sold for 5,000 donated dollars.

Once Josef Fashions took the runway the debonair dress designers 2017 collection took stage with celebrity models like: New England Patriots girlfriend Ciera Liguori, legend fashion icon Yolanda Cellucci, singer Alya Brown, WCVB Channel 5 Boston reporter Nichole Berlie, the one and only Janet Wu and more. The fundraiser has had many influential guests from Boston's fashion network and raised the largest amount of money yet for this amazing cause.

October 2017 Scene&Style Magazine bosfw LaFauci Shines on Color in Couture Runway

Boston Fashion Week 2017 came to a close at The W Hotel with Color in Couture. The evening was hosted by an America's Next Top Model Bre Scullark and Joshua Steele with production from Junior and Rose Vipent of VOGE FASHION RUNWAY to support The Autism Program at Boston Medical Center.

Guests gathered in a hall of the hotel where VIP seating lined the walls and a runway came right down the middle. The show started off with a warm welcome came from celebrity host Bre Scullark expressing her excitement to be in Boston. The fashion got going with; Josefa Disilva, a local Boston designer showing a worldly inspired collection of exotic dresses, furs, using plastics and glitter to pull it all together. Another local Allexandra Bianchi who took her studies of stitching to Italy and brought back to Boston a line that was worthy of a Milan runway. Bianchi highlighted dresses, crop tops, skirts even a wedding looks that featured a beautiful, embroidered patterns. Other collections showed such as Shaco Couture, Janabay, Yannery Burgos, and even designer Joe Malaka made time to hit the stage while showing off his personal outfit for the event.

The attention of the evening went to designer and city sensation Ann Marie LaFauci. Known for designing high end energetic pieces and her bathing suit lines LaFauci gave the guests not only swimwear style fit for an A list Miami pool party but took it casual and to the club with her metropolis looks. She featured sheer tops, patterned miniskirts, leathers, glitter, and even stylish relaxed jumpers fit to still stand out on a Sunday. The staple of the collection was for a night out in the city with a sequin skirt, a black crop top paired with cuffed jewelry, rocking heels and hair and makeup from Salon Viari in Malden.

Color in Couture was one of the final shows to present for Boston Fashion Week 2017 with support to The Autism Program at Boston Medical Center. For more information visit bmc.org and search Autism program.

October 31st, 2017, Scene&Style Magazine Annual Halloween Gala was Boston's Best Bash

Boston is known for many things; sports, accents, chowda and of course the Annual Halloween Gala. This year the cities two most lavishing holiday personalities; Managing Editor of the Boston Herald, Gustavo Leon and King of Darkness Designer Samuel Vartan gathered forces for the weekends best bash. For an event not to be missed, Scene&Style threw on some glamour and was on site in gladiator form.

The A list evening came together by Jena Tang of Prestige Communications and stage production from Pete Paraskevas. It began with a classy cocktail hour of passed hors d' oeuvres and music from Internationally World Famous Dj Liz Ladoux that gave guests time to arrive at the Boston Exhibition and Convention Center. Master of Ceremonies Gustavo Leon took center stage looking fabulous in his custom coat and hat from Marilla Designs by Mae Horak. Always with his intoxicating presence Leon welcomed and acknowledged ticket goers with gratitude as the evening was a benefit for the Red Cross Hurricane Relief.

The vampire fashion presentation by Samuel Vartan Collections and head pieces from COCO designs by Coleen Galvin Yaroshenko started with a black velvet stare in a full length deathly deep dress. The freaky fashion continued with Vartan vixen looks of, metallic golds, busty black leather, a detailed off the shoulder burgundy dress. A laced look of all white with the model strategic placement had death lurking in the shadows on the walls. Following was a feathered expression fit for an evil queen and a bold red finished out the ghoul and glamour meets sex goddess collection.

In traditional manor Vartan the Vampire arrived in his famed casket style entrance for an epic live performance with the Natalie Joly Band. From there the night was opened up to dancing, and judges Laura Ladd - CEO of Click Boston, Michael L. Carucci – Executive Vice President of Gibson Sotheby's International Realty along with Vanessa Farino – President of Boston Businesswomen giving out 12 golden tickets nominating them for the best costume contest. The grand prize was an all-inclusive VIP package for two to the choice of either Punta Cana or Cancun Hard Rock Cafe Resort. The winner was Marta Mohammadi who made her costume Spanish inspired flower fantasy attire. Three other awards were given out to two Marie Antoinette's and one mermaid with each a $100 gift certificate from the Briar group.

The evening was a spooky success between the masterminds behind the event, the creative costumes, sponsors and raising money for the Red Cross. It will be tuff to top the event yet the word is out that their collaboration is already planning to set a standard for 2018.

10-26-2017 Scene&Style Magazine "Vogu Featuring; Josefa Disilva, Allexandra Bianchi, Shaco Couture, Janabay, Yannery Burgos, Ann Marie LaFauci."

Boston Fashion Week 2017 came to a close at The W Hotel with Color in Couture. The evening was hosted by an America's Next Top Model Bre Scullark and Joshua Steele with production from Junior and Rose Vipent of Vogu to support The Autism Program at Boston Medical Center.

Guests gathered in a hall of the hotel where VIP seating lined the walls and a runway came right down the middle. The show started off with a warm welcome came from celebrity host Bre Scullark expressing her excitement to be in Boston. The fashion got going with; Josefa Disilva, a local Boston designer showing a worldly inspired collection of exotic dresses, furs, using plastics and glitter to pull it all together. Another local Allexandra Bianchi who took her studies of stitching to Italy and brought back to Boston a line that was worthy of a Milan runway. Bianchi highlighted dresses, crop tops, skirts, even a wedding looks that featured a beautiful, embroidered patterns. Other collections showed such as Shaco Couture, Janabay, Yannery Burgos, and even designer Joe Malaka made time to hit the stage while showing off his personal outfit for the event.

The attention of the evening went to designer and city sensation Ann Marie LaFauci. Known for designing high end energetic pieces and her bathing suit lines LaFauci gave the guests not only swimwear style fit for an A list Miami pool party but took it casual and to the club with her metropolis looks. She featured sheer tops, patterned miniskirts, leathers, glitter, and even stylish relaxed jumpers fit to still stand out on a Sunday. The staple of the collection was for a night out in the city with a sequin skirt, a black crop top paired with cuffed jewelry, rocking heels and hair and makeup from Salon Viari in Malden.

Color in Couture was one of the final shows to present for Boston Fashion Week 2017 with support to The Autism Program at Boston Medical Center. For more information visit bmc.org and search Autism program.

10-26-2017 Scene&Style Magazine "Fashion on Fire Featuring; Maddy Ventresca, LaFille Colete, Tina Melo, Marilla Designs, Daniel Hernandez, Solo Jubin."

The Hilton Boston/Woburn took part in Boston Fashion Week 2017 with Fashion on Fire. The A list event had guests arriving early to enjoy the pre-cocktail party with desserts, passed appetizers, and shopping from local vendors and began the bidding on silent auction items.

The show began with Host for the evening Erika Tarantal from Channel 5 news and Production Director Olga Kwasniewski welcoming guests, thanking sponsors and praise donations that went to benefit "Project Smile."

The opening number came from Dance Artists Ballet Academy with their magnificent movements that left you feeling like you had been whisked away in a fairytale. Then the fashion began; the first collection from Maddy Ventresca featured a silk Chanel look of a soft pink, a beige baby doll dress with a vintage white jacket and retro pinned back hair. Next was LaFille Colete Collection with strategic cuts on the simple black and white cocktail dress and a deep turquoise also purple floral pattern. Tina Melo Collection took to the runway with, winter furs in a warrior look for men and women both showing ancient patterns and leathers. Finishing out before intermission was a Lewis Flores performance playing modern radio hits on his violin while the Marilla Designs Collection showed a female princess gown with a gothic dark night appearance for men.

After guests were given a break to bid on more items or grab a cocktail the second portion of the evening began with the mesmerizing Dance Artists Ballet Academy for a final performance. The fashion continued with internationally known, Daniel Hernandez. His collection started off in fan favor with Managing Editor of the Boston Herald and our industries Master of Ceremonies Gustavo Leon being the first model to hit the runway. Hernandez wowed with his artful eye for putting together must have contemporary looks. Following was a unique musical performance from Issam El Hadouti on the keyboard and George El Bacha on hand drums. Solo Jubin Collection kept the style hitting the runway with deep burgundy, reds paired with black leathers for men and women. Continuing with off the runway talent was Francoise Voranger and her steady strength acrobatic presentation. Miss Liya Atanasova won over the audience with her voice and originally written song. The event came to a close with Lewis Flores again taking stage with his stunning violin melody and the ruby red themed collection from Isabel Lopez. The sexy chic designer with her classic lace ended the evening with elegant style.

Fashion on Fire was filled with high end style, entertaining performances, the city's finest fashionistas all brought together to benefit Project Smile. They are a non-profit organization dedicated to bringing comfort to children who have been victims of traumatic events. They donate stuffed animals, coloring books/crayons, and books to police and fire departments to be given to children immediately following a traumatic situation. For more information on how to donate or become involved visit projectsmile.org

10- 19-2017 Scene&Style Magazine "THE CUE Collection Marveled the Liberty Runway" - Lindsay Tia Styled by KB Fashion Productions

Bravery Brand beauty Lindsay Tia is always finding a way to outdo herself. For Boston Fashion Week 2017 it was no surprise the designer again paired with the Benharris Production crew by taking over the Liberty Hotel's "Fashionably Late" and introducing "The Cue".

In the elegant and old jail house walls of the hotel guests began to arrive early in the lounge for cocktails and light shopping at Tia's pop up shop. It featured the seasons top handbags alongside the cities top traveling make-up and hair company, "MLR Artists" who had free goodies to give in addition to the styling for the show.

"The Cue" Collection began with a black and white affair; A chic classic look of a white button down and stretch black pant paired with a platform shoe and a fur flavor for fall in a crop jacket finished with a Lindsay Tia camo shoulder strap bag. Followed was a funk feel; of a high cut leather skirt, classic T, fringed jean jacket also rocking the versatile camo purse. In more of a satin finish; on a sleeveless midnight top, classic black pant with a ruffled 60's rock look and leather LT bag. Also showing in the "The Cue" Collection was a comfort fit stretched overall paired with a bold red LT shoulder strap original, a sheer ruffled retro look on a long sleeve mini, a solid gold and beige "baby" was the highlighted tone of a flared top, classic black bottom, and staple clutch. The final look to hit the runway was a midnight velvet glamour gown with peekaboo thigh cuts, finished with an initial necklace and bold red LT clutch all brought to you by "The Cue." There was the expected catwalk closing where Tia posed alongside the Model Inc. ladies to take a bow for her fresh fall funk and chic style that hit the "Fashionably Late" runway.

Lindsay Tia Reilly is the Founder and Owner of THE CUE, as well as the creator of the popular Lindsay Tia brand. The fashion fighter lives by her motto; Inspire, be brave and empower. Originally from Quincy, MA she started sewing at age 10 and is known for her Bravery brand, being Massachusetts made and now her latest venture "The Cue" a style lounge carefully curated for the trendy professional. Tia explains, "It's for all of us that want to look our best, whether you're going from the boardroom to the bar room, from day to night, or from busy weekdays to lazy Sundays. The Cue has everything we need to feel confident in our look - anytime, anywhere."

10-13-2017 Scene&Style Magazine "What They Didn't Teach You in Fashion School, Presented by Jay Calderín"

Professor at the School of Fashion Design - Boston, Founder of Boston Fashion Week and Fashion Group International Boston Board Member Jay Calderín took center stage at The Boston Public Library for an intimate lecture on his upcoming book about the finer points of being in the fashion business.

With a lengthy resume not even fully listed, Calderín's many style goers were eager to grab a seat for his Boston Fashion Week exclusive speech with ears and eyes open to soak up all the knowledge that the classroom may have left out. His FREE presentation was intoxicating with his strong presence at the podium taking guests through each chapter giving the finer points of creativity, reproducing masterpieces without being a knockoff, having a sense of play in your work, be a lifetime learner, keeping an eye on what's next, taking time off for a sexy comeback and more.

Calderín brought visuals to a big screen by highlighting greats; Anna Wintour, Edith Head, T.S. Eliot, Henri Matisse with quotes like "Fashion never stops. There is always a new project a new opportunity" by Carolina Herrera.

It seemed as if the hour was only a few minutes being there was so much more to consume from what The Boston Globe refers to Jay Calderín as, "a budding designer's best friend." He ended the evening with a gracious question and answer portion and attended to as many of the curious minds as he could.

Jay teaches a wide variety of fashion and professional development courses at the School of Fashion Design and has graced readers with the opportunity to learn outside the classroom walls. Scene&Style being captivated by his new book's introduction, "How do you navigate the confusing and competitive fashion world after the relative comfort of fashion school? How do you learn to adapt to an industry that constantly evolves and throws new challenges your way? And above all, how do you play to your strengths as a designer and build a successful career in business? What They Didn't Teach You in Fashion School is your survival guide to the fashion industry. Providing expert advice, and lots of inspiration, Jay Calderin shows you how to get the best out of the exhilarating world of fashion.

10-12-2017 Scene&Style Magazine "Carbon Concepts" showing the "Elements of Fall Beauty – Styled by KB Fashion Productions."

Carbon Salon in Boston's theatre district brought a different take to Boston Fashion Week with holding "Carbon Concepts" showing the "Elements of Fall Beauty" brining a runway right to the salon floor.

The evening began with VIP guests pouring in the door to tasty food and drink with time to mix and mingle before a warm welcome came from Producer Kathy Benharris. Kathy, who is also a client, testified she may not walk in like her strongest self, but the staff has her leaving feeling superhuman. She continued with introducing MC for the event and Co-Owner Justin Robey also bringing on stage Matthew Waldron the other half of the debonair duo.

Once Dynasty, Model Club Inc. and Boston Models representation hit the runway MC Robey gave a full head to toe and tips on each look. Shown were a modern pinup, autumn tones of undone textured fishtail braids, amped up teased and volume with a twiggy 60's inspired makeup stare, handbags by Oliver Thomas, body pieces from De La Becca, bracelets from Wear Your Music, leggings by Irina Gorbman and the funk flair of T*Racy chain link designs. "Carbon Concept" looks weren't only for the ladies; gentleman took front and center with poise and styled with a round brush for a natural everyday appearance finished with an Oliver Thomas duffle bag that was from his unisex line.

Even once the fashion came to a close the night still wasn't over. Guests got the opportunity to see live tutorials and grab tips on how to create "Carbon Concepts" at home. Master Stylist Lindsey Grenier showed that braids are always in style with a transformation in under five minutes into a full up do. MC Robey took it to the chair with giving client pointers on a quick curl to add volume and texture. The last lesson was on; find your flattering brow through shades and shaping.

The highly ranked salon paired with Benharris Productions for some of the hottest styles and must have for fall looks for an evening of success. Carbon Salon's talented team enjoys making their guests feel and look their best.

10-6-2017 Scene&Style Magazine "LIQUID ART HOUSE SHOW Takes on Swimwear"

The event began with a day party for the guests to mix and mingle over a tasty cocktail at the chic Liquid Art House before the pink carpet was rolled out for the show Pose featuring Makuwa Swim Wear.

When the style started to take place two pieces like; a classic white look covered with a pink patterned jacket and finished with a Jewelinga Designs tassel necklace hit the runway. Followed were a camo flair with fish net wrap wowed and a teal and maroon crochet knitted two piece paired with a layered stone necklace work the room as it was complimentary to the painted colors on the walls. The showstopper was a heightened statement of a black classic two piece with a full-length fish net wrap finished was a bold diamond choker from well-known Hairstylist and Makeup artist Racine Bell making her accessories debut.

The scene welcomed some of the city's finest of fashionistas; The center of stage ceremonies Gustavo Leon and the debonair of the duo Patrick Dwyer, Designer Samuel Vartan, Stanley Connie Diforo from Mesese TV, Top photographers; Dan Minicucci, Robert Paris, Jay Lamour. Also, Amber Lu, Angelina De Jesus Solomon, handbag designer Shaunt Sarian, Yemi

Sekoni, Joe Malaika and more with Prive's pro team in place alongside head honcho Tail Coat Times tying everything together.

The Boston Fashion Week opening night was a success in more ways than one with Makuwa Swimwear taking a stand with her handmade creations. One of the primary goals for the line is to give back to the specific region of the Congo where Francine is originally from. The focus is to build opportunities for the young people of the Congo to find independence and success through their artistry. To learn more about her mission visit wearmsw.com.

10-6-2017 Scene&Style Magazine "Benharris Brings Style to Sowa for BFW17" – Styled by KB Fashion Productions

Boston Fashion Week 2017 officially began on Sunday October 1st and the SOWA Art + Design District transformed their gorgeous outdoor space with roped off shopping paths into runways for an afternoon of style.

The fashion got going with a retro rock appeal; rugged jeans, a tight tank and classic leather jacket was shown for a gent. A simple T with bold cherry red lettering over deep blue along with matching pant and finished with Chuck Taylor shoes complimented a ladies look all to be found at Bobby's From Boston.

A little on the lighter side, an athleisure approach from Ash and Rose with a comfy pink cape hoodie paired with basic leggings. An effortless style, of a Sowa t-shirt and velvet bark colored skirt with a pop of culture in a Zainab Sumu Primitive Modern head scarf. Many of the looks showed Ser Verde Shoes from Spain and one of a kind couture hat made by Marie Galvin. Bobby's from Boston also carries men's suit lines that can be dressed down for a casual event and sent out a sexy relaxed business poise. The tone was taken up a notch for ladies to "shake it off" in a red-hot leather dress that rocked the runway and many other looks from the Sowa Vintage Market.

More styles ranging from funk, furs, chic, gowns, deep culture, natural easy looks and more came to life from the Benharris Productions team. With their styling and grace sent down the runway they brought in a solid crowd to spend the rest of the afternoon shopping at Boston's SOWA Art + Design District.

October 2017 Boston's Top Designers Open Fashion Week 2017 Scene&Style Magazine Issue #11

Boston Fashion Week Opening "A Maven's World Produced by KB Fashion Production Featuring; Denise Hajjar, Zjajah Creation, Intriguing Hair Extensions, Early Birds, Envu Bridal, Chevalier Homme's, Angelica Timas, I AM KREYOL"

Fashion is a power all throughout the world. Showcasing in many venues, cities with their own style and Boston has taken on a new venture with a melting pot of talent collaborating to create a face demanding to be seen.

Boston Fashion Week 2017 opened with Anna Foster and her mogul brand A Maven's World produced by the queen bee of styling Kathy Benharris. Her right hands Grace Goodearl, Billi Francis and production team.

The evening began with Master of Ceremonies and Managing Editor of the Boston Herald Gustavo Leon grabbing guest's full attention with his charm and style to welcome celebrity host Naturi Naughton star of the hit show Power to the stage.

Opening the show were timeless and elegant designs from Denise Hajjar that brought beauty and class starting with a sheer hombre look that flowed with the dominant piece of music played from Donna Summers. The collection ranged from glamour gowns, strong business looks, cocktail attire, furs and finished with a striking pose from model Tachou in a classic beige beaded dress from Hajjar.

Following were budding Boston talent like; Zjajah Creation whose bold creations of traditional African looks showing golds and teals. Next up was Intriguing Hair Extensions who took a runway risk with some models wearing only strategic body paint and hair which most certainly gained the attention they were seeking. Coming out after was, Early Birds with pieces focused on winter wear highlighting leather snakeskin jackets in jeans and boot rugged outfits. Envu Bridal attire gave an isle showcase of lace, sequins, also silk with high hip cuts and deep low dropping busts. Finishing the segment was Chevalier Homme's tight spandex bottoms for men, button down slack ensemble with a prep feel, also statements of a classic T and hombre scarfs that brought a European style to a classic white pant look.

After Intermission, Designer Angelica Timas opened her portion with an upbeat and inspiring Beyoncé dance number from her daughter Naysa Kaira. Commanding down the runway were sheer and sparkled dresses along with all white dramatic cuts. Fitted mustard and floral jumpers with sex appeal and classic couture taste showed for Timas's Spring/Summer 2018 collection.

The A Maven's World fashion show closed with I AM KREYOL featuring a collection fresh off the runway from London Fashion Week. KREYOL brought together shades of deep and floral greens pops of yellow in a beautiful dresses, leathers, and pencil skirts. All while making a statement of silence with each model wearing a teal sequin cover over their mouths yet spreading love when hitting the end of the runway by showing the stenciled heart on the palm of their hand.

The evening came to an end with Anna Foster Founder of A Maven's World taking stage to thank guests, participants and Boston for bringing our fashion industry a successful show. The event set the standard for

Boston Fashion Week from the celebrities on stage, in the audience and back of the house to the famed designers that took to the runway.

September 2017 bosfw preview Scene&Style Magazine Issue #10

Fashion is a power all throughout the world. Showcasing in many venues, cities with their own style and Boston has taken on a new venture with a melting pot of talent collaborating to create a face demanding to be seen.

Boston Fashion Week 2017 is October 1st-7th with events taking place beforehand and after. The season's top show opens on Sept. 30th at Royale produced by the queen bee of styling Kathy Benharris and brought to you Boston's busiest entrepreneur Anna Foster and her mogul brand A Maven's World. The show will feature the cities top designers all from different spectrums; timeless elegance from Denise Hajjar, edgy yet classic. Also, Angelica Timas looks, eccentric bold designs by I Am Kréyol, modern men's wear from Chevalier Homme and a budding breakout like Envieu. Naturi Naughton, Star of the hit show "Power" will be hosting alongside local celebrity Gustavo Leon with proceeds for the Boston Arts Academy.

With the amount of trendy talent behind the scenes and glamour set to hit the runway, this display of design is sure to be the talk right into 2018. The week is full of fashion, charity cocktail events and more. A few highlights include SoWa Style 10/1, an outdoor fashion show featuring the SoWa Art + Design District's designers and retailers.

Models Against Cancer on 10-02, Models fighting cancer through fashion & photography at the Beehive FREE contact deerodrigues4@aol.com to get involved!

Carbon Concepts. Elements of Fall Beauty 10-02, Explore the beauty of science and sustainability with Carbon Salon and experience the fusion of fashion paired with next level hair and makeup artistry. info@carbonsalonboston.com.An

Evening with Isaac Mizrahi at MFA Boston 10-04, In a unique conversation with Michelle Finamore, Penny Vinik Curator of Fashion Arts. Fashionably Late: Featuring THE CUE by Lindsay Tia & MLR Artist Management at Liberty Hotel 10-05, www.shopthecue.com FREE.

Fashion on Fire at the Hilton Woburn Hotel 10-06, A gala featuring a fashion show hosted by Erika Tarantal of News Channel 5 to benefit Project Smile contact cpisacane@projectsmile.org for tickets.

KID KOUTURE Platform Downtown on 10-07, Closing will be with the kids! A public display of the fashion and art created by student k-8 with Boston's Bridge to Excellence - at the Tobin School and a helping hand from Jay Calderin, the Founder and Executive Director of Boston Fashion Week.

BFW2017 has set the stage for excellence and a full schedule can be found at Boston fashion week.com.

May 2017 Summer 2017 Swimsuit Trends Scene&Style Magazine Issue #6

What time is it? Summertime! Well… almost. Are your one pieces and bikinis from last year just not going to cut it for 2017? Then it IS time to get your bikini body ready to hit the mall. You can expect high neck and wrap around swim tops, high leg bottoms, plunging necklines, and straps everywhere. In terms of swimwear, Miami Swim Week is the foremost authority on what's hot and what's not. The high neck swimsuit dominated the runway appearing over and over in crochet, mesh, and prints.

Wrap around styles followed suit, crisscrossing in front, and securing in back on both bikinis and one pieces. Brands such as HAH (Hot as Hell), Cirone Swim, and Love and Lemons debuted slinky bottoms that were so high cut they deemed themselves "frongs." In case you're not hip with the lingo, a frong is a swimsuit so high cut that it's almost a front thong, hence the name. To contrast some of the more demure top styles, designers showcased cleavage baring suits, some plummeting almost to the belly button. Pushing barriers even further, some designers paired the deep neckline with the high leg to create a few very daring looks. Strap detailing on bikinis and one pieces was also a common thread among the designs whether it was a caged two piece or just decorative bands.

Where can I get these amazing swimsuits, you ask? Urban Outfitters, Nordstrom, and Topshop are your go-to spots to snag some of the hottest styles. Their inventory will embody the trends from Miami but will prove to be a little more wearable for your upcoming days on the beach.

May Magazine Link https://madmagz.com/magazine/1084450

April 2017 Spring Summer Hair Trends 2017 Scene&Style Magazine Issue #5

As spring and summer approach, women are looking to change up their hair and their look. The top five hairdos of 2017 are inspired by celebrity and runway styles. The half-up half-down bun or "hun" has become the go-to style for this season. Hailee Steinfeld and Youtuber Zoella have sported the updo on the red carpet and the street respectively, showcasing this style's versatility. Straight and sleek strands have also reappeared and can be paired with whatever suits the wearer, the options are limitless. To further prove that old trends are coming back, the classic ponytail has received a reboot. Celebrities like Ashley Graham have been spotted with their hair chicly secured at the top of their crown. The high pony can complete any outfit, day, or night. The high double bun style of the 90's just recently resurged at Coachella in 2017. While this 'do looked great with festival attire, it would look just as cute paired with joggers or a bomber jacket. Lastly, accessorize, accessorize, accessorize. Clips, ribbons, or hair pins can instantly transform any outfit. Just ask Katy Perry.

Although all of these styles are beginner friendly, the top five salons in Boston can help with trickier hairdos or a more permanent change. Salon Capri, located on 11 Newbury Street, is a modern salon that boasts many awards including Best Hair Salon in Best of Boston 2016. Contact the salon at 617-236-0020 for an appointment. Bradley & Diegel, another beautiful salon at 77 Newbury Street, has successfully distinguished themselves from other salons nearby, resulting in high praise from Boston Magazine. They can be reached at 617-266-7707 or 77@bradleyanddiegel.com. Salon Mario Russo's two Boston salons at 9 Newbury Street (617-424-6676) and 22 Liberty Drive (857-350-3139) are equipped with either four stories or a fantastic view of the waterfront. They have been featured twenty-one times in Best of Boston. James Joseph Salon and their talented staff are located at 30 Newbury Street and can be contacted by phone (617-266-7222). The company has received major recognition from several high profile magazines. These four salons offer amazing hair services including wash, cut, color, styling, and various treatments. The Loft Salon and Day Spa at 253 Newbury Street specializes only in hair coloring and has been recognized by Boston Magazine for their craftsmanship. They can be contacted by phone or email, 617-536-5638 and hello@theloftsalonboston.com.

April Magazine Link https://madmagz.com/magazine/1065633

March 2017 Spring/Summer 2017 Nail Trends and the Top Five Salons in Boston Scene&Style Magazine Issue #4

Ladies spring is just around the corner and with the breakout of pastels and sequins styles here is a quick look at the seasons nail trends that hit the runways.

Modern Metallic; is a fresh look to move from a winter white to a soft Phillip Lim look. A hint of black; high-shine black polish with just an accent is a must have spring accessory that designers like Vera Wang are showing in collections. Color blocking; stripes, dots, and patterns of bold bright colors. A funk french; the classic manicure makes a move into multicolored tips and diagonally painted edges. Nude and neutral; a lady like almond shade and an oval nail shape is always an in. A cool cuticle: peek at looks inspired by Rodarte Spring/Summer 17 with a glittered outline for subtle edge.

If you're a busy lady on the go, where can you grab these hot new nails? Here is a list of Boston's top five salons to take a time out and leave looking fabulous! Hollywood Top Nails: Beauty is always what women covet to own, but not all women know how to make up themselves. Visit Hollywood Top Nails, their professional staff will make you more beautiful and charming than ever. 585 Columbus Ave Boston, 617-536-3635 hollywoodtopnailsboston.com. RelaxSation; Staying ahead of the competition is important in any industry. That is why RelaxSation Massage Therapy & Nails makes it part of their policy and business ethics that their staff never stops learning. 25 Kingston St Lower Level Boston, 617-482-6800 RelaxSation.com. MiniLuxe; It's their mission to help you feel your best everyday with mini moments of luxury. Don't think of it as selfish to focus on yourself, because putting yourself first feels so good. One Faneuil Hall Square Floor 7 Boston miniluxe.com. Treasured Hands: provides a VIP experience that leaves you feeling relaxed and even more beautiful. 715 Boylston Street Boston Suite B, treasuredhandssalon.com. G2O Spa & Salon; water is acknowledged as a life force that sustains, rejuvenates, and cleanses. Water, of course, is a common denominator for us all, making up 80% of the human body. Providing The Formula for the Essentials of Life, G2O is at 278 Newbury Street Boston, 617-262-2220 g2ospasalon.com.

February 2017 Diva Kelly Dempsey Releases RACK ADDIK Line Scene&Style Magazine Issue #3

Boston bred Kelly Dempsey is a self-taught fashion designer and former contestant on Season 14 of "Project Runway" where she landed runner-up. She is the founder and creative force behind Rack Addik, a newly launched clothing line focusing on fashion forward streetwear. Dempsey embraces fashion as a creative outlet and as a child, her mother ran a craft store out of their home in Western MA. She spent countless hours watching her mother create anything from wind-chimes made of forks to custom hand sewn purses. Kelly felt a desire to create at a young age, and her original true-to-self vision is distinguished through her consistently eclectic design motifs. A product of a creative space, her visceral instinct for fashion is quickly making a name for herself throughout the fashion world.

1. What are you aspirations for 2017? My aspirations are to expand my brand to retail beyond on my online website. Keep building and growing!

2. Do you have any big projects in the work? I am constantly creating new collections and looking to do some even bigger things this year! Always working on big projects but nothing I can mention right now :)

3. Are you launching a spring collection and if so, what is the inspiration behind it? Right now, I am getting ready to show my Fall Winter 2017 collection in February and hoping to pick up some contracts with major retailers out of it. I am waiting to see if I will be showing during NYFW right now, but I will have spring clothing up on my site before that!

4. Are you doing any fashion weeks or are there any ones on your radar to show? I find out this week if I am showing my FW2017 collection in NYC for fashion week in February. I am also doing a fashion show on Saturday the 28th of January in RI for Runway For A Cure. (flyer attached)

5. What is the hottest item listed on your website? Fanny Packs! They are back and in full swing, I would say to be specific: Plenty of Fish in the Sequin.

6. What is the story behind your style and what inspires you? I am a huge hip hop music lover and I think that that is a big inspiration for my designs. I have always loved to wear bright funky and fun colors because I really think the way you dress reflects your personality. I never really worried about what anyone thought about my bold choice of colors and prints and I think if you like something then you should follow yourself and not worry what other people think. I am a total girly girl too so I

figured I needed to add a bit of glam to my street wear. I believe there is a serious market for glamours street wear and I am ready to bring it!

When people ask what inspire me, I find that to be the hardest question, because I think that my inspiration is deep inside me and I cannot tell if it is a curse or a gift that I can never shut my brain off. I am constantly coming up with designs and ideas in my head, but I would never change that.

Dempsey is set to take on 2017 and you can dig in more on the designer by visiting her website where you can also shop her current collections and grab a high in demand fanny pack at www.rackaddik.com.

Chapter Nine – 2016

**"After all, computers crash, people die, relationships fall apart. The best
we can do is breathe and reboot" - Carrie Bradshaw**

**December 2016 In Depth With Angelica Timas Scene&Style Magazine
Issue #1**

1. You showed for the first time at Boston Fashion this fall, how was the
experience and can you compare it to others cities you have shown in?

AT: Yes first time showcasing at Boston Fashion Week, if I had to sum it up
to one word I'd say 'Extraordinary'.   It would be unfitting to compare
Fashion Weeks. Each collection showcase has a number of factors that
defines my experience. The production team, hair & makeup, models, the
aesthetic of the collection, the audience, etc. each of these collectively
embodies an experience, and each experience is completely different
form another. I'll advance you that showcasing at Boston Fashion Week
for the first time and having a fantastic outcome, an oversold show it was
surreal.

2. What was the inspiration behind the collection you showed?

AT: The theme of the Spring/Summer 17 Collection was Flamboyant vs
Bourgeoise, 2 Friends, 2 Styles a fashion rivalry. This concept came about
a joke, I'm a Gemini and people often correlate Geminians as having 2
personalities as a joke with friends when I am not in such a pleasant
mood, I say my Evil Twin is out. Based on that I concocted 2 imaginary
personas one bold, hard worker a humanitarian, the other nouveau rich,
elegant and with a more refined taste in fashion. Each look was reflective
of the 2 personas.

3. What piece of that collection seems to be catching the eye of the
industry and what are the aspects to its appeal?

AT: Soon after the presentation I had a voting poll that took place on Facebook where the public decided who was the winner. It purposely presenting 19 looks, so that that the 19th would be the tie breaker, it was equal as to what the audience's preference was, the tie breaker gave the win to the Flamboyant looks. The audience was drawn to the butterfly print looks just as they were drawn to a simpler and elegant look like the Off-white two-piece silk pants and side-tie dress, I believe we all have bit of the flamboyant and bourgeoise in us.

4. What fashion week was your favorite to show at?

AT: Ask me this question after I attend New York Fashion and Paris Fashion Week

5. Your company name and logo have been playing on billboards in Time Square NYC, how did that come about and what is the focus of the promotion?

AT: After I picked up representation by Brinks212 Showroom, they are working diligently to bring awareness to my brand, and it included to my surprise, billboard display. The focus was Fall/Winter 16 campaigning as we are in the season and timing is optimal, as the seasonal buying and traveling starts, they hope catch shopper's attention.

6. What's next for Angelica Timas? - shows - collections - business plans

AT: With so many invitation to fashion weeks, New York, Los Angeles, Paris, London, Cannes to name a few, I really haven't decided which one I'll go next, but Paris sounds so inviting, remains to be decided.

Next collection will be Fall/Winter 17 I'm usually a bit more reserved with the aesthetic, but the theme will be "No Fear. No limits. No Excuses."

I am now represented by two showrooms Brinks212, NYC and Eccplise Management, LA, and since representation I have caught the eye of some buyers, and am currently working on getting my brand ready for manufacturing on a larger scale to suffice retail ordering. Who knows what the future brings, but for now the focus is brand awareness.

Since Vancouver Fashion Week my brand has been featured on British Vogue, British Glamour and Glamour Italia, several magazine have my garments featured, such as Dopeness Magazine with Milania Vyantrub, Ellements Magazine, Elegant Magazine to name a few.

The business aspect of the brand Angelica Timas is requiring more of my time, expansion and outsourcing certain task is order right now. I think I may have snagged a nomination for Boston Fashion Week. Let's see!!

November 27, 20242016 Scene&Style Magazine - Benharris Brings the Runway Back to the Boston.com Ski and Snowboard Expo

The Queen Bee of fashion production and a ski bunny herself Kathy Benharris will be bringing the runway back to the expo by popular demand.

With 40,000 plus snow obsessed industry folks from around the country piling into the Seaport Area this week to catch all the latest resort deals and will also have the opportunity to see this seasons coolest slope style.

Benharris productions will once again be hosting multiple runway shows each day of the expo featuring brands like; Obneyer, Volkl, Scott, Spyder, Marmot and more. This is a can't miss opportunity to get first hand styling tips for the weekend getaways to cozy up or meet someone new all thanks to the style you picked up from a winter outfit expert. You can visit www.skisnowexpo.com click on "Boston" to view a daily schedule for the runway action.

The 35th Annual Boston.com Ski & Snowboard Expo is where winter dreams come true. Skiers and snowboarders may not have gotten their "fix" of winter last year, but like any sports fan, there is a "wait'll next year" optimism that has winter lovers ready to surge to the slopes this season. Expo boasts the best deals of the new winter. It kicks off on Nov. 10 and runs through Nov. 13 at Boston's Seaport World Trade Center. The big event is presented by Subaru of New England. Boston.com Ski & Snowboard Expo has been produced for 35 years by BEWI Productions, Waltham, Mass. For a live-action video, click on www.skisnowexpo.com.

NEW Retail Support: Metro Boston retailer Country Ski & Sport has moved into the forefront with a huge pop-up store inside the Expo hall. It's the perfect place to kick off the holiday shopping season. Country Ski & Sport has stores in Quincy, Westwood, and Hanson, Mass.

NEW Aerial Extravaganza: Flippenout, Boston's own extreme trampoline show, takes center stage at this year's Expo. Performances are scheduled throughout Expo's four-day run, presented by the NFL and Killington Resort.

NEW Mountain Activity Center will incorporate the popular Slackers Slackline Demo and Competition arena, and energetic fun and games for youngsters of all ages.

NEW hours: In honor of the Veterans' Day holiday, on Friday, Nov. 11, the Expo has expanded hours, with doors opening at 10 a.m.

Hundreds of ski resort and travel companies will be offering Expo-only specials and giveaways plus a range of lift tickets, season pass and vacation packages at some of the best prices of the coming winter. Tune into Twitter: https://twitter.com/BOSkiSnowExpo daily the week of Expo and discover the many specials that abound at Expo.

Expect hours of entertaining action, from athletic exhibitions to musical performances and interactive fun centers. Children-centric activities include kids' learn-to-ski/snowboard arenas, games, and entertainment.

Expo is the place to shop for winter savings and gives a whole new meaning to the word "deals," including skis and snowboards, boots, and bindings, to clothing and accessories. Expo exhibitors offer up shopping surprises down every aisle to kick off holiday gift buying. New England Patriots fans will find all the logo gear they could want at a special NFL booth in the Expo hall.

Fashion and aerial trampoline shows plus musical performances of top regional groups scheduled regularly every day and evening. Ski businesses based in the greater Boston metro area that are having an impact on local economies AND on the Snowsports business nationally, even internationally.

10-16-2016 Scene&Style Magazine - Anne Fontaine Brought Brazilian Style to Boston by KB Fashion Productions

A Boston Fashion Week 2016 highlight was the esteemed Brazilin born designer Anne Fontaine showing her Fall-Winter 2016 collection at the Four Seasons Hotel in the Back Bay.

The night began with the cities top glitterati gathered in a polished ball room inside the hotel for a cocktail hour that came to a close with welcoming remarks by Amanda Blynn, the glamorous manager of the Boston store. Amanda also thanked attendees as a portion of the show's proceeds were to be donated to The Crohn's & Colitis Foundation of America New England Chapter, a 501c3 charity.

The collection began with Fontaine's classic white blouses; the Alizea piece had a ruffled old-world royal appeal. Blouses were paired with modern leather looks and, in a Scene&Style favorite, the Adja skirt. The structured pants and a Boston specific heeled boot were also shown. Feminine yet tailored jackets showcased Fontaine's Brazilian flair for fall. As the show continued, winter jackets made their debut in a chic white and black zig zag Arla piece alongside an eye catching Awena poncho in a honeycomb pattern.

Fontaine's focus on romanticism bloomed in a portion of the collection that featured breath taking stitching in ruby shade velvet that was applied in multiple patterns over a solid black base dress. Closing out the collection were seductive and luxurious furs, silk, suede, and butter soft leathers paired with jackets, little black dresses, leggings, and cocktail attire.

Her Fall-Winter presentation featured strong themes of retro-graphic, dark romanticism, and the house signature of playing with masculine/feminine to create pieces for the most discerning women. Versatility was at the heart of the collection with creative transparency and flattering silhouettes. Inspired use of unique collars continues to be her signature touch, but the shoes, bags, and other accessories are equally noteworthy.

The evening ended with Anne Fontaine making a loop with her models down the runway where the fashionistas in attendance responded with a very enthusiastic applause. The designer absolutely glowed; you would never know she had just arrived in Boston from Paris that very day.

Anne Fontaine and her husband decided to take over his family's clothing business after discovering an old trunk filled to the brim with white shirts. With 70 retail shops around the world, being distributed in several hundred high end retailers and her first U.S. store being right here in Boston, this beautiful Brazilian's newest line is the perfect place to source classically beautiful and gorgeously made clothes. To learn more about the designer, view her current collection or purchase online visit www.annfontaine.com.

10-14-2016 Scene&Style Magazine - Official Boston Fashion Week Opening Hosted by A Mavens World Hosted by Gustavo Leon and Eve Marcelli

The official opening night for Boston Fashion Week 2016 started off with high-end class integrated with stylish shopping. Anna Maven CEO/Owner of A Mavens World stepped outside the box of her successful online boutique, on air radio personality and the lengthy list of other contributions she is making in the community and set the stage for runway shows through the week.

The evening began with a shopping lounge full of local city boutiques like Pink Shoe Lounge, Zodiac Fly, Tasha Michele, Lulu Roe, The Throw Back Clinic and so many more. The red carpet welcomed the city's top fashionistas, celebrities and the VIP area roped off for classic cocktails and delicious bites was a hot spot.

The night was hosted by local socialite and Master of Ceremonies/Editor of the Boston Herald Gustavo Leon alongside America's Next Top Model and Maven herself Eve Marcelli. The duo ruled the room and had the guests eating out of the palm of their hands with their professional chemistry and striking beauty between the two.

The fashion portion began with Ortega Jewelry designs and captured the audience with a stunning blue warrior look. The collection featured an edgy take on gold chest and neck pieces. Following was esteemed Claude Michelle with his resort wear. It had a take on vintage patterns focused on bold and powerful colors with floral and funk flair. His line highlighted a sexy swim wear with bold cuts and beach vacation appeal. Chicly Klosets rocked lace and stripes looks with a sequence silhouette.

Pink Shoe Lounge showed with a stapled pink high heel, seasonal boots and the full outfit to match leaving the shoe as the feature of the looks, Beauty Rockx Boutique brought their version of the little black dress and sequined bustier , Couples Therapy Boutique had a detailed Arabian themed take meshed with lace and velour , Tasha Michelle Closet ranged from gorgeous gowns to fly street wear with class, Intriguing Hair wowed from beautiful curls to jet straight blue locks, Zodiac Fly with an all-black collection from body suits to business wear, and TNT closed the show with their casual t-shirt line.

The evening ended with a heartfelt speech from our queen bee Anna Maven and then off to the after party held at the chic W Hotel. Scene&Style was able to catch up with Maven post show and got some insight to her wildly successful opening for Boston Fashion Week.

What made you choose opening night for Boston Fashion Week? "It's a signature event for us! Every year, for the last 3 years, we have offered an amazing Opening Night experience for Boston Fashion Week! It sets the tone for the rest of the week and we bring out all the bells and whistles! We want to make sure the guest has a fabulous time in Boston and that the event is high energy and definitely more exciting than the year before."

Was there a specific focus or even fundraiser that inspired the night for you? "Yes! Tailored for Success was our nonprofit partner for the event! The percentage of the proceeds from the A Maven's World Lifestyle Brand, Boston Fashion Week kick-off event being donated to Tailored For Success, Inc. will help make a difference in the lives of many individuals striving to re-enter the workforce, especially women. My team and I are proud to be able to make that kind of impact."

What is it that made you chose your designer lineup? "The choice of designers consisted of a lot of our brand affiliate businesses, so I'm awfully familiar with the amazing products and designs that they offer! For most of them, it was their first experience opening Boston Fashion Week, so we felt it was a great fit and it was an opportunity for these boutique owners and designers to showcase their brand and gain some new fresh eyes to their products/designs. With Ortega Jewelry, I love the rawness of Ortega. Claude Michelle, love the custom designs. ChiclyKlosets, very mod looks. Pink Shoe Lounge, I love that they stay on trend and the fact that they have a physical location in Boston. So, if you saw it on the runway, you can actually stop right into their retail location."

What was your attraction to having Gustavo Leon and Eve Marcille host the evening? "I've known Gustavo for a few years, and he has such an amazing personality! No one else came to mind but him for this event, as I knew he would make Eva feel comfortable and be a great Master of Ceremonies for our amazing guest. "

What is next up on the schedule for AMavensWorld? "Well as a Lifestyle Brand, our events are always different. Our mission is to connect people thru fabulous events, so we have events coming up in November, December, and January. They range from the "Bridge to Everywhere" motivational event with Best Selling Author Trent Shelton, our 6th Annual Holiday Bazaar with over 40 vendors and crafters and our Women's New Year Conference, theme for 2017 is "year of the ask"."

10-5-2016 Scene&Style Magazine - Kelly Dempsey Kicked off Boston Fashion Week 2016

Local Boston based designer and Project Runway diva Kelly Dempsey opened the festivities for #bfw2016 also The Liberty Hotel's season of Fashionably Late.

Dempsey was back to the bean fresh from her time trending at New York Fashion Week where she showed pieces from her new RackAddik collection which is a fashion forward based streetwear line. Dempsey mentioned prior to New York that she had never really shown in Boston and was looking to get closer with the community.

Dempsey has a style that demands attention and the night's vibe ranged from a pop princess look of a glittered sequence pant with pom styled hair to suit the style, a metallic zebra top with a rainbow sequence overall and all pieces being finished off with her staple fanny pack.

Scene&Style was able to catch up with the producer of the show Miss Kathy Benharris for a one on one to kick off her filled Boston Fashion Week. How was it working with Kelly Dempsey? "Amazing! She has a clear vision of the fashion story she wants to tell, and I love that. "

Which was your favorite piece of her collection? "From apparel standpoint it was the pink tiger suit. I am a fool for animal print. That combination she put together I can see young celebrities wearing to a fun event and will be expecting to see that piece as a cover photo. Her staple of the brand is the fanny pack and was roped in by the Swarovski crystals used. I never had fanny pack love until I met Kelly."

What is next on your fashion schedule? "I am right back in the game after fashion week with Fashion Gives Back tomorrow night at the South Shore Plaza. After that will be the Halloween themed Fashionably Late at the Liberty Hotel on the 27th. That show should be fun! It's not a costume party is a runway show focused on the dark, sexy danger, glamourous side of fashion. Then will be one of my favorite productions, the Boston Ski and Snow Expo November 10th through the 13th. It's a nationally attended event with over 40,000 ski industry folks looking for slope gear. We will be having multiple shows daily featuring brands like; Obneyer, Volkl, Scott, Spyder, Marmot and more."

"Kelly from the Delli" is how she referred to herself through Project Runway season 14 being she is a self-taught designer who pays her way through the expensive threads at Mood in New York City by slinging sandwiches at a local deli where she grew up in Monson, Ma.

You can catch all of Dempsey's designs on her website at www.rackaddik.com also read up on the back story of this runway rock star and see what is up next for the local Boston gal. You can follow Dempsey on Instagram at @_kellydempsey_

9-28-2016 Scene&Style Magazine - Angelica Timas Closes Boston Fashion Week

Boston fashion is emerging with many thanks to designers like local Angelica Timas. Her ready to wear collections have hit the runways of major cities like New York, Vancouver, Providence at fours season of StyleWeek and current invitations to L.A., Paris, Chicago, and Cannes.

Her European background can be seen in her stunning cuts and sexy design that still hold to a classy look fit for a lady. Timas is taking her first shot at Boston Fashion Week in staying true to her roots and being more involved with the community style here in the city.

Timas is a go big or go home type of gal and will be closing out the week with by far the best venue to host a production at the Old South Church in Boston's chic Back Bay.

The show is next to sold out with VIP pre-entertainment at 7pm, a mix and mingle with their handmade leather clutches by Timas herself filled with the city's hottest trinkets from accessory designers Nicole D'Andrea and more. The evening will begin at 8pm with a special performance by Dance Group Soldierz with Daumos following at 8:15pm. There will be an 8:30pm intermission with Motown Recording Artist Danielle Andrews.

At 9pm the "battle of personality" Timas designs will take the runway in the breath-taking church. To end the evening a post after party at GEM night club with champagne and reserved tables for the guest list invites.

The theme of the show is two beauty women with style and completely different personality going head to head on the runway.

#Flamboyant; A true humanitarian and activist constantly involved in her community. She is caring, nurturing and intelligent. Worked her way to pay for her law degree yet refuses to leave her community behind.

#Bourgeoise; A dreamer, notorious for her profligacy and service. Smart but prefers the easy way out. Her ambition didn't allow her to remain in the community for long. She marries a wealthy businessman.

Guests are encouraged to vote on social media using the #hashtags for their favorite designs.

Designer Angelica Timas moved to Boston, USA as a teenager, where she completed high school, undecided between voices of passion and a reason, a degree in fashion was not an option early on in life.

Angelica earned two master's degrees in Professional Studies in Informatics and Computer Science though her plan to pursue her PH. D in the same field was place on hold when she decided to pursue her passion for fashion. A full time Senior Software Developer, wife, mother and CEO of her brand Angelica Timas, her dream is surely a reality.

With no formal training in fashion Angelica has mastered her skills by self-taught knowledge and true passion for what she envisions in her work. The aesthetic of her collections is inspired by various passions: Her culture, her history, nature, her love for architecture and the simple things that life has to offer.

At the heart of the brand there's an alter-ego her name is Chikke, she is confident, she is high spirited, fun, strong, she is on the go but slows down to enjoy the night, she has a versatile yet a unique taste which makes her have a style all her own. The concept behind the label, is "low maintenance," "simple," and "versatile" fashion. Each collection features edgy yet classic, while the aesthetic is a fusion of asymmetry, minimalism, and color.

Angelica Timas is a clothing label that offers its clientele limited collections of luxurious pieces. Each piece is unique and hand-crafted, made in small quantities giving a real exclusive and individual feel.

"I design primarily for the woman who shares the same traits as Chikke, the versatile woman who is also a trendsetter who is bold, simple, but very elegant and chic." Angelica Timas

7-2016 boscFW Caribbean Dreams at the ICA Boston Post Gazette Socially Scene Column #133

Socially Scene Reviewed… Fashion went waterfront recently when the Elevation Collection showed at Caribbean Dreams First Friday held at the ICA Boston.

It was the start of the season for ICA First Friday summer events with a colorful night put together by Althea Blackford owner of VStyle Productions and Creator of Boston Caribbean Fashion Week. The night featured live performances, DJ Mikey D, a pop-up oyster bar from Island Creek Oysters, and Carnival costuming with a festive flash mob that broke into traditional dance so authentic videos from the evening went viral.

The showcase designer of the event was KREYOL with a preview of the Elevation Collection being launched in August 2016 at the AfroPunk Festival in Brooklyn. Being known for her powerful speaking pieces the collection did not disappoint. A floral fabric dress gave the collection a sense of simplicity, her stapled black and white checkered pattern made an appearance in a crop top, paired with a seasonal florescent skirt. The two statement pieces of the line were risky see-through white lace dresses that any women wearing would be gleaming confidence.

The theme behind the collection is; "We landed here, never quite assimilated to the culture. An alien among the natives, we sought to fit within the folds of the landscape: unmuted the contrast and lightened the shadows to blend within the background. But we failed at mastering the formula. We could not dim our light- failed to settle within the comforts of normalcy- failed to become one of them. Over time, we have come to understand that we were not created to adapt- to adjust. We were born to be free- fashioned to manifest the power within us. Having taken the fruits of our past, we rise above, molding the future- Sankofa. We landed here to elevate."

Socially Scene was able to catch up with creator Joelle Jean-Fontaine and get some insight into the recently crowned Boston Best Clothing Designer. When asked why the name Kréyol, is it just a Haitian thing? Jean-Fontaine expressed, "The influence behind the name is of course our Haitian heritage. However, when one looks into Creole elements, we find that there are so many people from different parts of the world that consider themselves to be of this culture. Our food, music, customs, style, struggles, and strength are very similar. It matters not that you are from Haiti, or New Orleans, or Cape Verde, or Brazil we all see life in color.

Joelle Jean Fontaine added; "Kréyol is a movement. We aim to enlighten, educate, and empower by using fashion to increase awareness of social causes affecting people domestically and abroad. When one thinks of Kréyol, they think of audacious individuals who fight, and aspire to be more. They envision warriors in A-line dresses and combat boots. Revolutionaries; the Kréyol woman is not bound by generational or ethnic backgrounds. She is simply one who lives boldly and walks in her purpose."

This breakout Boston designer had shown at New York Fashion Week this year and is power steaming forward alongside her brother Stanley Rameau doing public relations and mother who flawlessly does most all the sewing. For more on this fashionable family or to purchase pieces from the collection you may visit www.iamkreyol.com.

The evening was a preview to get the city excited for Boston Caribbean Fashion, a weeklong event of diverse festive fashion shows. The week takes place in August where there are a lot of Caribbean events are happening in Boston. It is a dedication of celebrating fashion and Caribbean culture. This year's events will be held from August 9TH through 13th. For more information on all the week has to offer visit www.bostoncfw.com.

June 2016 Scene&Style - Modeling Against Bullying is Back at Emerald Lounge Boston Post Gazette Socially Scene Column #132

Creator of the Modeling Against Bullying Campaign and Fashion Publicist Crissy Ford-Leatham is back at it again on Wednesday June 22nd in collaboration with Emerald Lounge for Lucy's LOVE Bus. The bold, bright looks and fun editions of 2015's fashion show left an impact on all in attendance. This year with Bill Dwyer performing along with the city's top athletes, entrepreneurs, and stunning models the event is one not to be missed.

The Models against Bullying Campaign has been growing and gaining momentum over the past four years. It has put the cause in the fast lane and now will show the stand to fight against bullying for the second year in a row.

The Models Against Bullying Campaign consists of fashion and beauty models who have either been bullied or are bullying advocates. Each model shares their story with the campaign. Crissy Leatham started the campaign with a focus of wanting the world to see that models are not perfect, they are individuals who have seen life today and realized bullying made them stronger. The models have made a solid statement through their personal endeavors, community outreach and a variety of editorials shot over the past four years.

Creator of the campaign Leatham stated, "The Models Against Bullying Campaign is more than a representation of models. It's an example of how individuals can overcome trauma they faced and strive for the peace that life should bring. The Emerald Lounge and Fulgenzio Coppola Image Design Salon have partnered with the Models against bullying campaign to bring our campaign's vision to life. Our goal together is to work and raise funds for Lucy's Love Bus. The outcome is to help both the victim and the bully understand that a relationship is more valuable to life than hurting one another."

A highlight to this year's event will be the live performance by Bill Dwyer. Scene&Style was able to catch up with busy musician for an interview on; how he met Crissy to be involved with the evening and what projects are up next.

Dwyers commented, "I met Crissy about 2 plus years ago and then I went to a fundraiser she put together at a salon on Newbury Street which a blast, we became fast friends. Crissy kicks serious ass!!! She is a beautiful human being! Her first MABC event at The Emerald Lounge last year was off the hook

FUN! It's for a SUPER cause and I'm honored to be a part of it. I'm looking forward to all the beautiful energy there this year. I will be performing three songs at the event, South Caroline, Boomerang and Chemicals In My Brain.

Bill closed out the interview by saying, "My upcoming projects include: preparing for a 2-week tour of Europe in the fall 2016. I am writing and finishing a bunch of brand new material for our 2nd full length record. Also having an exhibition of my photography in Cambridge, Ma (opening date TBA probably July-August 2016) and helping out humanity to be the best it can be as much and as often as I can."

You can catch Bill live on June 22nd at the fashion show or for a link to record samples visit http://www.cdbaby.com/m/Artist/BillDwyerBand You can check out their new record 'Renaissance After Sundown' on iTunes or CD baby or for more on the artist visit http://epresskitz.com/kit.php?u=35270431

The Modeling Against Bullying Campaign in collaboration with Emerald Lounge for Lucy's LOVE Bus will take place Wednesday June 22nd. The event details are listed as follows:

Event Location: The Emerald Lounge Event Time: 7:00 PM - 12 AM Live Performance by Bill Dwyer Door Prizes and 50 VIP Gift Bags with full size products, Kristi Vosbeck - Designer - New York, Angelica Timas - Designer – Boston, R.E.D - Rabia ED - Designer – Paris, Claude Michelle Sanon - Designer – Boston, Cooper 9 - Gianni Valentino - Designer - Los Angeles, AMavensworld.com: Anna Maven – Boston, Madison Avenue Accessories - Diel Louisgene

HAIR and Makeup Team: MakeUp: Janeen Jones and her team, Leslie Patrock, Jill Fontaine. Hair: Eurayshia Reed - Shi Shi's Lounge, Elza Rosa - Blowdry Bar. Technician - DanaLynn Owner of Fun Fancy Nails.

For tickets visit https://www.eventbrite.com/e/models-against-bullying-campaign-in-collaboration-with-emerald-lounge-for-lucys-love-bus-tickets-24719953045

June 2016 Scene&Style - Date Night Rentals with Date My Wardrobe

Anyone involved in the consumer business is well aware of the quote, "fashion is never finished". As the trends and styles emerge convenience is becoming a must to make your clientele return. With the online craze to purchase anything and an app available for everything Boston has a new option for "borrowing an outfit for an evening."

Date My Wardrobe is bringing the sharing economy directly to the fashion designers, giving them a mobile platform to be discovered based on users location and make it easier to rent out from their high-end collection for a 4-day rental period. If you happen to love what you rent, you have the option to buy in the end.

The purpose of Date My Wardrobe is not just saving money but convenience is a huge factor too. Imagine being invited to a black tie event. Instead of buying something new for that one occasion or wearing something you have worn in the past, you can now rent from local fashion designers.

They also have ready-to-wear listings (retail $250+) which professionals can rent for conferences, meetings or just trying on something different. For example; they had attendees of Boston Business Women conference rent from their ready-to-wear collection for the day of the conference.

The current designers on the app include: Denise Hajjar - Evening/Cocktail, ready-to-wear and clutches (from Iris Lane) | Location: InterContinental Boston, Candice Wu - Evening and bridal, Colette Chretien - Ready-To-Wear into evening | Location: Newton Center, Shaunt Sarian - Leather clutches | Location: Newton Center, Maria Bablyak - Hand painted silk scarves | Location: Boston.

They are launching many more designers in the coming few weeks/months including Providence based Jeffrey Dickerson, well-known Boston based designer Daniel Faucher, Ella Tang (from Tangoella) etc.

Date My Wardrobe is also a great way for locals and travelers to find the local fashion designer community - who might be otherwise hard to find.

Amrita Aviyente, founder and CEO of Date My Wardrobe, is giving the local, high-end designers a mobile platform to be discovered and giving them a new revenue stream by introducing rentals. "The future of rentals in the fashion space excites me," says Aviyente. "It is not just about saving but also convenience, giving users the ability to find these designers near them. Users have more options to choose from for special occasions or even ready-to-wear without having to commit."

In building Date My Wardrobe, Aviyente combines her software engineering background with her passion in the fashion space. She produced the idea trying to solve her own problem – having access to high end fashion without having to buy it. "I wanted to make access to high-end collection easily accessible and affordable," said Aviyente.

Date My Wardrobe is a Boston based, mobile first, consumer/fashion Tech Company focused on bringing the sharing economy to the fashion designers and giving women access to high end fashion through an iOS app. Date My Wardrobe was part of Babson College's Butler Venture Accelerator program.

This budding business woman reached out to Scene&Style mid-March just looking to get to know our local fashion scene and seek insight. I was immediately impressed and knew the idea was going to explode. It just a few shorts months Date My Wardrobe has become a hit and demanding attention for the city's top fashionistas.

If you are not aware of this must have app you are behind the game yet in luck. Date My Wardrobe has teamed up with Ma Cherie Studios an elegant boudoir photographer and a top ten website to check out ASAP, www.macheriestudios.com They are hosting an event on June 22nd for Fashion Rack Night Out Boston at Liquid Art House. From 6:30pm to 8:30pm you will have the opportunity to shop and meet local designer that are featured on the app while mingling over cocktails.

For more information on this innovative idea, you can visit the website at www.datemywardrobe.com or download the Date My Wardrobe app on the app store.

6-2016 T*Racy Shows Fashionably Late Boston Post Gazette Socially Scene Column #130

Socially Scene Reviewed… Recently the Liberty Hotel welcomed designer Tracy Belben at a Fashionably Late presentation featuring new and classic pieces in her T*Racy collection.

The show began with the more casual portion of the line in all black dresses paired with easy accessories for an effortless everyday look. The show transitioned into more of Belben's style with her trademark chain link skirts, stunning dresses, and a flirty bikini top for a little fun.

You can always count on T*Racy designs for a stunning, cohesive fashion show and the evening delivered. The event was flawlessly executed from Benharris productions under Grace Goodearl and Billie Francis's direction.

Socially Scene was able to catch up with Designer Tracy Belben before the show to catch up on what is new with her collection. Belben stated, "Things are really great right now, I have been busy literally linking everything together. I am currently rebranding and have taken on a business partner, Mel Ellard." Belben mentioned, "We are focusing on breaking my collection into two divisions; ready to wear and runway/red carpet designs".

For more on these original pieces, to shop or get to know the designer visit www.t-racy.com.

June 2016 Bravery Brand Honors Local Hero's Boston Post Gazette Socially Scene Column #129

Recently Lindsay Tia Reilly held a Patriot Week presentation and themed runway show, "Mass Fallen Hero's" at Copperfield's for support of our local troops in Afghanistan and Iraq.

The South Boston pub was a perfect location with its garage door walls opened for the waterfront breeze, the warehouse high ceilings and space to fit the masses that piled in for the show. The scene was set with American flags draped on the walls along with service nets, a Lindsay Tia pop up shop and three handsome U.S. Marine's to escort the models through the event.

The evening began with pride for all as local favorite; "Scully" took to the stage and sang The Star Spangled Banner. From there the fashion took to the runway. Tia was showing her spring 2016 collection and her "Bravery Brand" themed styles for the occasion. Each look walked was accessorized by Tia's own merchandise and accompanied with a "LT" branded handbag which is the focus for the designer.

The line featured fun and flirty crop tops, flowing skirts, beach attire and red white and blue color choices. The statement piece of the collection was an army green parachute dress worn by bombshell model Sophie Weidhass. Tia personally took to the stitching of the garment and with the rip cord still attached she stayed true to the fabric. Tia felt it was a tribute to all the hard work our service troops and veterans have done for our country.

The night was flawless with production by Kathy Benharris and her team, Grace Goodearl and Billie Francis. The Bravery Blog creator and Lasell College Fashion Merchandising graduate Lindsay Tia had every reason to take a bow from success. The night was a homerun for the "Mass Fallen Hero's" charity in which proceeds were donated to.

Lindsay Tia has her own boutique located at 407 West 1st Street in South Boston. Her American made and Boston designed handbags represent to inspire, encourage bravery, and empower others. You may visit www.lindsaytia.com to see more on this "Change the World One Bag at a Time" designer also shop and be connected to her Bravery Blog.

April 2016 Scene&Style - Josef's Runway for a Rescue Boston Post Gazette Socially Scene Column #128

On April 12th fashions finest came to the rescue at West End Jonnies to support Aimee Takaha's Animal Sanctuary.

Last year iconic dress designer David Josef created a runway event, "Fashion to the Rescue" after falling in love with Petunia, a pig on Amiee's Animal Sanctuary. The heart of gold designer brought in top designers and models to The Beehive and raised approximately 20,000 which in turn went into buying a new truck to transport food and the rescued furry little critters living on the farm.

This year Josef brought the show to a new venue at West End Jonnies. Josef again called on elegant and timeless designer Denise Hajjar who walked in the previous show as a model and this had designed a special collection just for the event. Also added to the lineup was I am Kreyol a new local company making their way in the industry recently showing at Macy's for New York Fashion Week. By the night of the show tickets were completely sold out and the RSVP list from the cities glitterati was the classiest of the year.

The wall to wall packed event began with host and creator David Josef taking stage by thanking all of the amazing support here in Boston from the industry and friends. You know the fabulous fashionistas are out when faces like top photographer Iggy Barskov, Gustavo Leon his partner in crime Erica Corsano, Angela Menino, and the lovely Yoland Cellucci along with many more. Following was a heartwarming video on all the work that Amiee does all from the heart and left the guests in tears.

The runway portion of the evening started with Denise Hajjar stetting a standard with her cohesive spring collection created just for the show that featured pink and stunning patterns. Next to hit the runway was emerging designer I Am Kreyol with their modern and urban styles for the season. Closing out the fashion portion was the elegant dress designer and sanctuary savor David Josef. Josef also produced a collection exclusively for the show. The line featured special occasion gowns and dedicated presentations in-between each piece. The show was high class all the way and designer threads were draped on the cities celebrity models like; Jane Conway Caspe, Linda Cole Petrosian, Kathy Benharris, Simone Aptekman and many more.

Closing the event was an live auction featuring animal paintings from Aimee's Farm, reservations for six at West End Johnnie's legendary Sunday Brunch, trip to Las Vegas for two, which included airfare on Jet Blue, two nights at the Bellagio Hotel and two tickets for Magician Mat Franco, Winner of America's Got Talent that included a backstage meet and greet with Mat.

Scene&Style caught up with David Josef post show and was able to get insight of his gratitude. Josef expressed, "The love that was in the room was palpable. To be surrounded by 300 friends all there to salute Aimee and help her with her sanctuary work for these beautiful animals, was life-changing. My amazing friends and clients Brian and Kathy Stevens were so generous in matching all of the donations that we took in last night to tap out our evening at just over $200,000. Last year's fashion to the rescue 2015 benefit took in a total of $20,000 so we really did make a great big jump."

Josef praised on by saying, "To have dignitaries from both side of the aisle represented last night from Senator Scott Brown to the entire Thomas Menino family was profoundly humbling. Every top model in the city celebrities and even my clients worked the room last night to raise funds for Aimee and the farm."

The benefit fashion show for Aimee's Animal Farm was a huge success and even more a big staple event in the city of Boston and the generosity of our community. Aimee's Farm Animal Sanctuary is a Non-Profit 501(c)3 entity. All funds raised at this event go directly to Aimee's Sanctuary which Rescues, Rehabilitates and Rehomes neglected, abandoned and abused animals. The sanctuary provides them with temporary and long-term shelter In a caring, safe environment with proper nutrition and medical attention. If you would like more information or to make a donation please visit www.amieesfarmanimalsanctuary.com

3-2016 Project Runway Sensation Takes Over Apple Boston Post Gazette Socially Scene Column #128

Recently fashion met up with technology at the Boylston Street Apple store where local designer and Project Runway finalist Kelly Dempsey and fanny pack specialist gave a tutorial on how she uses apple products in creation of her designs.

Apple Boston was the place to be for RackAddik fans and fanny pack followers as the creator of it all Kelly Dempsey made her way home from her busy New York City styling to host an interactive session on how technology is giving a helping hand in her latest design methods.

The celebrity guest appearance got started off with her giving fans insight into her background in the fashion industry. With so much success it was most certainly a surprise to find out she has no formal education in fashion, is a self-taught seem tress with style and has worked her way to the top slinging sandwiches in a local sub shop right at home in Massachusetts.

She continued on about her time with the hit series Project Runway. She gave in-depth details on her experience with the challenges. Also giving inspiration with how no matter how hard things got, the designer drama or politics she knew what she wanted and never gave up. With all the hard work Dempsey was also able to list all her accomplishments from the show making it to the final four and showing a collection at NYC Fashion Week also receiving a hefty cash prize for being the designer to win the most challenges on the show during Project Runway Season 14.

From there Dempsey dove right in to the technology based demonstration with her Mac laptop, hooked up to the massive store desktop all accessible from her Apple iPhone. As most anything in this day and age fashion design also has an "app" for creations and daily use. Dempsey walked her fans and hopeful future designers through the options of creating a garment from start to finish. The selections seemed endless as she displayed everything from choosing a neckline, skirt length or from simply putting in measurements from a customer for a custom piece to forming her own unique patterns.

The evening ended with a question portion answer session and her fanny packs fans were able to get a personal photo with the designer. Kelly Dempsey is a local lady who took hold of her passion in design, taught herself and is making way in the fashion industry with her RackAddik brand. Dempsey's 2016 spring collection will release in the upcoming weeks, her fanny pack stock will be replenished and all can be purchased at www.rackaddict.com

**March 2016 Scene&Style - Angelica Timas Shows Spring Collection
Boston Post Gazette Socially Scene Column #127**

Recently The Liberty Hotel held their most recent "Fashionably Late" featuring South End's, Angelica Timas.

The Liberty Hotel is always a classy spot for a designer to show their latest collection line. The Hotel's high ceilings and chic décor is a great compliment for the multi-floor show. Guests gathered on the main level in the lounge. Whether it is from the VIP tables or mingling through the spacious area the models were front and center for all with the strategically stages set.

Angelica was presenting her 2016 Spring/Summer collection and the pieces made you want to toss your boots to the back of the closet and dig out those open toes. The line featured soft silks seen in a full V-neck cut beige jumper, a full length spring green dress, silver toned pants, a sexy black lace cocktail number yet the highlight of the show was a high neck dress with long sleeves and a stunning peacock dress.

Angelica Timas is making quite a stir in the city. At the heart of the brand there's the alter-ego Chikke, she is confident, is high spirited, fun, strong, is on the go but slows down to enjoy the night, has a versatile yet a unique taste which makes her have a style all her own.

The concept behind the label is "low maintenance," "simple," and "versatile" fashion. Each collection features edgy yet classic, while the aesthetic is a fusion of asymmetry, minimalism, and color. The evening was a class event and the collection really showed Timas and her talents.

Angelica Timas is a clothing label that offers its clientele limited collections of luxurious pieces. Each piece is unique and hand-crafted, made in small quantities giving a real exclusive and individual feel. To view more of her collection or to purchase merchandise you may visit her website at www.angelicatimas.com

3-11-2016 Fashion Power Play by KB Fashion Productions Boston Post Gazette Socially Scene Column #126

Recently the center of Copley Place was transformed into a chic catwalk that held the second annual "Fashion Power Play" to benefit the Bruins Foundation and The Friends of Dana Farber.

Kathy Benharris and her amazing production crew brought the "B" puck back to show Neiman Marcus's hottest spring styles and usher in the cities top fashionistas for a charity event. This year's event was larger than last after what a success it had been in 2015. The evening was a hit from cocktail hour to final struts of style. The 110 foot runway was an expansion from the previous year and a must for the 250 seat sold out show. The second floor was a new edition and blocked off for a VIP cocktail reception with donated treats from the cities tastiest restaurants.

The red carpeted event was hosted by Jenny Johnson, two time Emmy award winning and co-host of NESN's Dining Playbook. Johnson was just the beginning of the A-List attendance; the Bruins Coach Claude Julien and their front line sat right on the runway, NESN, Channel 7, Dirty Water TV, The Boston Breakers Rachel Wood and their ESPN Analyst also Olympic Gold Medalist Cat Whitehill along with Owner John Powers and General Manager Lee Billiard were amongst a few of the celebrity faces seen.

The Bruins wives, girlfriends, Maggie Inc., and Dynasty models took center ice for the Neiman Marcus styled show. MLR Artist Management and Owner Lou Rodriguez returned to highlight the beauties of the runway showing a classic and flawless feel with hair and makeup.

Spring season is upon us and the styling by Benharris and her team featured looks like; casual ripped jeans with a sleeveless turtleneck sweater, a flashing orange knee length fitted dress for the office yet with a bell bottom arm for a little flair, off the shoulder full length pastel patterned dresses for a Sunday flow, sexy chic all black jumpers for a cocktail evening in the Seaport and more.

The event was a success in its second year and an original creation by Boston's best productions, Kathy Benharris. Socially Scene was able to catch up with Benharris who commented, "The Fashion Power Play was my concept that I brought to the Bruins and then connected with Copley. This year we brought in Dana Farber and their involvement has been amazing. I am very proud that this event has grown and excited to continue to see it do so. I have to admit my production staff is amazing and I couldn't do it without them and my right hands, Grace Goodearl and Billy Francis along with this year's lead intern Meghan Borges. I am so grateful to all the sponsors and donors throughout the city of Boston for their contributions, this is a charity show so the generosity makes an important impact."

The "Fashion Power Play" at the center of Copley Place was all class whether it was the spring styles modeled by Bruins beauties or the face of 12 year old Paris being treated at the Jimmy Fund Clinic who was the last lady to hit the runway. Once again Benharris brought fashion and charity together for a night not to be forgotten.

2-2016 Designer Candice Wu Opens New Boutique Boston Post Gazette Socially Scene Column #125

Recently Boston designer Candice Wu opened a new location for her wedding gown couture in the South End and welcomed the city in for an evening of fashion and treats.

The event began with a warm welcome of a specialty sparkling cocktail and a tour. The basement space is located directly next to the famed Ash&Rose boutique for shoppers to get a full experience. Once inside you could feel the design talents of Wu come over you: from the exposed brick that gave it an urban appeal to the walls honored in her accomplishments. It was a very clean look that gave the draped wedding gowns from wall to wall their own spotlight. Wu is known for her fabrics yet was prideful is mentioning to guests that she also had done all of the interior design.

The night saw many of Boston's social scene come through from the cities top hair dressers, fellow designers and to promote the event Miss Massachusetts and Miss Maine, Miss New Hampshire and Miss Connecticut. The company to chat with for the evening was high end as to be expected with the event being produced by Cat Walk for a Cure leader, Bryan Finocchio and 33Monroe Events.

Candice Wu has featured on Fashion TV, voted a Boston Best and most recently with a spread in Marie Claire is known for her dark couture dresses and the past year has been focusing on wedding design. Socially Scene had the opportunity to sit with Wu and when asked about her current projects commented, "I have been doing wedding dresses for over a year now. I still do everything but am focusing on the couture wedding collection with a lot of Swarovski crystal in the gowns. Most all of the dresses are convertible from church ceremony to reception comfort."

The evening was chic with tasty cocktails, desserts and mingling with some of the city's top fashionistas. Candice Wu has made a name for herself with evening wear and looking to expose her talent with wedding design. Wu's new couture wedding dress store is located at 460 Harrison Ave in Boston suite C-3. To view more of her collections or to read more on the designer visit www.candicewucouture.com.

1-2016 SKEA Slopes Down Fashionably Late Socially Scene Column #124

Recently the Liberty Hotel got style started off for 2016 with their Fashionably Late presentation featuring Skea.

Now that winter is officially here, the ski resorts are open it was Kathy Benharris and her production crew to showcase the coolest slope styles for the season.

The current collection focused on bright pink and turquoise pastels tied together with the classic winter white. The Dynasty models flaunted the must haves for your trip to the resort; fitted ski pants with matching jacket, a cozy vest and mini skirt for a pop to an outfit for the lodge and most every looked was finished with fur. The design to top the runway show was a tiger print skin suit that is sure to grab attention on any slope.

Boston's fashion community flocks out in support of Benharris as her reputation holds strong with always putting on a quality show. In attendance for this edition of Fashionable late was CEO of Skea Diane Boyer and former U.S. National team skier Pam Fletcher. Socially Scene was able to catch up with Boyer and when asked about her role in the company she commented, I took over the business from my parents in the 90's and love what I do. Our tag line is, Follow your passion to your dream. I live everyday by those words and will continue to for myself and the Skea lifestyle."

Skea was founded in 1972 which is based out of Vail Colorado and is a family owned business. They are a ski and winter lifestyle brand for women made by women. Their clothing line is meant to give a stylish look to the ladies while hitting the slopes with the boys. You can view their current collection, blog and even shop on their website at www.skealimited.com

Chapter Ten – 2015

"Never use the word 'cheap.' Today everybody can look chic in inexpensive clothes—the rich buy them, too. There is good clothing design on every level today. You can be the chicest thing in the world in a T-shirt and jeans—it's up to you." - Karl Lagerfeld

12-11-2015 Fashion's Finest Gather at DVF on Newbury Boston Post Gazette Socially Scene Column #123

This past week Boston's fashion community gathered together at a Newbury Street store to see industry legend Diane Von Furstenberg's new collection revealed.

The Boston Fashion Meetup paired up with store manager and Boston brand ambassador Meghan O'Brien along with staff welcomed in the city's finest for a shop, mix and mingle event with all brining donations for the Newbury Street based, " The Women's Lunch Place."

The evening began with a bubbly cocktail and a tasty cupcake from neighboring "Georgetown Cupcake" that was designed especially for the event with an editable DVF logo. As the VIP guest list of fashionistas like; debutant dress designer David Josef, leading lady of production Kathy Benharris, Samuel Vartan and Kiki Papadopoulos from Vartan Collections, pageant producer, Iva Nicole, fashion marketing beauty Anna Maven and many more fabulous faces that make our fashion community what it is.

The guests mingled amongst themselves in their holiday attire and then to be pulled together for a brief presentation from manger Meghan on the store's current collection and the history behind Von Furstenberg and her 40 plus years in the business. The December line is called, "Miami Vice" being in the fashion world the month is the beginning of resort wear being released. Von Furstenberg's line focuses on a bold zebra print, floral placements, striped jump suits, chiffon dresses that show her innocent side and the result for the collection is a delivery fit for a debutant or a dreamer.

O'Brien then moved into some background information on Von Furstenberg and her journey through in the business. Dianne began her career by stating, "I didn't know what I wanted to do when I first started out but I knew the women I wanted to be." With her 40 plus years in the business has only had store fronts for the past ten years, only five here in Boston and were happy to welcome the guests for the evening as they find many residents aren't aware of the store and have been doing their DVF shopping at Sak's. Her current focus for the future of her business is, "If you get the millennial women you will get their mother and then get their daughter." The story could go on for days with the past, present and future of this icon in the fashion industry and it can in her newly released book, "The Women I Wanted to Be."

The night was a fashion success for the city; the brand and the amount of donations to "The Women's Lunch Place" were heartwarming. If you are looking for great gift ideas Diane Von Furstenberg has them all. The staff can help you find that perfect handbag, a dress to make a statement at a holiday cocktail party of even help you build a custom gift box with DVF swag. You can visit www.dvf.com or pop into the store located at 73 Newbury Street. The evening took in so many donations for "The

Women's Lunch Place" and if you were looking to make a ladies life a litter better you can view the suggested list at www.womenslunchplace.org/donate or visit them at 67 Newbury Street, Boston.

11-27-2015 Slope Style Hits the Ski&Snow Expo Runway Boston Post Gazette Socially Scene Column #122

This past week Boston welcomed in one of the most anticipated events of the year, the Boston.com Ski & Snow Expo. The 34th annual expo held at the Seaport World Trade Convention Center brought in all of the top mountains in New England and around the country to showcase their powder appeal. The convention always has an upbeat vibe the second you enter the door. There are rows and rows of resorts to visit like; Stowe, Steamboat, Vail, Big Sky, and many more.

The event has more to offer than information on the ski slopes but plenty of entertainment like; the Skyriders who are a traveling trampoline team that showed off their flip and fly skills also displayed behind the scenes practice tactics for snowboard professionals per trampoline training. The team had no problem drawing in a crowd yet seemed to steal hearts being they were decked out in Patriots gear for the big game against New York that Sunday.

Each isle offered its own amusement with interactive snow board demonstrations, the fitting of ski and snow gear, spin wheels games, Jeep giveaways and even Stowe Mountain Resort had their kitchen on site for samples of their sushi rolls that are on their five star menu.

Returning this year was Boston's top stylist and ski queen herself Kathy Benharris with her flawless production crew for the Fashion Spectacular

Runway Show presented by Country Ski&Sport. The four day expo was host to multiple fashion shows throughout the day that gave attendees the opportunity to see models strut the seasons best slops styles down the runway. The show highlighted top brands; Burton, Volkl, Skea, Scott, Karbon, Spyder, and all were paired with accessory style of goggles, poles, backpacks from Benharris and her keen eye for the season's coolest slope looks. A highlight for the fashionistas of the scene was when a legend made an appearance for Fridays Fashion Spectacular, Barbara Alley Simon. Simon was the first lady in ski fashion doing shows all over the country, appearing on Oprah and The Tonight Show, was the fashion editor for Ski Magazine and now in her 70's still making it down a runway or two.

The Boston.com Ski & Snow Expo was once again a success and continues to be an event New England looks forward to with attendance growing year after year. For more information on lodges, slopes, or the event itself you may visit www.bewisports.com.

11-13-2015 Frank&Oak Opens on Newbury Boston Post Gazette Socially Scene Column #121

Recently The Boston Fashion Meetup held an event at Frank & Oak's Newbury Street location to give the gentleman in the city a taste of this season's trend.

With all the amazing designers to show their latest collections at Boston Fashion Week it was clear that most focused on women's wear, yet this evening gave a little insight for the gentleman of the city on how to stay on top of their wardrobe and Socially Scene was on site.

Although Frank & Oak is a men's clothing store it was a night welcome to all by brand Ambassador Jeff Lahen's to introduce the franchise's newest location. The evening began with fashionistas mixing, mingling, and meeting a new in the store's spacious and appealing to the eye design. Once the chatter came to a calm brand ambassador Lahen's took center stage and gave an in-depth tour of the Newbury location.

He walked guests through the primped sections of the store while pointing out that the focus of the fall line is to bring class to an outfit for the office that can transition with a loss of a layer and a button or two down for an appropriate after work cocktail or dinner date. The brand is geared to the everyday guy with pieces they can dress up and dress down all while each month the entire collection changes in the store for fresh new looks.

As Lahen's educated about this season's style he expressed that Frank & Oak are more than just a clothing store. They are a multi-purpose modern day spa for the men! Not only are customers able to grab simple pieces like undershirts but can make an appointment for a personal shopper consultation, an online option to have a head to toe look sent to you, grab your accessories and even come in for a coffee and personal barber pampering with a call ahead.

Frank & Oak proved that fashion forward is just for the ladies on Newbury Street but the newest spot to bring the best for the men. The night was a success and brought a new brand to hit Boston into light. As the holiday season rolls around Frank & Oak located at 220 Newbury Street is a great place to grab a gift. To view the recent collection on the shelves visit www.fankandoak.com or call 617-778-2373 to set up a personal shopper appointment.

Riot Theatre Reenacts… Most anyone in Boston knows the names Matt Damon and Ben Affleck since they are our hometown heroes on the big screen and The Riot Theatre is brining you a hilarious on stage rendition of their road to stardom, "Matt & Ben: The Gender-Bending Parody" with select dates.

It's no surprise that Matt Damon and Ben Affleck became movie stars after showing off their acting skills in Good Will Hunting. The shocker is that they also wrote the critically-acclaimed screenplay. Unable to believe that claim, comedian Mindy Kaling and actress Brenda Withers created this hilarious comedy that explains the "true" origin of the Academy Award-winning screenplay. In this clever re-imagining of the events that led to the creation of the film, the screenplay for Good Will Hunting drops mysteriously from the heavens and the boys realize they're being tested by a higher power. This affectionate riff on the legendary bromance stars Lauren Robinson and Libby Schap as Matt Damon and Ben Affleck, and follows them over the course of one long Saturday in Somerville as they fight, reminisce, and hallucinate a lot more than normal when confronted with the screenplay that will change their lives.

Who doesn't have a soft spot for the Boys from Boston! They have made such an impact in the industry yet have stayed true to the roots right here in Massachusetts. This is a great way to fall for these boys just a little more and there are only a select few dates left to do it! Grab your tickets for; November 20th, 27th or December 11th at the Riot Theater located at 146 South Street Jamaica Plain. To purchase your tickets or to see more of what is currently on stage visit www.theriottheater.com or call 617-650-7995.

10-16-2015 Socially Scene Column Boston Post-Gazette Boston Fashion Week Reviewed Column #120

"Denise Hajjar, Candice Wu, Earl Battle Designs, Kinda Touma, Firas Yousif, KB Fashion Production shows "FASHION + FITTNESS FIX and Benrus," MLR Artist Management, T*Racy, H.GrantStyle

Socially Scene Review... Recently Boston Fashion Week took to the runway for its 21st year and brought new and modern taste to the table.

This edition got started off with an opening party, "The Sixth Floor" at 100 Federal Street in a lofty open space where the walls were canvases for artists; Bob Packert, Sadie Dayton and Robert to give their version of design through paint while welcoming Boston's fashions finest to get the week underway.

2015 was the introduction of a new program called, "Platform Downtown" on the "Open Runway" which was a chance for budding designers to enter their collections in a show that took place in the revamped Downtown Crossing area and featured designers like; Chyna Pope, Jeffery Dickerson, Tatiana Tejedor and Carlos Villamil.

The week highlighted events like the classic Marilyn Riseman Luncheon Series, SMART Talk which were gatherings throughout the city with respected professionals discussing topics in the industry, the annual Hacking Arts presented by MIT that explores the intersection of art, science, technology and entrepreneurship, The Hand of Fashion that was an interactive seminar on the construction of garments and so much more.

Boston's stapled designers such as Candice Wu showed her bridal collection, Earl Battle Designs, Kinda Touma, and the king of the bridal couture Firas Yousif with his original evening wear. The introduction of the newest movement in fashion "Athleisure" made a debut with powerhouses Kathy Benharris and Lou Rod from MLR turning the new David Barton Gym in the Back Bay into FASHION + FITTNESS FIX. The future of Boston design came together with a collaborated event, JK x RG held in a chic space in the leather district from some of the city's favorites. Julie Kontos who brings a sophisticated style with edge to everyday looks brought her SS2016 collection. Accessory artist Tracy Belben showed her T*Racy line that wows the eye with her bold and well-made designs constructed from chain links into evening wear dresses and jewelry. The event was styled by H.GrantStyle who started out in the handbag making department and has evolved into a guru to get your closet ship shape.

Socially Scene was on site for two of the top shows to hit the runway and it was no surprise that the legendary Denise Hajjar was the first. Hajjar held her annual benefit show with Dress for Success at Royal and the night was class from start to finish. The timeless designer's 2015 Fall/Winter collection took to the runway with powerful print dresses that could be worn to the office then off to a flirty cocktail affair. From a consumer demand Hajjar had a series of jackets hit the runway that had an everyday appeal and inner lining flair. The classic statement pieces made it down the catwalk with hints of leather that spoke to all women searching for that ready to wear look.

When Boston Fashion Week rolls around you can always count of Hajjar to put on more than just a show! Returning to the runway again this year was the fabulous dancing duo from Fred Astaire Dance Studio in Dedham, there was a newly vamped VIP area that gave an aerial view, a preshow cocktail hour, post-show dessert dish from Wicked Good Cupcakes and a live auction with proceeds from the evening going to Dress for Success.

Socially Scene was able to catch up with the elegant designer herself and when asked to comment on the inspiration behind the night said, "We don't dress head to toe in Chanel, it isn't our lifestyle anymore. I love showing that gorgeous look yet I'm selling to the real customer." Hajjar added, "I enjoy designing for the modern woman and my job is to show the woman how many different ways they can wear a piece, going from dressy to really casual. It is all about how they change it up."

The second showstopper of the week came at the Liberty Hotel's version of Fashionably Late produced by Kathy Benharris featuring Benrus. The night was a chic as to be expected from the queen of perfection with Boston's glitterati getting out in the former jail house turned hotel. Benharris came together with Rhode Island native and Chief Executive Officer for Benrus Giovanni Feroce to expose this earth toned line that is making statements in everyday outfits. The collection featured the classic all-American t-shirt and jean look with Bourbon&Boweties accessories. The stunner style of the evening to hit the runway was a cropped Bernus top paired with an authentic parachute skirt worn by brand ambassador Camille Kostek local lady and 2015 Super Bowl Champions New England Patriots Cheerleader. Benrus is a brand that has been around for ages yet has only been known to a select audience as they have been designing watches for our U.S. Military.

Socially Scene was able to snag a minute with the CEO Giovanni Feroce who was fresh from the plane. When asked about the rebranding of the company he commented, "We are moving into a full lifestyle brand. We are producing backpacks, denim, glasses made right here in

Massachusetts and the shirts are made in Fall River." Feroce added, "My focus right now is to get out there and see what the consumer is looking for and to incorporate it into our apparel."

Boston Fashion Week was once again was an innovative and educating. The community is growing, and the future of fashion is making a statement here in the city. There are new and exciting things on the horizon and 2016 will be host to a first in Boston Fashion, stay tuned!

9-25-2015 bosFW Preview Boston Post Gazette Socially Scene Column #116

The time of year has come where the leaves begin to fall and fashion takes priority in the social schedule. Boston Fashion Week will take place September 27th through October 3rd and the lineup of shows throughout the cities top venues are ones not to be missed.

Getting the week going is a Socially Scene favorite, Denise Hajjar who represents "fashion forward, timeless elegance." Hajjar will be hosting her annual Dress for Success charity show that focuses on "Powerful women empowering women" on Tuesday, September 29th 6pm at Club Royal located at 279 Tremont Street Boston. The evening will begin with a cocktail reception, followed by fashion show and live auction then end with a shopping event with dessert and dancing. The night will be swimming with local celebrities like host for the event Heather Unruh WCVB Anchor. Celebrity models will include; Adrianna Cohen from the Boston Herald, Tracey Noonan and Dani Valagie from Wicked Good Cupcakes, Ayanna Presley Boston City Councilor at Large and much more. The entertainment introduced last year will return with the dancing duo from Fred Astaire Dance Studio in Dedham. Hajjar is a staple in the Boston fashion scene and is always sure to bring a show. Mark your calendars for Tuesday September 29th and purchase your tickets at www.denisehajjar.com or to get a look at some of the stunning designs Denise brings to the runway each year.

Another must see show will be from a Boston best; Kathy Benharris, Stylist and Owner of K.B. Productions will be producing Boston Fashion Week's most attended show known as "Fashionably Late" a free presentation featuring BENRUS at The Liberty Hotel located at 215 Charles Street Boston on Thursday, October 1st with designs hitting the runway at 10pm. In addition to the fashion show, BENRUS will also be hosting a VIP party that will start before the fashion show and conclude at its end.

Kathy Benharris has built a reputation of class and flawless perfection when it comes to producing a show. Excellence is in all aspects of event execution also an obsession with styling is a vehicle to tell her client's unique fashion story. When Benharris is in charge there is a purpose to every fashion show and a business goal that it must serve.

BENRUS is mostly known for their military watch collection yet with the new edition of Giovanni Feroce, former Military Officer, State Senator and Entrepreneur left Alex and Ani in March 2014, after bringing the brand from $2.2 million to north of $230 million in a 36 month period the company is rebranding into a full line of clothing that has a military feel. For more information on the brand you may visit www.benrus.com.

Camille Kostek, former Patriots 2015 Super Bowl Cheerleader their brand ambassador / spokes model and will model in the Liberty Boston Fashion Week Show. The Patriots are on a bye week making it highly likely that Rob Gronkowski and other players may make an appearance. This show is a highlight in Boston Fashion Week and being produced by Benharris you can expect perfection.

Jump into the "athleisure" side of fashion with a no cost look at the brand new David Barton Gym located at 50 Park Plaza in Boston for a "Fashion + Fitness Fix". MLR Artists and Kathy Benharris will be brining you the comfort styles from Michi New York and G Star raw. The looks to create that strong physique will hit the weights at 6pm sharp. You may visit www.fashionandfittness.com for more information on the show.

Take look into the dark side of fashion with, "A Mask of Death." Boston based couture designer Ashley Rose will be debuting her new Fall/Winter

Collection for Boston Fashion Week on Saturday October 3rd at Cure Lounge located at 246 Tremont Street Boston free to the public with designs hitting the runway at 11pm. Her newest collection is inspired by a recent road trip through the Midwest exploring abandoned asylums and cathedrals that nature has taken rule over. Ashley's previous gowns have been featured in Paper Magazine & Vogue Italia. Her artistic vision has caught the eyes of Kelly Osbourne who recognized her exquisite craftsmanship, and love of art on her website.

Gorgeous pieces by Burial Ground will be paired with Ashley's Collection. Burial Ground is the collective vision of long-time best friends Jamie Mooers and Bill Crisafi. The pair met in 2004 while working part time at a coffee shop near their hometown of Newburyport, Massachusetts. They forged a lasting friendship over their mutual fascinations with occultism, magic, spirituality, and a deep nostalgia for old New England. You may view more on the collection at www.burialground.org

With countless numbers of shows, events, mixers and more through Boston Fashion Week this year there is a new edition; Platform Downtown. In the spirit of Boston Fashion Week 3.0 - which is all about changing how to define the role of fashion throughout the city and in our lives - Terri Mahn and the Downtown Boston BID team have spent the past several months building relationships and developing events that challenge everyone to think outside the box.

Socially Scene was able to catch up with the local fashionista Terri Mahn and get an insight to this new "platform" in Boston fashion. When asked, how did the introduction of Platform Downtown come about? Mahn replied, "I have coordinated and produced events for Boston Fashion Week since 2009 through my business thestylistcloset. This year I thought it would be great to show fashion outside-of-the-box — lift the curtain a little bit into how it works. I wanted to mix upcoming and established designers and give a forum for local photographers and filmmakers to express themselves about fashion. Downtown Crossing was the perfect location due to it being the transportation hub of Boston and an intersection of culture, arts, fashion, technology and lifestyles."

Digging a little deeper with Mahn Socially Scene inquired about; what Platform Downtown is and how it will benefit designers and attendees?

"Platform Downtown is a series of curated fashion events happening in Downtown Crossing during Boston Fashion Week 2015. Platform Downtown celebrates the diverse Boston fashion community. The Platform Downtown events will be the anchor and heart of Boston Fashion Week 2015," said Terri Mahn. "Fashion is an important part of the Boston lifestyle and history of Downtown Crossing. That being said, we want to shake up the landscape and introduce new ideas of a fashion presentation. We are hopeful this will yield innovative and alternative methods for how fashion will be showcased in the future."

Boston Fashion Week is on the horizon and these are just tiny tid bits of all the city of Boston will expose this 2015. For a full list of calendar events visit www.bostonfashionweek.com.

8-14-2015 Miss Central Massachusetts was Crowned Boston Post Gazette Socially Scene Column #115

Recently, the 2015 Miss Central Massachusetts was crowned and Socially Scene was on site at the historic Masonic Hall in Worcester to see the pageant. Every year, girls of all ages spend countless hours preparing their talent and style for one night in hopes of taking home the crown.

The evening began with celebrity hosts Gustavo Leon, managing editor of the Boston Herald, and Monica Pietrzack, former Miss Connecticut 2009, introducing the esteemed panel of judges and director of the event, Iva Nicole. From there, the contestants for Little Miss, Miss Princess and Miss Teen took to the stage and had guests gushing over the adorable future beauty queens. Even though only one was able to walk away Little Miss and Miss Teen, each contestant was given recognition of sorts with awards such as: Miss Photogenic, Miss Congeniality, Best Spirit, Best Dress and Best Model.

The audience was entertained during intermissions with performers such as Scott Isbell, who brought a pop-meets-rock sound to the stage. Wowing the audience was Ava Fratus, a seven year-old budding musician who writes her own lyrics and exudes a Gwen Stefani attitude.

The highlight of the night was the seven hopefuls that competed in the swimsuit, evening gown, and question portion of the event to become the next Miss Central Massachusetts. Each contestant was given the opportunity to show her class and beauty down the Masonic runway and prove to the judges why she was best suited to be the next queen.

Just before the winner was crowned, the current Miss Central Massachusetts, Roxanne Ribotgonzalez and Miss Teen Central Massachusetts Jessica Reyes gave their heartfelt goodbyes to the rein and wished well to the incoming contenders.

After much anticipation and being narrowed down to three, the new queen was announced and Jenna Kelly received the sash and crown to be the 2015 Miss Central Massachusetts. The night was full of glamour and prestige as beauty was put on display and given the opportunity to show the brains behind it all with their accomplishments along with what they give back to the community. New Queen Jenna Kelly will serve a one-year reign while also winning professional hair care, photos, and acting classes along with entry into the Miss Massachusetts pageant. If you would like more information on the upcoming associated events associated or to apply for next year, visit www.misscentralmass.com.

7-10-2015 BMC Catwalk for a Cure Boston Post Gazette Socially Scene Column #114

Boston recently hosted one of its most esteemed fashion shows, a charity event sponsored by Liberty Mutual and Macy's. The BMC Catwalk for a Cure was held at the exquisite State Room.

The evening began with a cocktail hour on the 33rd floor where the spectacular view reflected the VIP guest list, along with black tie and fashionable attire. Once the guests were seated, Emcee Kim Khazei from WHDH-TV Channel 7 News set the standard for the enthusiasm to follow. The show started off with figure skater, Olympic Gold Medalist, and brain cancer survivor Scott Hamilton introducing the heartwarming video that gave an in-depth view on what an impact the Boston Medical Center makes on the lives of its patients.

First to hit the runway were pastel swimwear pieces by Stephanie Raymond that were a cohesive combination from Boston's own Bryan Finocchio and Christina K. Pierce. Local celebrities were a highlight to hit the runway and a crowd favorite was Jonathan Soroff, from the Improper Bostonian, who strutted his stuff in Raymond's beach wear. Following was the showroom sensation, "Pierce," who brought her own personally bright, flirty, and A-List style looks to the stage. Next was "Kontos for a Cure," glamour gowns by Designer Julie Kontos, which were draped on Boston beauties and proud survivors as they all sashayed down the platform.

The Catwalk for a Cure benefit fashion show focuses on the strength these survivors project. Meanwhile, Kinda Touma brought a bold and powerful statement to the runway with her designs. Next to show was the very hands-on Director/Stylist Bryan Finocchio who continues to bring success to the yearly event. Drea Couture followed Finocchio with a collection that focused on the beauty of color with bold tones and a one-of-a-kind wedding dress.

Closing out the catwalk was Candice Wu with her classic dark inspiration of dresses, the grand finale being a flawless sheer fitted black number with the waist down being a layered ruffled look.

The night was a "cure" success and the BMC can put another well-made fashion show in the books! The evening was full of energy and tears of joy were shed while guests were cheering on survivors that walked the runway wearing smiles. The BMC Catwalk for a Cure is clearly a special event that Bostonians look forward to year after year.

Located in Boston's historic South End neighborhood, BMC is a private, not for-profit, 496-bed, academic medical center, and the primary teaching affiliate for Boston University School of Medicine. Consistent with its mission to provide the best in health care to all, BMC is the largest safety net hospital in New England and reaches into the community as a founding partner of Boston HealthNet, a network of 14 community health centers through Boston serving more than a quarter million people annually. If you would like to make a donation, become a sponsor or for more visit their website at www.bmccatwalk.com.

6-26-2015 High Society Fashion Boston Post Gazette Socially Scene Column #113

Boston's earliest high-fashion gown, an embroidery masterpiece, is now on view at the Old State House. Do you ever dream of living in a different century and being able to dress the part?

The Old State House in Boston is bringing you a chance to get a firsthand view of some of fashion's first looks. The prized hand embroidered 18th century wedding gown on display was designed and embroidered by Elizabeth Bull, Boston's original fashionista.

In today's society, it's all about the dress on that special day, as even wedding planners in the colonial era were evidently already well aware. In fact, Boston Designer Elizabeth Bull took the precaution of designing her own colorful, hand-embroidered silk wedding gown several years before she even had a groom in mind.

"America's colonial era schoolgirls were remarkably fashion-forward designers," observed Patricia Gilrein, Collections Manager at the Bostonian Society. "They were keenly aware of European fashion trends, and adapted these styles to suit their purposes."

Elizabeth Bull started designing, sewing, and embroidering her China silk gown when she was only fourteen, while still in school. Embroidery was often undertaken by young women at the time to practice and perfect the art of needlework, but Bull proved to be one of the most extraordinary embroidery artists of her day. By 1734, she had already been at work on her gown for several years when she met a handsome stranger, Roger Price, the Rector of Trinity Church in Boston. At the time, Rev. Price was busily making preparations to make his escape from the uncivilized colonies to assume a more gracious lifestyle in England. Yet, he met Miss Bull and his ship sailed without him. Within a year, he accompanied Elizabeth Bull as she walked down the aisle wearing her embroidery masterpiece at their wedding in King's Chapel.

The colorfully-embroidered, one-of-a-kind Elizabeth Bull gown, a stunning example of Boston's earliest haute couture, will be placed on temporary display through the end of this year at Boston's Old State House. The exhibition of the Elizabeth Bull gown was made possible by a generous gift from an anonymous donor.

The Bostonian Society was established in 1881 to preserve Boston's historic past and explain the revolutionary ideas born here. For 134 years, it has managed the Old State House, the oldest and most important public building in American history prior to the Revolution, where, John Adams insisted, "Independence was born." It now serves as a museum and historic site, open to the public seven days a week, from 9:00 am until 5:00 pm.

The Old State House and the Bostonian Society is located at 206 Washington Street, Boston and more information about the museum can be found at www.bostonhistory.org.

6-26-2015 Denise Hajjar Celebrates Two Years in Residence at the Intercontinental Boston Post Gazette Socially Scene Column #113

Reviewed…This past week one of Boston's most famed fashionistas, Denise Hajjar, celebrated her two years of residency at the Intercontinental Hotel Boston.

Hajjar usually holds her shows in the hotel's chic Rumba Lounge but with the wonderful weather finally in our presence, the event took place on the beautiful waterfront patio that overlooks the Four Point Channel. The evening was set to begin at 6:00 pm sharp and it was no surprise to see every table taken in anticipation of the first designs to show.

Hajjar's Spring/Summer 2015 collection started off strong with a bold neon cocktail number, and one

of the things that make Hajjar a clutch designer, the garment had just been made that morning. As models came down the waterfront runway, there wore vibrant dresses that focused on pastel patterns, Hajjar's couture taste keeps these young looks high-end with that classic appeal.

The evening welcomed some of Boston's finest in the fashion world, such as fellow gown guru David Josef; model/fashion photographer/luxury accessories designer Amber Lu; fashionista Sonia Garufi, and models AJ Williams and Simone Aptekman. Aptekman from Dynasty Modeling Agency is a rising star in the city. She had just returned from New York City that morning where she was modeling the fall collection of iconic designer Victoria Beckham.

The night was a stunning success with Hajjar herself glowing in a simple neon peach knee-length that brought out her gorgeous skin tone. This unique fashion show, where the models mixed and mingled with the guests as they showed the collection, was one to remember. Being on the Boston Harbor for a gorgeous spring evening didn't hurt.

I was able to catch up with the design diva and ask what her time has been like at the Intercontinental Hotel thus far. Hajjar said, "I can say after the two year mark I'm finally happy, it was an interesting start. I'm a staple fixture here now and the hotel got to know me. I love the customers and that I am able to provide service in the neighborhood."

When I asked Hajjar to comment on her current collection she responded, "I'm in a really good place, my clients are getting older, but still want to look young and fresh and this is a focus for me. I pride myself that tonight there is a size fourteen garment being modeled, it looks just as fabulous as the size four and these are pieces that never go out of style."

After spending 2006 through May of 2013 as the in-house designer for the Copley Plaza Hotel, Hajjar made the move to the Inter continental as their "Designer-in-Residence" in fall 2013. The new boutique enables Hajjar to have her retail store and design studio at the same location. The larger space enables her to expand her services, including custom designs, expert tailoring, couture alterations for men and women. Hajjar has also acknowledged that she is surrounded by residential real estate and has partnered with an ecofriendly dry cleaning company to provide the neighborhood and commuters with convenient drop off / pick up service five days a week.

Last year during the 2014 Fall Boston Fashion Week, Hajjar set a standard with an entertainment-packed show held at Royal. The setup was perfect and the runway was top-notch along with the guest list. Starting off the night were salsa pair dancers from The Fred Astaire Dance Studio who also performed in-between and along with models down the catwalk. Hajjar was all smiles yet secretive about what she has in store for this year's Boston Fashion Week edition (back at Royal, the date and time to be released.) Denise Hajjar's boutique is located at 510 Atlantic Avenue in Boston. Find out more about her services and collections by calling 617-266-2296 or visiting www.denisehajjar.com. Outdoor Tabata … This innovative style of breaking a sweat will be offered only two more times in the outdoor Faneuil Hall area — a summer must you don't want to miss!

January 2015 Scene&Style - East Coast Alpine Arrives Fashionably Late

This past Thursday was the latest edition of the Liberty Hotels "Fashionably Late" featuring East Coast Alpine styled by Kathy Benharris and Scene&Style was on site for the event.

The night was one of the below zero temperatures haunting the city but still brought out some of Boston's finest fashionistas; Shaunt Sarian a high-end handbag and accessories designer, Ivona Owens Owner of Ultima Moda Magazine, Sophie Weidhaas Dynasty Model and the Creative Director of Polished Magazine, budding designers and many more.

First to hit the redesigned jailhouse runway was a power couple's look with classic charcoal grey pant with flashy red jacket for the lady and a similar look with small tones of the red on the overall suit for her hunk to show off their synced style.

Following was a playful pattern for the ladies; the ensemble featured a fluorescent pant, fur lined hooded jacket and long sleeve top that had a paint brush splashed look of colors to pull in the paint and jacket for a slope stylish look finished with googles, a ski must accessory.

The power couple hit the runway for a final time in trendy and tasteful lodge wear. For the gals it was a skull baby tee paired with a slightly saggy pant, fitted snow hat, always complimenting fur lined hooded jacket and creative fox tail pocket pant accessory that finished the look with flair. Her handsome other half was draped in Oakley; a classic black hooded sweatshirt with a flaming full of color bandanna tied around his neck, a bold yellow parker and calming the look down forest green pant.

Benharris brought many ski and slope styles down the Fashionably Late runway once again showing taste and sex appeal in the most difficult of styles, bulky layers. You can find a full album of looks from the evening on Scene&Style Facebook page under albums.

This was the second collaboration in the current ski season between Benharris and Owner of East Coast Alpine, John Sullivan. They started off by bringing back a live runway presentation to the Boston Ski and Snowboard Expo that had multiple shows all weekend and featured many slope celebrities.

East Coast Alpine is a family owned business and has co-hosted the boston.com Ski and Snowboard Expo since 2010 and we continue to do so in the future. They have won the SIA (Snow sports Industries of America) "Retailer of the Year" award in 2010 & 2011, the Improper Bostonian "Best of Boston" award in 2011 along with Boston Magazine "Best of Boston" award for 2011, 2012 & 2013.

East Coast Alpine is best known for their large selection of diverse skis, snowboards and apparel, their popular ski leasing program for children, and their state –of- the-art tuning facilities to deliver you only the best service! They have expanded their product offerings to include summer equipment as well, with everything from bicycles, longboards, skateboards, and casual wear available. You can visit their Danvers, Boston or Newton locations or their website at www.eastcoastalpine.com for more information.

Be sure to stay tuned to Scene&Style social media for a HUGE styling announcement coming soon from Boston's best fashion show producer Kathy Benharris, it's a goodie!

Chapter Eleven – 2014

"Fashion fades, style is eternal" - Yves Saint Laurent

December 2014 Scene&Style - Timeless Tuesday "Skea" Styled by Kathy Benharris

Recently Bond in the Langham Hotel held their final "Timeless Tuesday" presentation for 2014 that showcased Skea slope wear styled by Boston's best Kathy Benharris.

Scene&Style was on site early to catch all the backstage action that had fashions finest perfecting the finishing touches; Arturo Draper was dolling up the Dynasty models like Sophie Weidhaas – Creative Director of Polished Magazine with hair and makeup. Close by was the Langham resident cosmetic queen, Amanda McCarthy giving Boston's top model Simone Aptekman tasteful beauty with her makeup brush that can only come from her creative hand.

Pulling all the looks together and steaming the final seems were Benharris's flawless team; Kim Dam and Billie Francis who are Beharris's top to-go to's. It also featured favorites like Megan Borges who can be found behind the scenes of top runway productions. Catching all the action was fashion photographer and industry favorite Dimonika Bray.

The night began with class that comes with Benharris, a VIP guest list that included a tasty cocktail from sponsor Kettle One. Luckily, Scene&Style was planning on the press pit as there wasn't an available seat in the lounge. The event drew in socialites like; the always stunning, Denise Dunbar, high-end photographer Dan Minicucci, the lovely and multi-talented Amber Lu, Daniel James Forrester, Rita Bean, Ivona Owens Owner of the chic Ultima Moda Magazine, President/Designer from Skea Diane Boyer and many more.

To Emcee the event and give away FREE lift tickets was Olympian Pam Fletcher and owner of Nashoba Vally resort.

The first set of slope styles to hit the runway; featured bright solid colors for the jacket and pant suits to keep you toasty warm on the "vertical runway" and perfectly styled by Benharris who can bring glamour to bulky layers. Next was a classy collection for the bunny slopes that brought a subtle touch of animal prints accompanied by a tasteful fur that brings every aspect of the winter weather in a flattering manor. Following was a piece by the gown guru, David Josef. His timeless shimmer couture dress was paired with that clutch winter jacket from Skea that would get you gorgeous to that holiday affair.

The dazzling diva Simone Aptekman hit the runway in a Julie Kontos original meant for that New Year cocktail affair finished with accessories from Race&Grant that give you flashy attention with obvious style. The finale and collaboration of the evening was a stunning metallic crop top with matching knee length skirt from Julie Kontos paired with a purple puffy jacket from Skea, accessories from Race&Grant along with a tiara that polished the look from Stephanie Pernice. The outfit was perfection from head to toe that brought class, style and comfort for a solid season look.

Nobody does it better than Benharris! She brought out the heavy hitters of fashion; David Josef, Tracy Belben, Helena Thorne Marrin Grant, Iam Kréyol, Stanley Rameau, EJ Battle, Julie Kontos, Stephanie Pernice and the one and only Iggy Barskov to demand and acquire a perfect runway production. She always holds herself to a standard and is the definition of a Gordon Ramsey in fashion.

The styling doesn't stop there; Give yourself more time for holiday fun and let Kathy take care of the gifts with her, "Shopping Gets Personal" a complimentary personal shopping service.

A personal shopper can shop with your guests or they can meet at the Copley Place after your personal shopper has located the perfect items on your wish list. Whether it's shopping for gifts, holiday outfits, or adding key pieces to a wardrobe, your personal shopper will help outfit your guests in the latest fashions that will fit their individual style.

Your personal shopper will shop with your guests at all of Copley Places' stores and knows what the stores have in stock just for you! Some retailors will even extend special promotions and benefits to guests when shopping with Copley Place's personal shopper.

With absolutely no sales pressure and a complete focus on delivering the highest level of customer service, this is all about providing your guests with an exceptional personal styling and shopping experience.

This is the ultimate shopping experience for your guests! Copley Place has a new personal shopper service headed by Benharris that will finish its trial run on January 31st, which will assist your guests with all their shopping needs. To schedule a complimentary appointment please contact dkonig@simon.com.

With the holidays here you can't beat the experience Benharris will bring. Be sure to follow **@SceneAndStyle** on social media for upcoming show updates and where to find us "on site"

November 2014 "Socially Scene" Bosfw Closing "Expressions the Faces of Boston Fashion" Boston Post Gazette Column #112

Socially Scene Reviewed... Boston Fashion Week finished in style with the closing being held at The W Hotel featuring "Expressions" The Faces of Boston Fashion.

The minute you would have walked in the door there were "faces of fashion" everywhere. The first spotted by Socially Scene was the catwalk queen, Denise Hajjar. From there some like Amber Lu photographer, Nathan Allen and Danielle Noel top stylists in the city representing Blo, Todd Lee photographer and so many more.

Of course, all were there to send off their beloved week of fashion yet there were so many looking to get a glimpse of their face flashing in the many rooms of the event. "Expressions" The Faces of Boston Fashion was an amazing slide show put together by local photographers including all fabulous Boston creativity that make up our world of fashion.

There were two main slideshows that featured some like; Nirva Derbekyan Stylist and Fashion Designer, Dana Duggan Fashion Designer, Cara Fratto Saks Fifth Avenue Public Relations Manager, Alexa Hall COUP Boston Editor in Chief, Marc Harris from Marc Harris Salon, Sam Mendoza Fashion Designer, Dimonika Bray Photographer, Michael Diskin Photographer, April Riccio Public Relations Manager Neman Marcus Natick, Michelle Bearse-McGrath Makeup Artist, Dava Muramatsu Jewelry Designer, The woman the week was dedicated to the late Marilyn Riseman Fashion Icon and honored man of the evening Jay Calderin Boston Fashion Week Founder.

The Party was buzzing with the names listed above and a mass more being that was just a short list mentioned of all the faces that bring Boston its fashion. You could have sworn there was a runway nearby based on all the top designs floating around the room.

There was a break in all the mixing and mingling to recognize Mr. Jay Claderin for bringing Boston Fashion Week into its 20th year in 2014. The chic crowed paused to appreciate the imaginative Calderin throughout his speech thanking everyone in the room and all who give their heart and soul to making this industry thrive in our city.

Upcoming for this fashion fellow Jay Calderin, he will be honored by YOUTH DESIGN as 2014 Mentor of the Year at their 2nd annual CARNIVAL celebration and fundraiser at the W BOSTON on Thursday, November 13th from 6p.m. through 8:30p.m. Join them for a fun and engaging evening set against the backdrop of a series of interactive carnival games, cocktails and celebration. Guests pay to play and win fun, buried prizes from local design-driven, retail partners celebrating Boston as a city of design. During the event, they will also present Youth Design's "Mentor of the Year Award" and you will have a chance to play and create alongside our Youth Designers!

After the heart felt thank you the energetic crowd took back to sashaying the glitter around the party and taking photographs that were sure to make the top Facebook Pages in the city. It was an important night for the city and the fashionistas of it. As Boston Fashion Week likes to encourage, "shop locally and we will see you in the front row 2015".

October 31st 2014 "Socially Scene" Denise Hajjar, David Josef, KRÉYOL, Julie Kontos / KB Fashion Productions Reviewed Boston Post Gazette Column #111

Socially Scene Reviewed… The grand finale of shows that were attended for Boston Fashion Week was the Fashionably Late presentation at the Liberty Hotel.

The Fabulous, Fierce, and Fashion Forward event was hosted by Boston debonair Denise Hajjar and designer showcase styled by Kathy Benharris with a portion of bar proceeds from the event donated to the Susan G. Komen Foundation.

The Liberty Hotel is always an amazing place to hold a fashion event with the jail house structure creating sky high runways. The main floor space is cosmic yet that evening there was barely room to move as the crème de la crème of the Boston fashion scene were on site for the show and many in anticipation of the iconic closer for the night.

The first to designs to hit the runway were Joelle Jean-Fontaine with the KRÉYOL collection that had a playful pattern with classy appeal and was perfectly coordinated for the fashion forward lady seen in the streets of the Back Bay.

Second to hit center stage was award winning apparel designer Julie Kontos. Her collection featured dark soft tones layered with lace and metallic. Each piece was paired with luxurious handcrafted accessories from Race & Grant. The editions to the outfits were over the top with the punk edge that brought a wow factor from the creative construction. These ladies are sure to start a buying war between designers.

The grand finale was none other than the sophisticated red-carpet designer David Josef who was making his first Boston Fashion Week presence since 2003. He started off his show with a pink number that is meant for a night spent amongst Manhattan's finest style.

He transitioned into a classic black cocktail dress with flair perfect for that high-end social affair. Following was an all-white ball gown sewn with a refreshing fabric, flawless stitching for a timeless look.

The collection closed with spectacular showstopper. Josef proved to the fashion world that glamour is not gone. A perfectly pleated black gown with a fitted gold shimmer V-neck top and matching clutch showed high class is always a product of Josef's designs. In the final piece his extraordinary talent exuded Judy Garlin with a fresh face on fashion.

David Josef has been creating breathless special occasion dresses for celebrities and honorable clientele for over 30 years. There wasn't a classier way to close the show then with red carpet looks and celebrating his first Boston Fashion Week appearance since 2003.

Stay tuned next week for the closing cocktail party of Boston Fashion Week and the celebration for 20 years by honoring creator Jay Calderin.

October 24th 2014 "Socially Scene"JJP Collections and Revs Reviewed Boston Post Gazette Column #110

Socially Scene Reviewed… Boston Fashion continued last week with Bond hosting two top shows; The New England Revolutions annul show and StyleWeek sensation Jonathan Joseph Peters.

Boston Fashion week was jam packed with multiple venues, catwalk callers, style swaps and trunk shows but Bond in the Langham Hotel featured some of the region's top athletes and a Project Runway legend in the making.

Last Wednesday The Langham Hotel welcomed the New England Revolution for their annual show yet this time with a twist. The soccer superstars invited their wives, girlfriends, and fiancés to join them on the runway in the London based looks by Boden.

The host for the evening was the magnificent NECN Meteorologist Nelly Carreno. Hair and makeup were complementary from Dellaria Salons and proceeds from the event were donated to The Ellie Fund.

The night was filled with plenty of personality and anything but that serious strut. The players and ladies showed smiles, winks for the press pit and a boisterous athletic pep. The crowd really turned up the volume when the U.S. National Team and recent World Cup star Jermaine Jones hit the runway. Jones is a fresh face in New England with barley being signed a month with the Revolution. The night was a hit and how could it not be with the flattering designs and the sexy cliché of professional athletes and the lovely ladies on their arm.

The following evening, Thursday was a fashion week first. The innovative and masterful StyleWeek stud Jonathan Joseph Peters made his Boston debut. However, the Providence based Peters is no stranger to the style scene. He is known for his time spent on Project Runway, closer for the exceptional StyleWeek fashion presentation and has a store with fellow designers called Nude in Providence.

Peters brought the wow factor to fashion goers with the successful risk he took at StyleWeek in August. This time around he showed his latest collection "Noir." It was a dark and seductive collection of evening, special occasion, and day wear. Peters show had a collaborative transition with the pieces having similar textiles and patterns that moved from a chic day design to mysterious sexy cocktail attire.

The show was flawless, and Peters once again exuded technique and professionalism. Although he made the trip from Providence, he did not make it alone! StyleWeek is an extraordinary event all its own but they are also a family off the runway.

The fashion forward thinking crew traveled together to show support. In attendance were colleagues from Nude; Jess Abernathy, Amy Stetkiewicz also StyleWeek designer Nick Pini alongside creator Rosana Ortiz and Amanda Doumato owner of accessories retail Flaunt Boutique.

StyleWeek 2015 will take place in February and Socially Scene will be on site to see what is next from this unforgettable collaboration of the industry's best in the North East. For more on Peters and his collections visit www.jonathanjosephpeters.com or for information on the upcoming show www.styleweek.com. Stay Tuned to next week's column that will feature an onsite review from Fashionably Late at the Liberty Hotel show casing the amazingly talent Davis Josef.

October 10th 2014 "Socially Scene" BosFW Denise Hajjar Review Boston Post Gazette Column #109

Socially Scene Reviewed… This past week marked the 20th annual Boston Fashion Week and Socially Scene started it off right.

The events began with the opening cocktail party at the W Hotel showing faces for some of the scene's top designers and Boston's best glitterati. The shows took off from there and all in the style loop received the "dailies" email from creator Jay Calderin informing of the many must see events that the day would bring.

Socially Scene got going on Tuesday with dear to our heart and fashion guru Denise Hajjar's annual "Dress for Success" benefit at Royale. Hajjar is far more than just the brand name she has created but the definition of high-class style for the working woman.

The evening was all you would expect from the runway goddess and each year she finds a way to top the last. The show was more than just a fashion presentation but a spectacular stage show opening with a couple "dancing with the stars" ballroom type team from Fred Astaire Dance Company. The duo was mixed in with models as the hit the runway and their flawless talent was a showstopper.

Hajjar has a special place in the heart of Socially Scene as two years ago was my first week show to be covered and feel that it was her extravagant aura that pulled me into the scene for life. I would not think it were possible to feel anymore blessed, yet it was such an honor to be standing next to Jay Calderin who had the look of a proud father in the press pit.

As the superb and tailored head to toe looks hit the runway they were worn by professionals like the city's beloved Simone Aptekman. Also, celebrities like; Janet Wu, Simone Winston, Tiziiana Dearing, Charolette Golar Richie, Linda Cole, and the everyday beautiful women.

Between the dancers and obvious signature fashion show one would think that was the best it could get. The night was taken away as legendary designer Yolanda Cellucci a timeless diva took her strut to stage. Cellucci is being honored this season with her "50 years of high heels, headpieces and haute couture". The crowd couldn't get enough of the socialite who has branded our city.

The chic designs and polished seems brought some of Boston's most fashionable together. Designer David Josef was spotted on the runway; Miss Massachusetts United States was accompanied by pageant director Jena Tang, Top stylist, and manager of Blo South End Nathan Allen and more.

Hajjar is always top class and the night went to benefit the Dress for Success foundation. She also gave an up and coming designer her Boston Fashion Week taste with a showcase of fashions by student designers from Denise's alma mater, the School of Fashion Design.

For all who are a part of the fashion community here in the Hub know what a sophisticated and fresh look Denise Hajjar bring to the scene. The night was flawless, and many were buzzing, "How is anyone to top that." Boston Fashion Week had only just started so stay tuned to see if it was a mission that was accomplished.

October 2014 bosFW "Socially Scene" Fashion Meets Science Boston Post Gazette Column #108

This past week science and design came together in honor of art week to create the first ever DESCIENCE at MIT.

Research on the Runway was proof positive that Boston Fashion is SMART! Yuly Fuentes-Medel, Patricia Torregrosa, and Claire Jarvis creators of the event brought creative talent and brainpower together. However the night was whisked away by 9 year-old Junior Sartorialist Toby Otting who presented throughout the show.

I am sure many of you are a bit confused as to what the event was all about. It was a special edition to Boston Fashion Week and the first ever so let me bring you up to speed on Descience.

It is a project in which the world of scientific discovery offers inspiration for the innovative minds of fashion designers. Descience creates collaborations between designers and scientists and brings research to the runway, providing a platform both for emerging designers and for science.

"The difference between science and the arts is not that they are different sides of the same coin… or even different parts of the same continuum, but rather, they are manifestations of the same thing. The arts and sciences are avatars of human creativity." – Mae Jemison (doctor, dancer, first African American in space)

The breakdown of how this fabulous event unfolds is as follows; Scientists provide ideas and images of their scientific research. Scientists' submissions include images taken from their discoveries and descriptions of their research, noting the greater implications of their findings. Scientists describe what makes them passionate about science and why they are interested in participating in Descience.

Next the designers "shop" for inspiration from scientist profiles, choosing their top three collaborator choices. Designers are inspired by the strong ideas and images provided by scientists. If a scientist receives more than one request, they create their own designer ranking. Descience creates the final teams of one scientist and one designer.

Then the designers and scientists collaborate to create a runway look, inspired by science. Teams brainstorm and agree upon a creative vision and execution for the project. The designer creates a sketch or visual representation of the team's concept, to be approved by the scientist and submitted to Descience. Designers then create a research-inspired garment through continued collaboration. Teams submit photographs of completed looks to the website, where they compete for votes.

The design with the most votes will be named "People's Choice," featured in the runway show as a finalist, and receive a $500 cash prize. Descience showcases submitted looks at Descience Runway, the capstone fashion show event. Final teams are chosen by a panel of advisors to be part of the Descience Runway Collection.

The fifteen runway finalists are featured in a final runway walk, displayed by models during a reception following Descience Runway, and showcased in a second runway show at the Liberty Hotel's Fashionably Late Thursdays event which Socially Scene will keep you updated as to when. An Overall Winner is chosen, and a cash prize of $1,500 is awarded to each member of the winning team.

Did you get all that? What an amazing and innovative event but what else can you expect from the creative minds at MIT.

Back to the show itself, The big winner of the evening was Team Cytocouture: Carlos Villamil (design) and Laura Indolfi (science). People's Choice went to Team Orphacure: Candice Wu (design) and Christopher Gibson (science).

The panel of judges was so impressed with the collaborations that they had to single out two of the design teams for honorable mentions. Those honors went to Team Quorum54: Tatiana Tejedor (design) Tal Danino (science), and Team Interwoven: Margaret Jackson (design) and Pedro Parraguez Ruiz (science).

The night was filled with fashion, art and collaborated design. For a full listing of the winners or more on this fabulous event you can visit www.fashiodescience.com.

10-3-2014 "Socially Scene" BosFW 2014 Break Down Boston Post Gazette Column #107

Here we are again another week closer to Boston Fashion Week! The designers are sewing the final stich and the events are beginning to unfold.

Socially Scene was on site this past Saturday for The Design Museum "Five" Gala at the W Hotel to celebrate five years. It was a creative black tie event to say the least. The guests were draped in ball room attire that was "redesigned" to suite the affair.

It was amazing to see what The Design Museum has done for the city of Boston and fun is an understatement for the dynamics of the evening. The live band, signature cocktails, silent and live auction, it was just one fabulous evening. Be sure to tune back in as Socially Scene will be making a personal trip to The Design Museum with an onsite review!

Moving closer to Boston Fashion Week there is an endless line up of events to compliment the upcoming runway shows. Here are just a few; YOLANDA: Innovative Fashion Icon, 50 Years of High Heels, Headpieces, and Haute Couture will run through November 30th. "YOLANDA: Innovative Fashion Icon; 50 Years of High Heels, Headpieces, and Haute Couture" is a textile and fashion arts exhibit featuring extraordinary designs and accessories from the late 20th century.

The exhibit celebrates fashion icon, brilliant business entrepreneur, and innovative marketing genius, Yolanda Cellucci. On display will be an array of couture ensembles and high fashion accessories on loan from Yolanda's private collection, the Lasell College Fashion Collection, and the Museum of Fine Arts Boston. This fine selection of garments features pieces by celebrated designers such as: Bob Mackie, Givenchy, Oscar de la Renta, Stephen Yearick and more. For all this extravert fashion visit the Charles River Museum of Industry & Innovation located at 154 Moody St, Waltham and can be reached at 781-893-5410, ext. 11 or visit http://crmi.org/ for more information.

Beginning Friday, October 3rd through November, 28th at 12p.m. Marilyn Riseman's Fashion Luncheon Presented by Brasserie JO at the Colonnade Hotel. Each week will highlight a different designer while you can treat yourself to a delicious lunch, stylish atmosphere, and a fashion design presentation. Brasserie JO at the Colonnade Hotel is located at 120 Huntington Avenue. You can make your reservation by calling 617-425-3240.

Also on Friday, October 3rd at 5p.m. is First Fridays "Fashion Fusion" presented by The Institute of Contemporary Art. Join Boston's most chic for a night of fashion, music, cocktails, and dancing where art and style collide.

The Boston Globe's Style Magazine team joins the ICA for First Fridays: Fashion Fusion! Contributing Editor Rachel Raczka and independent stylist Sarah Benge, with other members of the team, give us the behind-the-scenes scoop on how the Bianca Jagger-, Glam Rock-inspired "Fall Fashion's Cooling Trend" feature came to life. Also get personal advice on how to put together these looks for fall with models on hand dressed in the fashions featured in the magazine.

MLR Artist Management will join fashion forces with stylist Kathy Benharris, Model Club Inc., and various student designers to present a Fashion Fusion Installation. Guests will also have an opportunity to pose with models in photo booth and visit beauty bars.

This 21+ event does sell out; advance tickets are recommended. ICA Members can attend the event for free, but are encouraged to make advance reservations. The museum will not be open to visitors outside of the First Friday's event. The Institute of Contemporary Art is located at 100 Northern Avenue. They can be reached at 617-478-3100 and more information by visiting http://bit.ly/1pJE99e.

Saturday, October 4th at 3p.m. enjoy an Afternoon Tea Fashion Show with Ted Baker London presented by The Reserve at The Langham. Celebrate Boston Fashion Week with an afternoon tea fashion show featuring the latest men's and women's looks by Ted Baker. For reservations call 617-451-1900 and the event will take place at The Reserve at The Langham, Boston located 250 Franklin St Boston. INFORMAL

School of Fashion Design, Celebrates 80 at City Hall presented by City Hall. They say if you don't like the weather in New England, just wait a minute, so stylish Bostonians must be prepared! The collection of stylish outerwear on display at Boston City Hall is the result of collaboration between the School of Fashion Design and Newbury Street neighbor Marimekko. Student designers took inspiration from the brand's signature fabrics resulting in these bold and colorful garments. Be sure to stop by

Boston City Hall, 1 City Hall Square, Boston for this FREE ongoing event. For more information and specific times visit www.schooloffashiondesign.org.

Ladies and gents be sure to clear those calendars for Boston Fashion Week October 5th through the 11th. There are numerous runway shows and cocktail gathering to be "Socially Scene" at. Visit www.bostonfashionweek.com for a full listing.

9-26-2014 "Socially Scene" Looking Forward to BosFW 2014 Boston Post Gazette Column #106

Once Labor Day has passed and temperatures take that shocking drop it only means one thing, Fashion Week's around the world.

This year Boston Fashion Week will take place October 5th through the 11th and will be dedicated to the late Marilyn Riseman, a fashion legend in our city. The Boston Fashion Week organization is inviting this year's designers/event producers to keep one front row seat open as a tribute to Marilyn Riseman's lifetime commitment to the art of fashion and her tireless support of our creative community.

The School of Fashion Design will be creating an installation called "Marilyn & Me" in the lobby of their Newbury Street location. It will be unveiled during Boston Fashion Week in honor of Marilyn Riseman, and be on display throughout the month of October.

Getting your photo taken with the local fashion icon was a rite of passage for many. Anyone fortunate enough to have shared a moment and taken a photo with Marilyn is invited to share it with the School of Fashion Design. The project, equal parts heart, history, and haute couture is meant to represent the many lives Marilyn Riseman has touched in our community. You are able to email photos to marilynandmesfd@gmail.com. Please be sure to include your full name, email address, and any message you'd like to share.

I will be listing the full and official schedule in next week's Socially Scene column; you can also access what is currently in place at www.bostonfashionweek.com. For now here are a few highlights; currently at the Museum of Fine Arts through March 8th 2015 is, "Hollywood Glamour: Fashion and Jewelry from the Silver Screen".

"Hollywood Glamour: Fashion and Jewelry from the Silver Screen" presents designer gowns and exquisite jewelry from the 1930s and '40s—the most glamorous years of Hollywood film. The exhibition focuses on the iconic style of sultry starlets of the period, including Gloria Swanson, Anna May Wong, Greta Garbo, Marlene Dietrich, Mae West, and Joan Crawford.

Hollywood style in this era was a blend of on- and off-screen fashion and accessories, including dramatic costumes created for the screen by famous designers such as Adrian, Travis Banton, and Chanel and dazzling jewelry from makers of the era like Trabert & Hoeffer-Mauboussin and Paul Flato.

Along with eye-catching gowns once worn by famous figures and the sparkling jewels that contributed to their allure from the MFA and private collections, photography by Edward Steichen along with period photographs, film stills, and film clips capture the style of the silver screen era. Enjoy a glimpse of Hollywood in the Golden Age of glamour.

The exhibit will be on display at the Museum of Fine Arts, Boston in the Loring Gallery of Textiles (Gallery 276) located at 465 Huntington Ave, Boston. You may visit www.mfa.org/exhibitions/hollywood-glamour for more information or call the museum at 617-267-9300.

Thursday, October 2nd at 6 p.m. enjoy Descience – Research on the Runway, Presented by Descience and The Koch Institute for ArtWeek. You can explore Descience, a project that fuses the world of science and fashion into a unique symbiotic relationship. Exclusively for ArtWeek, Descience and The Koch Institute will allow the public to attend an interactive exhibition where designers and scientists will be on hand to discuss and answer questions related to their science-inspired fashions.

Mix and mingle, watch videos about the creative process, and see how deeply art and science can collide to make something beautiful. All featured designs will have recently been shown at a runway show in the MIT Media Lab judged by experts in the fields of science and fashion, and you get to see a few of them now! The Koch Institute, Massachusetts Institute of Technology is located at 500 Main Street, Cambridge and for more information email info@fashiondescience.com.

Let the must see shows begin with a fashion favorite on Tuesday Oct 7th 6 p.m. at Royale Boston Nightclub. The night will benefit Dress for Success Boston. For more information visit www.dressforsucces.org/boston, www.denisehajjar.com even grab a sneak peek at her boutique located at the InterContinental Boston 510 Atlantic Ave Boston or call 617-266-2296.

Get into the groove with the new editions to Boston Fashion Week on October 8th at Emerald Lounge from 8 p.m. to 10 p.m. for a luxury high fashion brand called Latoré.

A Boston legend in the industry Firas Yousif is surprise SOLD OUT! Maybe you can talk your way in into his show that will take place on Friday October 10th at 7p.m. in The Algonquin Club to unveil his 2015 couture collection.

The Boston debut of the Carla Fernandez will be on Thursday, October 9th at 6:30p.m. on the Catwalk in Calderwood Hall, Isabella Stewart Gardner Museum located 25 Evans Way, Boston.

Space is limited and there will be an after party in the courtyard with music by DJ Ricardo De Lima. To purchase tickets you may call 617-278-5156 or visit www.gardnermuseum.org/calendar/events/6022.

That was just a tasty tid bit of what Boston Fashion Week has to offer! As always, the event crew encourages you to continue to seek out fashion professionals in the area, buy local, and be instrumental in helping our local fashion industry thrive. Stay tuned to next week's column for a full listing of shows and events.

8-15-2014 Alistair Archer Painted the Bond Runway Socially Scene Column #99

This past week Bond Boston resumed their "Timeless Tuesdays" fashion show, but this one with a twist of a painter's pattern.

The evening featured well known painter, who has now taken his brush to the sewing room and created his own identity on the runway. Alistair Archer evolved from the unique experience of its founder, Robert F. Merton, a contemporary painter who has exhibited his artwork in Boston, Miami, New York, and Washington, D.C. The night started off with some of Boston's most fashionable sipping cocktails and enjoying the complimentary Aperitivo Peroni that is always a part of the show.

Backstage was AGW makeup dolling up the Dynasty models to blend well with the fantastic wearable art that rocked the Bond runway. Some of the first looks shown were simple cut dresses that caught attention with colors of vibrant turquoise blue, deep poppy purples and a design that had you thinking you were bidding at an art show. The casual dress suitable for the office also came in a stunning orange and pink combination toned down with that brilliant turquoise color.

To compliment these beautiful styles and take them into a different season were similar style rain jackets with matching umbrellas and solid boot color as to not make the outfit busy on the eye. Every few models or so one would walk with a complex painting by the designer that demanded attention itself and had each wondering if they were buying a dress, jacket, painting or just the whole package!

The story behind this fashion and art guru is warm and inspiring just like his collection. The premature birth of his first son, Archer, served as the catalyst for change. Life became the priority, both literally and metaphorically, mso Merton had absolute faith in redirecting his own path to become Archer's primary caregiver.

Before entering toddlerhood, it was clear that Archer needed the focused love: his dyspraxia, a motor planning issue, made verbalizing nearly any sound an arduous task and the related weakness in manual fine motor skills made sign language impossible. Fatherson communication focused on art: sitting side-by-side on the painting studio floor, Merton and Archer listened to music and created large, free-form abstract art.

To Merton's surprise, Archer influenced his own paintings as much as vice versa; Merton's subsequent

work included luminous and textured rich jewel tones that communicate his passion for life and serve as the basis for all of the Alistair Archer textile patterns.

Alistair Archer targets a highly successful female population who balances strong responsibility in the workplace, family and community. Their clothing and accessories are "wearable art" that may be worn in layers as well as individually. The designs range from complex, colorful images to bold, geometric patterns, with titles embodying femininity, such as Chloe, Citron, and Blythe. Much like the artist wielding a paintbrush, the clothing serves as a canvas for savvy women and may be enjoyed for generations to come.

The 2014 collection featured a dress line that dazzled everyone in the audience with the unique presentation and a fun appeal. Timeless Tuesdays are always a great production but this specific show was one to remember. Fashion is about expressing yourself and creating looks to suite your target audience, yet this designer found a way to appeal to many. You can shop online at www.alistairarcher.com, view more of his collections and art and see upcoming shows.

8-8-2014 "Socially Scene" Seaside Allure Revere Rooftop Review Boston Post Gazette Column #98

Socially Scene Reviewed… This past Thursday the Revere Hotel was back in action with their rooftop fashion shows.

The event has been held every Wednesday night but due to our out of the ordinary stormy weather a few had been canceled. The well attended shows resumed with, "Seaside Allure" boutique that is based out of Marblehead, Ma.

It was a gorgeous evening with many of Boston's glitterati already sipping cocktails on the fantastic rooftop pool when Socially Scene arrived on site. The Revere Hotel is a more upscale venue with light bites to complement their mixology beverage list.

Back stage is always a pleasure as you get the opportunity to catch the last minute preparations that go into making these social events a success. Or even get a sneak peek at items that weren't able to fit in the show like a fabulous beach bag that included its own wine key!

Hair and makeup was created by Pyara Aveda Salon currently located in Harvard Square but are moving to a brand new "secret" location. They did an amazing job of highlighting the features on each of the Maggie Inc. models.

First to hit the runway, was a collection of fun and flirty dresses that would have made a great look for a backyard BBQ or a cabana cocktail party. Casual and comfy hit the runway next for Seaside Allure that would be fitting for a summer Sunday spent at the beach. Closing out the rooftop show, chic evening wear that brought a bold solid color and poppy floral appeal that would catch attention at any cocktail party.

It is always a fashion success when the event is managed by Christina K. Pierce Fashion Agency. The styles were a hit with the packed cocktailers on the Revere Rooftop. There are still more shows to come from Pierce and you can visit her website at www.christina-pierce.com. If you are interested in purchasing any of these summer styles, Seaside Allure is located at 7 Pleasant St, Marblehead can be reached at 781-639-0617 or visit www.seasideallure.com to purchase right on line!

7-25-2014 "Socially Scene" Miss Central Massachusetts Review Boston Post Gazette Column #96

Socially Scene Reviewed… This past weekend Miss Central Massachusetts held a meet and greet at Emerald lounge in the Revere Hotel.

Iva Nicole, Miss Central Massachusetts pageant coordinator put together a "mix and mingle." Photographers, pageant organizers, family members and contestants were able to get to know each other and make memories before next Sunday's pageant in Worcester.

The gathering gave the opportunity for guests to find out a little more about how the pageant works behind the scenes as they were able to sit in on the review and rules for the breakdown on the big day.

There was plenty of entertainment in attendance with Miss Massachusetts, Miss Teen Central Massachusetts, Miss Rhode Island Belleza Latina, and the current Miss Central Massachusetts all giving the future of beauty pointers from their own personal experiences. The evening even brought on site a little shopping with "Jewelinga" unique jewelry made by Inga Puzikov.

The Miss Central Massachusetts took place on Sunday July 18th at Mechanics Hall located at 321 Main St, Worcester. The evening began with a 6pm cocktail reception that was open to the public. The pageant showcased contestant talent and reigning Queen Scarlette Florian began the program by singing the national anthem followed by the Teen and Ms. Teen competition before leading into the main event of Miss Central Massachusetts competition. To find out whom our new 2014 Miss Central Massachusetts is visit their website at www.misscentralmass.com

7-11-2014 "Socially Scene" SDF at the Langham Review Boston Post Gazette Column #93

Socially Scene Reviewed… Recently Timeless Tuesday's at Bond in the Langham Hotel welcomed a special runway presentation, The School of Fashion and Design.

The future of fashion took the Langham runway with fifteen student designers' featuring 24 unique looks. The School of Fashion and Design is celebrating 80 years of creating quality fashion designers and that night highlights from their 2014 collection hit the runway.

Each dress was anything but similar to another as the evening brought multiple styles into one show. There were many summer sensible outfits for an evening spent out having cocktails on a private roof deck. They varied from bright poppy fluorescents to soft pastel floral patterns. There were gorgeous bodysuit type jumper mini dresses that were shown with flowing wraps to keep it classy. Also were a few fall pattern hooded knee lengths that had you waiting for the leaves to change and a few classic gowns fit for a high end charity ball. The emerging designers were so focused on perfection that they even paired the looks up with the skin tones of the lovely Dante models.

The night was a proud of one Boston Fashion Week Founder Jay Calderin also Director of Creative Marketing and Special Projects. Also in attendance and running the looks from backstage was director James Hannon who also was very expressive about what amazing designers were growing under their wings. The School of Fashion and Design is located at 136 Newbury Street and you can check out their website at www.schooloffashiondesign.org for upcoming shows and more on becoming a student.

7-4-2014 "Socially Scene" BMC Catwalk for a Cure Review Boston Post Gazette Column #92

Socially Scene Reviewed… This past week Boston had another one of its high end events, Catwalk for BMC Cancer Care.

The breathtaking State Room was host to the third annual Catwalk for BMC Cancer Care in partnership with Open HeARTS and Clappazzola. Thirteen Boston Medical Center cancer patients, professional models and BMC staff strutted their stuff. Also local celebrities like; Kennedy Elsey for Mix 104.1 FM, Jonathon Soroff with The Improper Bostonian, Sam Chambers Assistant to Mayor Marty Walsh and Janet Wu from Channel 7 News walked down the runway last Thursday night. The evening welcomed all of Boston's best and socialites like; Yolanda Cellucci, Denise Dunbar, Erica Corsano, Marjorie Clapprood and Chris Spinazzola just to name a few.

The evening started out with event emcees Kim Khazei and Adam Williams from WHGH-TV Channel 7 News introducing a heartwarming video of patients and their struggle to survive all while showing a smile. The perfectly placed rows and rows of glitterati in attendance were in tears by the end of the recording.

As it always can; fashion brightened the vibe back up and the first designs to hit the runway were by one of Boston's staples in the industry, Denise Hajjar. Her line was a classic business style with an expected colorful appeal. Following was, fashionista herself Amber Lu who hit the catwalk in

DreaDesigns Couture collection that was sparkle chic fitting for the finest cocktail hour. Next, was a surgeon with BMC who rocked the runway wearing stylists Brian Finocchio Macy's men's collection. Sashing right behind was, emerging designer Lori Kyler Christensen most recent looks with a pop of fluorescent pattern in her dresses perfect for a night on the town or summer cocktail event. Strength was the message of the evening and comes in all forms. The next was Boston's finest fashion industry agency Christina K Pierce who was not only in attendance but walked the runway proud four days after the birth of her daughter. Her collection brought bold styles with perfect pops of accessory color to the show from Liberate Apparel. After was, Candice Wu with her catwalk couture where you can always expect the best from her styles that express a funky feel and high end cuts. Man of the evening and closer of the show was the one and only David Josef. His collection is known for timeless beauty for women of all ages and that night the strongest of women, cancer survivors.

The show was full of energy with so many emotions. Every time a survivor stepped out to walk the runway the guests were on their feet cheering with tears of admiration. The event raised over 22,000 and left so many feeling hope, pride and wanting more. How lucky they all were being the evening didn't end there. After there was a live DJ for dancing, two bars for countless cocktails, cupcakes and plenty of people ready to party.

The Boston Medical Center is a private non-for-profit, 496 bed, academic medical center located in the South End. The largest safety net hospital in New England, Boston Medical Center provides a full spectrum of pediatric and adult care services, from primary care and family medical to advanced specialty care. The BMC is the largest and busiest provider of trauma and emergency care services in New England. Upcoming event for the BMC are as follow; Kids Fund Golf Tournament on July 28th at Belmont Country Club, Mayo Bowl on September 8th at Kings Dedham and Rodman Ride for Kids on September 20th in Foxboro. For more information on these events or how to make a donation visit their website at www.bmc.org.

6-27-2014 "Socially Scene" StyleWeek Swim Review Boston Post Gazette Column #91

Socially Scene Reviewed… Recently the cast of StyleWeek were at it again with a rooftop fashion show "Swim" at the brand new Providence G in downtown.

These fashion forward bunches of ladies are well known for their bi-annual shows in the early spring and late fall. This season they took a stab at a Sunday fun day focused on summer trends. Rohde Island has some of the Northeast most emerging designers and a few established with the boutique "Nude."

The cabana like roof deck was prepped to perfection with pop up shops along the back wall like; Esmeralda Lambert Designs, Bound by the Crown that brought a new red carpet ready look also children's wear, Ash and Willow accessories along with favorites Restored by Design and Flaunt Boutique. There was a bar right in the middle of the action, personalized seating along the runway for all the glitterati in attendance and as to be expected, set for success.

Showing first was the original styles of Stetkiewicz that hosted a metallic hint perfect for your favorite beach café. A new edition to the lineup Eight Optics Swim Wear took to the runway with a rock, retro and funk style with bold neon colors. The look was great for that VIP pool party to make a unique statement. Following was Jess Abernethy spring designs that showed a sporty and casual look fitting for the first date with that new summer crush. Walking last in the StyleWeek Swim event and the show stopper himself was Jonathan Joseph Peters. His summer 2014 collection that featured poppy glamour and a style fit for any occasion. Peter's designs are truly one of a kind and are the Nude Boutique shelves.

The event was another StyleWeek success in Providence. The hottest fashion to hit summer 2014 has been presented and most available at

Nude Boutique Providence also. The creators of StyleWeek are expanding every season and bringing the Mercedes Benz Fashion Show class to the Northeast. If you are interested in attending their next fabulous show visit their website at www.styleweeknortheast.com.

6-6-2014 "Socially Scene" South Shore Swim Review Boston Post Gazette Column #89

Socially Scene Reviewed… This past week was a Timeless Tuesday production we have all been waiting for, swim wear.

Designer Dana Duggan took her South Shore Swimwear styles to the Langham Hotel runway last Tuesday. The collection was fierce and brought smiles all around signaling it's time to break out those bikinis.

The summer line had a little bit to offer every taste and size. There was a solid focus on this seasons trendy colors; prime pink, bold turquoise, poppy pastels, a satin mint along with a classic zebra and metallic leopard print. The collection also offered some VIP pool party attire. There was a cutesy deep blue tennis outfit, picnic pattern cover-ups and even a bedazzled dress or two.

The show was a hit as always with top stylist Jana Rago on site from Salon Acote on Newbury Street but well known for her work with Mercedes Benz Fashion Week in New York as well Paris. The flawless models from Dynasty Models and Talent added to the designs of the evening, great vibes came from DJ Kuppa James and always a favorite the Appertivo promotions by Peroni.

You can find Dana Duggan and South Shore Swimwear designs on Facebook and at www.pintrest.com/southshoreswim. Also there is still another chance to catch the styles live on June 10th as they are joining in on the collaboration fashion show with "The Women of Boston" at Bond. The show will feature Rough House Style, Luigi and Lola shoes, Amber Lu "Smart Luxury" Designs, EyeStarr and many more. There will be a shopping Plaza where you will be able to purchase items in the show also Blo from South End and the new Seaport location will be on site doing complimentary dry styles. For information on the show or to find out more about The Women of Boston visit www.WomenOfBoston.com

5-2-2014 "Socially Scene" Mass College Fashion Timeless Tuesday Review Boston Post Gazette Column #84

Socially Scene Reviewed… This past week The Langham Hotel was host to some of Boston's bright art and fashion future.

The Massachusetts College of the Arts and Design was given a great opportunity to shine from Bond Boston. Timeless Tuesday's fashion shows generally feature well established designers or boutiques. This presentation was unique with twenty-seven designers from the college fashion division being able to show one look a piece.

Socially Scene is a Timeless Tuesday regular and was very impressed with the professionalism from the budding stars that can always be expected from the event. The preparation of the Dynasty Models was top class from the ever flawless Benjamin James and new face for hair and makeup Jessica Feeley from Essentials Salon in Belmont. The buzz back stage made me feel like it was my first fashion show since each one of these designers was bursting with excitement. The large crowd was kept occupied with resident DJ Kuppa James and always favorite Apertivo Peroni promotion.

When the show began it did with nothing less than fresh fashion; the first look to hit the runway was a florescent green perfectly tailored dragon body suit with spikes and all. If the Massachusetts College of the Arts were looking to make a statement their mission was accomplished! The design demanded respect as it was truly a work of art. Following styles were more on the everyday wearable side like; hot pink dresses, classic lace corsets, chic evening wear and even a little lingerie slipped in.

It was very refreshing to feel the vibe that the stylish students had brought to their collections. There were priceless moments during the show that the up and coming designers could be found peeking through the window as their style was front stage. The show was classy, imaginative, and full of custom glam. These students will soon be able to call themselves stylist as they will have their graduation presentation on May 15th at the Park Plaza Castle. If you would like to attend this futuristic fashion show you can call 617-879-7676 or visit www.massart.edu.

4-25-2014 "Socially Scene" StyleWeek Favorites Show at Timeless Tuesday Boston Post Gazette Column #83

Socially Scene Reviewed… This Past week's "Timeless Tuesday's" at Bond in the Langham Hotel was host to some of StyleWeek North East's favorite designers from Nude Boutique in Providence Rhode Island.

Top notch preparations are always taken in high end shows and backstage were Boston favorites Benjamin James and Amanda McCarthy prepping Dante models for their "Nude" trip down the catwalk.

Jonathan Joseph Peters was the first designer to rock the runway. Peter's 2014 collection was part of the closing night for StyleWeek 2014 and a fan favorite. His collection had a chic twist to a look full of bold colors and prints. Jess Abernethy was next to hit the runway with a collection that featured poppy pastel dresses that were suitable for the office that transitions right into cocktail attire. Susan Troy showed a 2014 collection that highlighted a classic look perfect for a power business women yet with pieces to mix and match for a night out. The handbags carried by the Dante models were from the Kent Stetson collection. Amy Stetkiewicz rocked a funky collection with metallic fabric. The combinations of pieces shown were ones that could make a bold statement or suitable for a simple Sunday look all were paired with Kent Stetson handbags. Yellow Clover closed out the show in a playful floral pattern with stylish crops and edgy cuts to each style. The collection is a spring must!

The StyleWeek cast was on site as Founder Rosanna Ortiz Sinel, Vice President Christina Robbio and other production positions made the trip from Providence to give support for the designers they show. This group of fashionistas puts so much into this industry and will be personally responsible for the North East being put on the runway map.

This event was a fashion success where the featured designers from the evening were from "Nude" a boutique in Providence. The guest list was start studded and the vibe was intoxicating with the urge to shop. Timeless Tuesday's at the Langham Hotel generally fall on the second Tuesday of the month with a preshow Apertivo Peroni promotion from 4p.m.-7p.m. For more information on upcoming events visit www.bondboston.com.

4-18-2014 "Socially Scene" Miss Massachusetts Pageant Review Boston Post Gazette Column #82

Socially Scene Reviewed... Recently Boston was host to one of the most elegant events honored with rich tradition, the Miss Massachusetts United States pageant.

The Revere hotel welcomed some of the North East's finest in the fashion and entertainment industry to say good bye to Julianna Smith the 2013 queen and see who was to take on the title.

The competition was co-hosted by Chris Timoney a former ABC News member now a Sporting News Radio and Match.com event coordinator. Standing next to him through the night was the breathtaking and current Miss United States Candice Dillard.

The night began in the Revere Hotel Theatre lobby with cocktails and shopping as many of the designers and artists in the show set up shop to display their fantastic editions to the evening. Designer Colleen Ferry and owner of onsite Chantilly Place glamorized not only Miss United States but many of the contestants with her authentic gowns. They were one of a kind meant for a queen dresses and well worth checking out her store or visiting her website at www.chantillyplace.com.

When you enter into the theatre it is an amazing and modern space. The first five rows are beautiful tables with leather benches and were perfect placement to see the sold out show. The event started off with an inspirational and warming welcome to Boston with a highlight video of our amazing city and just how strong we stand.

After the celebrity panel of judges were introduced; Traci Bingham our local Baywatch babe, Amber Lu a designer of luxury leathers for iPhone and iPads along with an extensive runway resume from walking in shows from Milan, Paris to Hong Kong, Rocky Graziano the 1994 Mr. Pre-Teen pageant winner to only move up to national titles, TV appearances and currently on the Board of Directors for the Miss Boston Scholarship Organization, Reaz Hoque CEO of The SYNERGY and the fashionista herself Rosanna Sinel Ortiz Founder and President of StyleWeek a red carpet event that is going to be responsible how fashion will be perceived in the North East moving forward.

The competition started off with the swimsuit followed by evening wear to on stage interviews where a little humor crept in. The saying "pain is beauty" was put to truth. When each of these flawless ladies was asked, "How are you" the common response was, "Hungry, I just want a slice of pizza." The word "competition" is used often in pageants and that it is. Just like an athlete in a sporting event these women put in countless inspiring hours of training and perfecting that takes dedication. Just before the crowing of the 2014 queen then current Miss Massachusetts Julianna Smith took stage to give her heartwarming farewell speech.

The time had come for seven ladies to stop holding their breath and just embrace in holding each other's hands for the finalists to be announced. All of the women were unique, stunning role models yet it was Renta De Carvalho who walked away with the 2014 Miss Massachusetts title. It was an emotional moment for the freshly crowned queen and her large cheering section of family and friends. The closing of the evening was a performance by Push4171 who are rising up high on the pop charts.

The night was an elegant event that took many months of prepping and hard work from Assistant Director Monique Taylor, Co-Director Jeff Butterworth, Program Development Raquel Rohlfing, Operations Tony Hyppolit, Moderator Dacey Zouzas also the star of the show and one amazing women for all she give to the organization Director Jena Tang. Since 1937, the Miss United States Organization provides an avenue of achievement for women and girls ages 8-40. At the local, state, and national level, the program promotes each titleholder's platform for community service while acting as a national partner with Relay for Life and the American Cancer Society. The pageant process provides a positive and memorable environment, with focus on encouragement and community. The national Miss United States competition includes the divisions of Miss, Ms., Teen, Junior Teen, Pre-Teen, and Little Miss, taking place in Washington, D.C. during Independence Day activities. If you would like to see a schedule for the upcoming appearances for Miss Massachusetts United States or more information visit www.missunitedstates.com.

March 2014 "Socially Scene" Body By Blo Review Boston Post Gazette Column #80

Socially Scene Reviewed… Last week the budding Seaport District in Boston welcomed a new tenant. Body. BY Blo hosted a VIP "Pretty in Pink" event in anticipation of their grand opening.

One of the newest trends in the beauty industry is, "blow dry bars." They specialize in mainly blow dry's for the business women on the go, a special event or just a little pampering. With a location already in the South End "blo" has added a new edition in the Seaport "Body. By Blo."

The night started off with a warm greeting the second you walked through the door. The space was fabulous! It was a classy mixture of matte charcoal grey, fresh white walls, and décor with a pop of colorful products lines to highlight the room. Front and center was a long table for full nail services that featured "Morgan Taylor" professional nail color. The stations were innovative with perfectly placed mirrors to catch all the styling tips given throughout your session. You can bet this location will be receiving a Boston's Best "Customer Service" award being Socially Scene was five minutes in the door and already with a fantastic beverage and getting styled. There is bright cursive lettering right above the wash area that reads "Hello Gorgeous" and that is exactly how they sent Socially Scene into the party.

Chief Style Boss of South End location Nathan Alan and staff broke their backs with the little time they literally had to transform a back room in the newly built building itself to create the stylish party. There was a DJ, dancing, photo area, tasty treats, and fruity drinks. There were plates of passed sweet potato puffs, mini tacos, raspberry mouse and more. The caterer and owner of Matt Harker Events was on site himself preparing the delectable delights for the guests to indulge in.

The night was filled with some of the Hub's hottest glitterati like New England Patriots cheerleaders, former Miss Rhode Island Julianna Clare Strout now a great edition to Massachusetts society and future hopeful Boston City Council member were just a few on the lengthy list. I was able to get a chance to chat with Franchise Partner Gina Gesamondo and asked what was special about her new edition. She replied, "This is an extension of our already successful location in the South End. We offer more services like; full waxing, nails, deep conditioning treatments as well as our blo on the go, bridal blo and so much more. I am so excited to be in the Seaport District and service this growing community."

The VIP "Pretty in Pink" party was a tasteful event with a great look into the amazing business that is taking the industry in a new direction. Not only are they a top pick in the city but they give back to charity as well! On Sunday April 27th join them for "HAIRaising" at both locations. You can get a cat-walk blow out for a minimum donation with 100% of proceeds benefiting Boston's Children's Hospital. For more information on the event visit ww.hairaising.org. You can find Body. By Blo at 157 Seaport Boulevard and may book reservations by calling 617-426-0874. If you happen to be shopping around the South End pop into their location at 437 Columbus Avenue 617-262-0105 also both can be found at www.blomedry.com.

March 2014 "Socially Scene" Candice Wu Couture Boston Post Gazette Column #78

Socially Scene Reviewed... This past week Bond in the Langham Hotel held their monthly "Timeless Tuesday" fashion show and Socially Scene was on site.

The featured designer of the evening was Candice Wu Couture with her 2014 collection. I had arrived early to get some of the behind the scenes hair, makeup also last minute tailoring and even then Bond was busy and I knew this was going to be a great event.

The hours before a runway fashion show can be a bit hectic yet filled with so much creativity. Each designer has their own style and it is crucial that every detail leading up to the dress is a perfect fit. Benjamin James Beauty was there to start off each Dante model with a smoky eye look that was compliment to the collection yet had to give each one of the models a unique glow. Hair was being done by Viselli Santoro Salon, a new edition to Newbury Street. The stylists had to showcase some real talent being they were asked to make most of the models look as if they had a sort of short bob to highlight the edgy accessories from House of Cach that draped each gown. I had originally seen House of Cach and their edgy and exotic jewelry at StyleWeek and the Providence local was a classic match for the Couture collection.

Hong Kong native also Boston School of Fashion graduate now designer Candice Wu has already a high class resume. Her designs have hit runways like; Boston and New York Fashion Week, StyleWeek, Project Ethos in Hollywood, Ovations for the Cure, Red Cross charity events and the list goes on. Wu is also the back to back winner of the Boston Fashion Award for 2012 and 2013.

Just as the show was about to begin I took to the photographers pit and was able to catch a quick glimpse of what a great crowd Wu had pulled in. The room was filled with fashions most fabulous like; UpTemp Magazine editor Joseph Gualtiere, Nestor a local American Idol season 13 contestant, fashion designer Helena Martin, Denise and Stephen Dunbar, Amber Lu accessory and handbag designer along with so many more.

Once the show got going it became clear yet again what an amazing establishment Bond is being tables lined the runway perfectly for guests to enjoy the entertainment. The collection was brimming with imagination and Wu being known for her love to blend traditional elements with modern ideas had the runway filled with pure art. There were two walkthroughs and both were host to a combination of dark, timeless evil queen from a Disney classic also a lighter look with animated greens and soft silks.

Timeless Tuesdays at Bond in the Langham Hotel are always a quality event but I believe this was the best yet. They are generally held one the 2nd Tuesday of the month and always partnered with Peroni where before the show from 4:30p.m.-7:30p.m. you can receive a complimentary appetizer when drinking a Peroni, just another perk. You can visit www.bondboston.com for more on all their entertainment. Candice Wu is always up to something in the industry and with her studio right in the South End of the city don't be surprised when this talented designer is making her way to Paris and Milan with earning Boston a secure spot in the fashion business. You can find out more about her upcoming events at www.candicewucouture.com

February 2014 "Socially Scene" Venni Caprice Fashionably Late Show Boston Post Gazette Column #76

Socially Scene Reviewed... Last week CKPFashion Agency was host to "Fashionably Late" at the Liberty Hotel to debut Venni Caprice Clothing's 2014 Spring Collection.

The event was indeed, "Fashionably Late" being it didn't start until 10p.m. yet Socially Scene was able to snag a pre-show interview with designer Lori Kyler Christensen. She was happy to share her inspiration for the line that had hints of soft turquoise and her favorite color that worked well with the print. Lori also mentioned that she likes to take different patterns and use them together which gives her a unique angle in the industry. The night had a portion of proceeds donated to a charity that Kyler Christensen was very passionate in saying, "The Wounded Warrior Fund is something very important to me. It's a charity that gives back to the protectors of our country, we all know someone. Tonight's donation is in honor of my best friend Kevin O'Boyle who means so much to me." Lori was a clear professional but the most impressive part was that the fantastic piece she was wearing had been sewn at five that morning.

When the show began each of the "Dante" models started out on the second floor catwalk of the former jail house. After they would race to the lower entrance where they would come back in site by softly floating up the escalator to then show each piece on the four different platforms placed around the main room. The setup was perfectly put together by CKP themselves. You could see each design from every angle and the height the models were displayed at was a photographers dream.

There were two rounds of styles to hit the stages. The first; was a collection of dresses that focused on what Lori mentioned of the two different patterns coming together with bold poppy colors and a few classic black and white gowns. The second; were dresses assembled with bright florescent colors, floral print and fabulous comfort pants suits that had all the guests begging for spring to hurry along.

The "Fashionably Late" event was one of many glamorous shows the CKPFashion Agency put together and you can find a listing of their upcoming presentations at www.ckpfashion.com. The debut of the Venni Caprice Clothing 2014 Spring Collection was a hit and the local fashionista Lori Kyler Christensen is expanding fast and for a good reason. You can visit her website at www.VenniCaprice.com for the debuted line at the show but also for more on a custom, high end collection and store locations.

2-21-2014 "Socially Scene" Denise Hajjar Valentines Show Boston Post Gazette Column #74

Socially Scene Reviewed… This past Wednesday I was able to attend a fabulous and rather unique fashion event at the Intercontinental Boston's Ramba Rum and Champagne Bar.

Resident designer of the hotel and local legend Denise Hajjar held a "Valentines Fashion Show" to present her winter collection that is currently 25%-65% off through March 5th. The night was also to preview her Spring 2014 collection that will hit the runway for her annual show on February 25th in the Grand Ballroom at the Fairmont Copley Plaza Hotel.

When I first arrived I was a bit curious how all this would to come together being it was held in a very lovely yet hotel lounge. I quickly noticed layered steps, red lamps, fireplaces, and a long walk way where I could catch the models for a photo. To ease my night the Rumba Bar staff and promotions manager Allison were amazing with helping Socially Scene set up. This wasn't your average extravagant runway presentation that Hajjar is so very well known for, it was intimate and accommodating.

The models would come through the front entrance generally in pairs of two and took it table side through Rumba giving the guest the opportunity to see the designs up close and even get a full rundown on each piece they were wearing. Her winter collection was host to classic white furs, tailored leathers, professional pencil skirts and even some poppy red tones for the Valentine's Day theme. Her spring collection was only a little taste before her grand Copley Plaza presentation. It featured sheer dresses with a low cut in the back for a sparkling necklace to drape off the angle, bold poppy colors with a detailed design and breathtaking evening wear.

My favorite piece of the night was a chic knit design dress and holding the gold elephant clutch was model, Simone Aptekman. She has done a few different events with Denise but when I asked if she would be at the Copley she commented, " This is will be my first show at the Fairmont actually. I am so excited to be walking. I love her clothing; Denise is amazing to work with. She creates such unique pieces that are made to order." I also got a chance to chat with Denise herself about her new location. She was very excited when saying, "I love my new location! It is three times the size and I am able to sew right on site. I have my machines here in the hotel so I am really moving along with new designs."

The flow of the night was very timely and just what you can expect from Hajjar, fashion forward and timeless elegance. The winter collection will have a 25%-65% sale through March 5th at her new location Denise Hajjar Boutique/ InterContinental Boston 510 Atlantic Ave Boston. You can reach the store at 617-266-2296 or visit her website at www.denisehajjar.com.

Don't forget to mark your calendar on Tuesday February 25th for Denise Hajjar's Spring 2014 Fashion Show benefitting Big Sisters. The event will take place at the Fairmont Copley Plaza Hotel in the Grand Ballroom with cocktails and Hors D'oeuvres Reception from 6p.m. -7p.m. and from 7p.m.-9p.m. the fashion show and live auction. For tickets you can visit http://bit.ly/BigSisterFashionShow14 or for more information call Kira Ross at 617-236-5304.

2-7-2014 "Socially Scene" Style Week Boston Post Gazette Column #72

Socially Scene Reviewed… Recently an event so fantastic represented the North East with class and style. The Providence Biltmore Hotel was host to Style Week that took place from January 19th through the 25th.

The show was recommended to me by Boston's own fashion legend Denise Hajjar and the date must have slipped my mind. Opening night was Sunday the 19th and as I was browsing my Facebook I happen to come across photos being posted on their page. I spared no time in getting right on their website and contacting the head honchos to get Socially Scene on site!

I was able to schedule myself in for that Thursday from the speedy response within the directors of StyleWeek. When I arrived I couldn't help but be taken by the beauty of the Providence Biltmore Hotel. It had an elegant Victorian feel along with the décor to compliment it. Being an older landmark the stairs were not an option that I was willing to take to avoid an elderly elevator ride to the 17th floor.

I had made it safe, sound and a little on edge yet that didn't last long from the buzzing of this fantastic party taking place. I was immediately impressed when I approached one of two check in tables. I gave my name and the girls began to scramble through their many lists when a woman who I later found to be Toyin Omisore, reservations and event director had a spot in her memory where my placement was stored and sent me on my way.

When I actually arrived in the show room I was speechless. The room was flawless, the bright white runway, a timeless chandelier directly over it, the rows of chairs perfectly placed and Socially Scene right in front with my own labeled seat.

The show began with Martha Jackson's, "Restored by Design." The collection was highlighted with feathers and a turquoise touch. Next to walk was "Chevalier Homme" designs by Reginald Meromc that flaunted a Brazilian flavor and punk appeal. Closing out the night was Samuel Vartan and a fierce combination of leather with comfort class.

I had covered the majority of Boston Fashion Week and continue to pop in at style events throughout the city but this was nothing like I had experienced yet. The night had a very Mercedes Benz Fashion Week feel and I wanted more. I began to notice in between shows that there were a small select few of ladies running this show and I was sure to introduce myself to some with interest in attending the final show that Saturday night.

They confirmed my attendance for the closing of Style Week with enthusiasm and I couldn't wait. The time came and there were many Bostonites on site like; Boston Fashion Week Founder Jay Calderin, local designers Candice Wu also Amber Lu and to my surprise I was seated next to Gustavo Leon not only an editor at the Boston Herald but was voted the most Fabulous of StyleWeek. I had no argument with that being his ensemble for the night was one that couldn't be topped. Our own Post Gazette's editor is very classy and sheik with her power business suites and fabulous furs but who knew the editors out there were so fashion forward.

Saturday night's show started off with Nick Pini designs presented by Flaunt Boutique that expressed a dark look with lace and a fabric flow. Following was Selahdor by David Chum that gave a sheik sassy appeal. To close out the night and entire week was designer Jonathan Joseph Peters that won over the attendee's with his fierce Voguesque line for fall 2014.

Another fantastic addition to Style Week was, "The Accessory Showcase presented by Flaunt Boutique." It was open to non-ticket holders every day during StyleWeek from 5:30-9pm with goodies like; Boston's own Helena Grant and her "The Kitchen Sink Bag" who teamed up with T*Racy by Tracy Belben, Flaunt Boutique themselves where I couldn't help but purchase a beautiful handmade "Love" bracelet in gold and silver for an everyday accessory, luxury fur accessories by Zarusa, Gabrielle Lopez metals, Seams Couture Bridal Design, Ella Danla handbags, gorgeous reinvented finds from Restored Design and so many more on 17th and 18th floor of the hotel.

After the final show I grabbed the opportunity to chat with Christina Robbio VP of Business operations and a Massachusetts native to soak up her very loyal enthusiasm for this project. I could see the passion in her and the dedication of those surrounding Christina. When I asked what the most important thing for her with regards to the show, she replied "My Team!" "There is small board of eight members and heading the committee is Rosanna Ortiz Sinel, President and Founder. From there we only have a select few interns that are on site for preparation of the shows." She was very honest in saying, "We all have everyday jobs and truly care for this event so much that we make the sacrifices." I must say I was in pure shock to find that a small group was responsible for putting on a production of such measure.

StyleWeek, established in 2009, was created with the vision of connecting buyers and press with emerging design talent. They are a biannual fashion week focused on the business of fashion; StyleWeek is a true celebration of style and culture, which includes both formal fashion shows and community-wide events. They have showcased over 55 emerging designers on their runway since the inaugural week in 2010, including Project Runway alum and are one of the few regional fashion weeks, which have been visited by the CFDA.

Style Week North East was one of the most professional and fabulous fashion events Socially Scene has been on site for. I was blown away with the beauty of the event and loved all the detail to compliment it. I had an amazing time and recommend that Boston hop on that band wagon. The trip to Providence was very short and they were very welcoming and honored for those of us who made it from Mass. If you're interested in getting a full peek at all the pictures you can follow them on Facebook at "Style Week." The event will take place again in August and you can visit their website at www.StyleWeek.com to get more information.

1-24-2014 "Socially Scene" CKP Fashion Show Boston Post Gazette Column #71

Socially Scene Reviewed… This past week I attended a fabulous yet very educational fashion event at the Christina K. Pierce show room on Newbury Street.

The night was a planned peek at a spring 2014 G.Kim collection that was accompanied by d'andra handbags with proceeds going to a very serious cause through The Eva Center right here in Boston.

CKPFashion put on a sheik event as they always do that was host to cocktails, plenty of paparazzi, glamorous models with flawless faces put together with MakeupBy Anavaldi and of course a VIP guest list. There were tons of goodies to buy and Dry Bar chipped in on the charity event with blowout and cocktail gift certificates for raffle. I must say it was rather rewarding to know that the scarf I purchased had 100% of the proceeds going to Human Trafficking.

Most everyone has heard of "Human Trafficking" as it is a disturbing situation that has gone on for many generations yet I was shocked at the cold hard facts. Christina's agency was very committed to the cause and had printed out information on the actual statics and even personal stories from survivors. I truly had no idea of the kind of percentages that countries all over the world harbor including right here in the United States.

The night was incredible between the fashion, mingling, heartwarming giving and the blessing I felt for what kind of life God has granted me. CKPFashion is always giving back and making a great time of it, so if you would like to see what events are upcoming visit www.christina-pierce.com . The Eva Center here in Boston formally known as "Kim's Project" has plenty of awareness tactics as well as crisis counseling. If you have interest in volunteering or have questions they can be reached at 617-779-2133 or by email at theevacenter@gmail.com. Also if you would like more information on Human Trafficking you can visit www.equalitynow.org.

1-3-2014 "Socially Scene" TWOB Collaboration Fashion Show Boston Post Gazette Column #68

Socially Scene Reviewed... The day after Christmas I walked into a CVS and behold there was valentines and Easter candy on the shelves! Since the world of fashion is always looking forward and now with the holiday gone the industry is concentrating on springtime and the runway shows have begun.

Last week Rough House Style teamed up to help launch The Women Of Boston for a collaboration show at the Emerald Lounge in the Revere Hotel. Rough House Style is a brand with a focus on roughed up denim. Owner and designer Jamie Longo took a new approach to her spring 2014 collection with adding in superior leather to her look. The Women Of Boston are a premier network for business women in Boston who officially took stage that night with membership information, supporters that donated to the show and invited guests such as Denise Hajjar in attendance. Longo also a ground floor member of the group was happy to take her well known label and help this up and coming powerhouse get the ladies in the city interested.

The show was all I expected it to be with gorgeous models, one of a kind styles and professional photography by Ancelis Nunez Photography. The Women Of Boston and Rough House pulled out all the stops with heavy hitters putting their two cents in on the show. Model's carried "The Kitchen Sink Bag" designed by Helena Grant, hair courtesy of Blo South End, makeup-up by 437 and even Longo's brother Frank put together a little something for the gentleman in attendance with his own NOBULL hats for men. The swag bags sponsors like Scene Magazine, Eye Star lashes, Greyfree.com and Dreamlook had me going home with a fantastic smile from the lip gloss! Even though this was what they referred to as a "soft" show, I sure had a great time and was impressed with the trends and professionalism from Rough House Style and The Women Of Boston which have both struck an interest in myself for spring attire and membership to networking events.

Rough House is looking forward to their next show early spring yet is always customizing styles and can be contacted at www.roughhousestyle.com. The Women Of Boston are planning on a masquerade ball in February and monthly events for the business lady to have a fun while still doing a little networking in their line of work. You can find more information on them at www.TheWomenOfboston.com.

Chapter Twelve – 2013

"Fashion is part of the daily air and it changes all the time, with all the events. You can even see the approaching of a revolution in clothes. You can see and feel everything in clothes." —Diana Vreeland

11-29-2013 "Socially Scene" Diane von Furstenberg Boston Post Gazette Column #63

Socially Scene Reviewed... This past week Dress For Success teamed up with W.net for women's networking event held at Diane von Furstenberg on Newbury Street. It was an evening filled with high end shopping, business chat, cocktails and warmth from giving back to charity.

I have been a Dress For Success fan since I was first exposed to their cause during fashion week 2012 but was introduced to W.net for the first time and thought maybe best to give everyone the low down on just who they are.

The Women's Network in Electronic Transactions (W.net) is the premiere electronic transactions organization dedicated solely to women in the field. W.net's goal is to provide a forum to inspire and empower women in the electronic transactions industry through networking opportunities, mentoring programs, and the overall promotion of women by enabling them to maximize their potential and position them for greater success. More information at www.wnetonline.org.

Dress For Success is an international not-for-profit organization that promotes the independence of disadvantaged women by providing them with professional attire, a network of support, and career development tools. Young Executives for Success (Y.E.S.!) is a volunteer branch of Dress For Success composed of female professionals whose nine-to-five jobs make it challenging to volunteer and connect directly with clients of Dress For Success. Y.E.S.! members promote the mission of Dress For Success through volunteering and fundraising events that take place during off/after hours.

It was such a treat to hear about yet another organization that promotes the success of business women. The speech made by Dress For Success's Executive director Kimberly Todd was heartwarming to hear about the amount of work volunteers put into that charity, it has become my favorite! To close the presentation the stylist on site Drew gave us an informal show on the latest Furstenberg line and some insight on just what a wonderful career she has had. Diane von Furstenberg is a global luxury lifestyle brand and one of the premier names in American fashion that was founded in 1972 by the designer. Renowned for its iconic wrap dress and signature prints, DVF has expanded to a full collection of ready-to-wear and accessories including shoes, handbags, small leather goods, scarves, and fine jewelry. In 2012, its Founder and Co-Chairman Diane von Furstenberg was named the most powerful woman in fashion by Forbes

Magazine. The sheik vibe you get from the power white walls with strong print products, I couldn't argue with that title.

After all the introductions we were set free to shop a 20% discount with 10% of the proceeds going to Dress For Success. Throughout my mingling I was not surprised to see CEO/Founder Maria Paola from the brand new "The Women Of Boston" business network on site to choose their charity none other than Dress For Success. However, it was interesting to meet sisters and chief creative directors Candace (style guru) and Rachel (finance officer) Wilkes from "the Help Boston." They are a personal concierge, but are also so much more - offering a wide variety of services, tailored to your every need. From running your errands to updating your wardrobe, no task is too large or small. They founded The Help to assist others in managing the stress of a busy life. From moms and executives to young professionals; we could all use an extra set of hands sometimes, so let them be The Help that you need! The more I became familiar with the concept the more one of my favorite Sex in the City episodes came to mind. A hot new concierge service had just opened in the city and Samantha had homemade baby quiche, a movie and champagne delivered for their girl's night in! Good luck ladies the Hub can always use a little "Help."

All is all the night was fantastic from the networking to the glamorous designs and the true reason of the season, giving back. Diane von Furstenberg donated not only a percent of the proceeds from the evening but 2,500 dollars in cloths to Dress For Success. If you would like to become involved with the organization visit www.dressforsuccess.org

11-15- 2013 "Socially Scene" Style Fixed Boston Post Gazette Column #61

Socially Scene Reviewed… This past week was host to one of my all-time favorite events, Style Fixx! This premier one of a kind traveling shopping extravaganza made a stop at the Center for the Arts and impact on "The Women Of Boston."

Style Fixx is always at the top of my events to attend list based on all the swag and style that are on site to indulge in. When you first enter the room after strutting down the VIP red carpet it's like Christmas morning with presents everywhere and so much excitement not sure which one to open first. Thankfully, the Style Fixx staff makes that decision for you. After you check in the option to grab your swag bag full of goodies is in the back of the room, that's clearly where any girl would start. The next stop was to the Style Fixx bar for a little bubbly compliment of Barefoot Wines.

Now that I was all set up to start; There were designers local and nationwide that were in attendance. d'andrea handbags were one of the first to catch my eye since I fell in love with her product back at Boston Fashion Week when she was a part of the Christina K. Pierce fashion show at the Revere Hotel. Camille albane Paris was there to make you look modelesque with 20 years' worth of fashion week experience straight from Europe. Sazzy Boutique had classic accessories and expressive hats. SKM Jewelers had a trendy setup of necklaces, earing and more. Fashion and beauty are ones to complement each other and the European Wax Center was there giving complimentary brow shapes and discounts for more intimate visits. All this fashion and flair makes a lady think about her health; the one and only George Foreman III was promoting his grand opening of "The Club." It will be a facility with; power yoga, spinning classes and a training course for boxing. They will open in Southie this December so stay tuned!

When you were feeling a bit famished there was an entire corner for you to get back in the game with food and drink. Pretzel Chips, The Upper Crust, Luna Bars and Wicked Wines were there to help wash it all down.

Not only was it a shoppers dream but a great place to mingle with business women alike! I attended both nights as Socially Scene but was lucky to be a part of a launch on Wednesday with CEO Maria Paola and "The Women Of Boston." They are a premier network connecting business women one step at a time to; share and encourage growth through wine socials, fashion events seminars and more. If you are interested or would like more information on becoming a member you can visit www.TheWomenOfBoston.com. Thursday was just as fantastic with people to meet as I roamed the room with designer Jamie Longo from RoughHouse Styles who found inspiration from working at a boutique in her grandfather's hometown; Catania, Sicily. I actually met through a string of industry people that stems right back to my first Style Fixx Event last year. That particular night President/CEO Jason Roth was there with great conversation. He had such insight into the business world and really opened my eyes to opportunities for business women of all kinds looking to get started.

With an event sponsor like Improper Bostonian and many other local and national brands Style Fixx is an A+ event. You can shop, get some on site beauty tips and pampering also if you are business women this event is a great place to make contacts and learn from success in progress. Ladies if you missed the party not to worry the event will be back in Boston this coming May. You can visit www.stylefixx.com for more information.

10-18-2013 "Socially Scene" Firas Yousif Reviewed Boston Post Gazette Column #57

Socially Scene Reviewed… This week I am going to take a fashion flash back to Boston Fashion Week and highlight one of if not the top showcase of the week. Firas Yousif Originals held a very intimate and invite only runway presentation in Lindsey Chapel at Emmanuel Church on October 3rd.

The venue was breathtaking and fitting for the debut of his much anticipated 2014 Bridal & Evening Couture collection. The authentic artwork that filled the chapel was compliment to the elegance in Yousif's designs. The final piece to complete the setting was the music that filled the chapel walls; a soundtrack of ethereal vocals and rhythm of Middle Eastern instrumentals as the models strutted the runway in each gown.

The couture bridal wear featured a feathered texture, train in the back, knee length cut in front and the quality of fabric was to die for. The multi-talented Yousif also unveiled his most recent evening wear that showed an edgy shape, current patterns with a classic look and sheik appeal.

For close to twenty years, Firas Yousif has been living a double life. He is the successful professional in the pharmaceutical industry with an undergraduate degree in bio science – biotechnology and an MBA from Boston College. He is also known as a talented designer behind Firas Yousif Originals creating gorgeous one of a kind bridal and evening gowns as well as flirty cocktail dresses.

Firas Yousif was born in Baghdad, raised in Kuwait, and found a home in Philadelphia with his parents at the age of 13. Influenced by his seamstress Aunt in the Middle East and mother who always sewed, the self-taught Yousif began designing in 1993 all the while acquiring multiple degrees and launching a successful career in pharmaceuticals.

Looking for a something new he moved to Boston in 1999. His first showroom was opened on Huntington Avenue and he began generating a vibe via Boston Fashion Week shows at the former Gamble Mansion in Boston's Back Bay and the Boston Public Library in Copley Square.

Despite Firas' clear talent, he is an under the radar designer who works discreetly, yet diligently to produce the highest quality work for his discerning clientele. While he takes obvious pride in his finished designs, he is not one to sing his own praises to the masses in a shameless attempt to gain "it" status. Fortunately he has his partner of 10 plus years, Tom McGair, working as his public relations and marketing director.

As more and more women discover Firas, whether it be on his www.firasyousiforiginals.com, sitting in the audience during his fashion shows, or stepping into his welcoming Newbury Street showroom, it is safe to say that the secret will be out.

The Firas Yousif show during fashion week was one that has had many of the industry professional and followers buzzing. It was host to glamorous designs, fabric and the venue was a conversations piece itself. You can visit Yousif's site to see his designs also on Facebook at fj originals or pop into his studio located at 35 Newbury Street League, Dartmouth St and can be reached at 617-262-0100.

10-11 2013 "Socially Scene" BosFW Closes Boston Post Gazette Column #56

Socially Scene Reviewed... This past Sunday Boston Fashion Week came to an end just where it all began in the Langham Hotel with a runway show featuring National Jean Company hosted by COUP Boston.

Socially Scene was just that this past week in the city of Boston as I attended quite a few different shows! I was so impressed and excited to know what the city of Boston had to offer in honor of the fashion industry.

I started off last Monday at Bond in the Langham Hotel where the New England Revolution, Modest Clothing Connection and owner Santi teamed up with charity Friends Fighting Breast Cancer to rock the runway. The styles featured had a fun punk look with a casual everyday appeal. Monday was like a road race for Socially Scene as there were two more shows on list for that night. I rushed over to InterContinental Hotel – Boston for by far one of the top shows of the week, Denise Hajjar's fall/winter collection donating to Dress for Success. As always she puts on a fantastic night and this time there was a whole room filled with her styles on display and the handbags had me in heaven! On the rush again, I made it to the W Hotel for Candice Wu Couture & House of Cach fashion presented by Uptempo Magazine. Wu has really expanded in the fashion industry and the name she has made for herself definitely reflected in her high end styles.

Wednesday was at Taj Hotel that featured Luxe Boutiques' new fall collection of fur garments and fine jewelry, with complimentary wine from California's exclusive Ridge Vineyards and it was all I expected it to be.

Fashion and class go hand in hand and on Thursday afternoon back again at the Langham Hotel was afternoon teatime and cocktail hour hosted by Coup Magazine with Gregory Paul Designs. This was by far the most elegant event of the week and the dresses fit the scene. There were pops of bright green paired with a flat black or white that had everyone in the room wanting one piece or another.

Thursday night was a date I had saved months ago since I started covering the Revere Roof Top shows in August. Christina K. Pierce Fashions hosted yet again another fashion filled event at Gem in the Revere Hotel. The show started off with the Sefani fall collection that had in season tribal prints with classic formal wear that featured traditional turquoise and orange flare. I enjoyed every show I attended and each impressed me in their own way but by far this was the best runway view of the models and attire. The show closed with a launch by Susan Young that dressed with a silky sheik line of casual wear. The night also welcomed a braid and bun bar to spice up your up do along with d'andrea handbags that any fashion friendly lady would like to carry.

Just after the show I popped in downstairs to the Rustic Kitchen for an event being held by Jennifer Chen founder of Fashion Hubber 4 Life. It was a fashion networking event mixer that brought in some of fashions finest, models, bloggers, entrepreneurs and more. By the time I left I was excited to reconnect with all the industry professionals that have so much to offer.

Friday featured Rough House styles on Royal's runway. Rough House styles are an original to the fashion world with taking denim to a new level and rock it into a style all your own.

Eventually all good things come to an end and it did with Wrap Up Fashion Week back yet again at Bond in the Langham Hotel Sunday. COUP Magazine Boston brought in National Jean Company to feature "real people, real fun and the wardrobe you'll be wearing all fall."

I sure know I was busy and Boston, I didn't even cover half of what was scheduled. The city was host to multiple shows every day and one's that would earn respect for the Hub in the hottest fashion. Not to worry if you missed it, there are still shows going on after the fact. You can find them by visiting www.bostonfashionweek.com, so get out there fashionistas Boston has a lot to offer!

10-4 2013 "Socially Scene" BosFW Reviewed Boston Post Gazette Column #55

Socially Scene Reviewed… This past Friday Boston Fashion Week opened up at Bond Lounge in the Langham Hotel. It was a highly attended event for fashionista's to gather, meet designers, models, and founder Jay Calderin.

When I arrived fashionably late the place already had quite the crowd. It was great to see Bostonians at their finest wearing the top designers and prints of the moment. I was blessed to be wearing Michael Kors thanks to the good people of the North End that give a struggling writer/soccer player a chance to make money!

The organizer Jonathan was very public relations friendly and made it a point to introduce me to Mr. Calderin. It took a few minutes to find an opening since everyone in the VIP room was waiting for their chance to chat. When I found mine he was very excited and so well put together. He was more than happy to educate me on everything he does but I could see his mind racing with things to prep, promote and so on being this was just the beginning. I let him go on his way yet he made me promise to contact him when the week had passed so stay tuned for an exclusive with Boston Fashion Week founder Jay Calderin.

There were so many designers in attendance and how you could spot them out was that they had a tall glamazon walking next to them in one of their pieces to be presented through the week. If I had to pick a favorite of the night; Sasha Thomas and her elegant yet dark gown from her Til Death collection modeled by beauty Tracy Fiorillo.

Just as I came to realize I may have done my duties for the night I spotted a classic in the fashion scene, Denise Dunbar. I had never actually met her but the dress she had one was more than enough reason to approach her for a picture. Just as I asked and mentioned I was press she kindly agreed and to my surprise was sitting with designer Nara Paz and journalist Helena Martin. I had covered Nara is previous columns and thanks to them being dear friends of Post Gazettes editor Pam, I received an invite to join them.

At this point it was getting late and Bond is one of the more trendy night spots in the city so it began to take shape of a younger yet still very fashionable crowd. It was nice to sit and enjoy the sheik side of a fashion event as I felt honored to be sitting with very well respected names in the industry. It was also entertaining as they had a front row table for all the action. The models and followers pouring in began to get hyped from the DJ and started their own runway show. It was great to see their energy since it will be their passion that will carry on this week for years to come.

Fashion Week is still going and will come to a close this Sunday right where it started at Bond in the Langham Hotel. There are still plenty of shows to catch and a full listing is at www.bostonfashionweek.com. If you happen to make it out to one be sure to find "Socially Scene" I would love to meet you!

9-27-2013 "Socially Scene" BosFW Preview Boston Post Gazette Column #54

Socially Scene Exclusive… I generally like to start off with a review of an event attended the previous week but this issue is introduces one of the best things in Boston to arrive as the fall comes in; Fashion Week. Boston fashion week will start September 27th and continue on through October 5th.

Fashion week already speaks for itself with all the parties, runways and glitterati coming together. This year Boston lost one of our leading fashion citizens; a designer who dressed leading actresses (Audrey Hepburn, Julie Andrews) and First Ladies (Lady Bird Johnson, Nancy Reagan), as well as royalty (HRH Princess Maria Pia de Savoie). In honor of his exceptional life and extraordinary career, Boston Fashion Week 2013 will be dedicated to Alfred Fiandaca. To learn more about Alfred visit http://www.alfredfiandaca.com

The week-long event includes dozens and dozens of shows around the city and highlights some of Boston's finest and beyond. I have included a select few you should be able to find Socially Scene on site for and ones that are sure to produce a great runway show!

Boston Fashion Week Opens Friday September 27th with Kick-Off Event at BOND restaurant lounge at 8pm. BFW founder Jay Calderin launches the week's festivities with the city's many faces of fashion including designers, stylists, and models. Also at Bond; Monday September 30th at 6:30 p.m. Modus Collection Clothing Co. Runway Show benefiting Friends Fighting Breast Cancer. New England Revolution star Ryan Guy presents a charity fashion show with Modus Collection Clothing Co. Revolution stars, media personalities and more will walk the runway showcasing the company's latest designs. For tickets visit http://friendsfightingbreastcancer.org. 100% of ticket proceeds benefit FFBC, which raises money for Breast Cancer Research at Mass General Hospital. The Langham Boston is located at 250 Franklin Street and for reservations and more information call 617-451-1900 or visit Boston.LanghamHotels.com

Denise Hajjar Boutique will present her annual fall fashion show along with celebrating 30 years of business. Denise is a well-known Boston fashion icon and will be presenting her designs in her new home at the InterContinental Hotel Boston on Monday September 30th from 6:00pm to 9:00pm and the event EMCEE will be Dr. Mallika Marshall with proceeds benefiting Dress for Success Boston. Their mission is to promote the economic independence of disadvantaged women by providing professional attire, a network of support and the career development tools to help women thrive in work and in life. The InterContinental Hotel Boston is located at 510 Atlantic Avenue. For more information of the show, tickets, and Dress for Success visit www.denisehajjar.com.

Chirstina K. Pierce and The Revere Hotel present Boston Fashion Week @ Emerald Lounge October 2nd and third for complimentary signature cocktails, a braid and bun bar and runway shows featuring; g.KIM & Venni Caprice and Sefani & Launch by Susan Young on October 3rd. Cocktail hour starts at 6pm shows set for start at 7:30pm. The Revere Hotel is located 200 Stuart Street and for more information on the show visit www.christina-pierce.com

Boston Fashion Week was founded in 1995. The force behind the week has been dedicated to creating opportunities that increase the viability and visibility of the local industry. The series of fashion related events throughout Greater Boston and beyond serves as a platform for both established industry professionals and aspiring newcomers to showcase their work as well as network with peers and the public. This annual celebration of Boston style featuring a great wealth of local talent is unique in that it is designed to engage the community directly, at the grassroots level -- cultivating fashion as an integral part of the Boston lifestyle.

Boston fashion week is a time to dress and enjoy the arts of the fashion lifestyle. It will kick off on September 27th and will continue on through

October 5th. I highlighted just a few of many shows but you can visit www.bostonfashionweek.com for a full listing. Hope to see you there!

August 2013 "Socially Scene" Revere Roof Top Review Boston Post Gazette Column #51

Socially Scene Reviewed…. This past Wednesday I attended the finale of the month long Resort Runway at the Revere Hotel rooftop fashion shows that were all hosted by Christina K. Pierce boutique fashion agency. Themes for the events were cabana wear and the roof top pool decor with all white lounge chairs and cabanas were a perfect venue. The featured stylist was Heather Blond and these specific pieces were debuted at Miami fashion week. The models strutting the catwalk were none other than Maggie Inc. The view and service was great and the layout seemed almost built to host fashion shows and summertime festivities. Although the cabana wear is soon to find its way into the back of our closets doesn't mean the shows are at a close. Boston Fashion Week 2013 will take place September 27th through October 5th. This year the week will honor recently passed Alfred Fiandaca's exceptional life and extraordinary career. To learn more about this fashion legend visit http://www.alfredfiandaca.com. Also if you are looking forward to Fashion Week like I am you can find the current schedule at www.bostonfashionweek.com and I will be sure to keep all you "Socially Scene" followers up to date each week!

August 2013 "Socially Scene" Revere Roof Top Fashion Boston Post Gazette Column #49

Socially Scene Reviewed… August is a month I always compare to the holiday season; routine gets put aside being there are so many festive things to do and I tend to over eat outside my diet. This past week was jam packed for me with events and Socially Scene went into overtime.

I received a last minute invitation to a fashion show for last Wednesday at the Revere Hotel's rooftop. I actually got the info through a Facebook invite from Acote Salon on Newbury Street being they were the stylist for the event. I left a message on the invite about my column and would love some contact info. Before I knew it I received an email from Christina K. Pierce, a luxury stylist and owner of Boutique fashion agency who was hosting the event. I have had to embrace the social media movement and what a great thing it can be; within two hours or so I had booked a fashion show for Socially Scene and made plenty of future contacts in high end fashion.

I had never been to the newer and sheik Revere Boston Hotel it and its Roof Top pool were all I expected. It was very classy with all white furniture and the cozy cabanas. There were top hair, fashion and public relations buzzing around before the show. Lily & Migs from Newbury Street were the designs featured for the evening and the focus for the line was "Luxurious prints and bright knits." The show was very well timed with the sun perfectly setting on the models that were from Maggie Inc. It was a short but sweet show and a great way to slide into the fall fashion season.

It just so happens every Wednesday the month of August the Roof top will be hosting a fashion show. You can visit www.RevereHotel.com for more info and if you're excited as I for this fall fashion upon us visit www.christina-pierce.com for upcoming events and shows.

Now I love fashion almost as much as I love being Italian, it's the best! This past weekend the North End hosted their annual Fisherman's feast. I can pin point the exact moment of when my excitement began; I was headed to work on Thursday morning and just as I walk out my door, the street was blocked off and stage being setup.

The Fisherman's feast is a very traditional with the flying of Angels, the procession, and celebrations at the club. The vendors double in size for this event and so did my consumption of eggplant!

I had planned to just talk a little stroll Saturday night to enjoy the fun since it's was louder than my own stereo in the apartment. That was just a silly thought as five minutes in I am with friends and vino. From there I found my way to state Representative Aaron Michlewitz's annual backyard BBQ, then somehow off and sweating to the oldies with generations of all kinds down the Fisherman's Club. I have not had a night of so much fun in months and it was all right out front my door.

Sunday is a day I have come to hold high respect for all members involved. I have done my best to follow the entire procession but that is one long day and I'm not even carrying the saint on my shoulders, just skipping and singing along. The feeling I have while trailing down the North End streets in celebration is hard to describe but joy and honor fit the bill.

All the feasts have their own identity but the Fisherman's flying of the angels is one of a kind. The families, friends, and curious gather around the saint to watch a presentation in Italian by two angels on opposite sides of the streets to be followed by the VIVA chants and a final angel flying down to kiss the saint and end the celebrations.

I am so proud of my heritage and all the clubs of the North End do to preserve it. The feats will end out this weekend and Socially Scene will see you at Saint Anthony's. You can follow me as I post live at Socially Scene on Facebook or @SociallyScene_ twitter.

August 2013 "Socially Scene" - Rose Cherubini Boston Post Gazette Column #39

Socially Scene Reviewed... Last week I was blessed with the opportunity to experience an event honoring one of fashions finest. My editor Pam happens to be in the circle of the socialites and received a special invitation to an exhibition of custom bridal dresses and ball gowns by Italian American fashion designer Rose Cherubini and she brought me!

Our interest was piqued before we were even on the scene with our drive through the South End. It had us in such surprise with the preserved history yet so many things to see and new places to go all from the rebuilding process in Boston.

When we arrived I believe we both spotted Rose as she sat there was a soft presence and pleasant demand. It was hard to believe this woman had just celebrated her 100th birthday when she could pass for not a day over seventy! Pam went over and introduced herself being her rich family history has crossed with generations of designer Cherubini.

Pam and I were both impressed with what a great memory Rose had after putting the pieces together of her affiliation with the Donnarumma family. As Pam and Rose chatted I believe awe, wonderment, admiration were all understatement for how I felt listening to someone so unique. When Pam asked what do you attribute your youth to, Rose's answer was honest and simple, "Work, Work, Work and just keeping busy." After being introduced to me Rose held my hand while continuing to chat with Pam and I could just feel years of a well lived life from the aura surrounding her. The room was filled with family and shortly after Rose was accompanied home by one of her seventeen grandchildren RJ.

The event was being held in celebration of her 100th birthday recently. I couldn't keep my attention focused between just being memorized by a woman I felt so honored to meet or the breathtaking dresses I was surrounded by. I sometimes feel I was meant to of lived back in an era where I could look fabulous all day every day and each dress in the gallery represented that dream.

Pam and I began to sashay from dress to dress when we were intercepted by Joyce Hogan longtime friend of Cherubini. She began to tour us back around and give them most fascinating insight to Rose, her career and accomplishments.

There was a history behind each gown and one by one we learned of the personality traits that have helped create the art work throughout the years. Julia explained; Rose was very playful with her designs, spur of the moment women who is very particular with her designs. It was her way or no way; she would spin you around and took a quick gaze then design a look especially for you. It may not have been what you were looking for in the beginning but was always loved and adored in the end. Also, she genuinely enjoyed measuring real people with curves and length.

Some of her signatures to the styles produced were either a strategically placed rose, her name sewn into the gown or the handpicked jewels that she would travel weekly to New York for. All dresses were authentic, (I saw with my own eyes a legit long stitch inside the dress) and painted with care and she made lots of celebration dresses including one especially for when John Glenn walked on the moon.

She is a woman who is happy as the day is long and spends most of her time these days fantasizing in a room that overlooks the ocean from her house in Wareham. Her hair color is natural and the white tones have been there the full 20 years Julia has known her.

After we parted ways with Julia we ran into a dear friend of Pam's, a new fashion role model for myself and a women that stands out in the industry herself, the one and only Denise Hajar who will be celebrating 30 years of business this fall.

Just as everyone seems to be Denise was also very fond of Rose as well. Denise started out with Cherubini designs and contests that Rose taught her things she could have never learned in school. She mentioned she enjoyed helping out Rose when she was in a jam on an order and loved to hear that she praised the work she produced since it was always just what she was looking for.

I received such insight into a woman who found a way to build a business in a time where it wasn't "proper" for a lady and a family along with it. Although compliments of our guide Julia there is a beautifully written bio on Rose;

Rose Cherubini née Santeusanio was born in Boston, MA in 1913 and currently lives in Wareham, MA. Rose Cherubini Bridals, her first shop, opened in Quincy in 1946. Upon realizing most of the clientele was coming from Boston, Cherubini moved her shop to Newbury Street in 1951 until 1967. She closed to head the bridal and gown departments at Bonwit Teller's Boston outpost, Worth's and Hurwitch Bros. Rose Cherubini Bridals reopened and operated on Clarendon in Boston's Back Bay until the mid-1980s.

In operation for over 40 years, Rose Cherubini's designs gained popularity with a unique style incorporating hand embroidery, jewels, and beads. Her love of painting, color, and texture pushed her works into the realm of art. Ahead of her time, she refined the use of different materials in sync such as fine silk and burlap. She brought brocades into the field and designed coats for her dresses.

Cherubini created custom dresses for many celebrities and notable figures of the time. John Glenn, the 1st American to orbit the earth, requested Cherubini to create the "Orbit Dress" for his wife. The Chandler Burlap Company commissioned a burlap dress to which she responded with a pink burlap cocktail dress, which was photographed for Life Magazine. Rose Cherubini (while raising two sons) mounted several fashion shows around the Boston area including multiple shows at the famous Blinstrub's Nightclub.

Her work was also pictured and featured in articles including the Boston Globe, the Quincy Sun, The Boston Traveller (then known as the Boston Herald), the Patriot Ledger and The Hellenic Chronicle, among others. Her work touched many women and the generations that followed. In order to design a wedding gown, she was allowed access to the union of families. These intimate public moments her work was a part of, attests to her cultural contribution as an Italian American woman. Her designs were worn to major cultural and social events where high society, politics and business met, but also to the most popular nightclubs and dance halls where the moment's best musicians amongst other creative and colorful characters resided. Rose Cherubini's works, prized family possessions, are still worn by daughters and granddaughters to only the most special of events. In addition to the exhibition there will be a catalog developed with photos by Julian Cherubini and a text by Nicole Cherubini.

The gallery presentation was all I imagined it could be and more. The timeless pieces on display, the thrill to meet Rose herself and the glitterati in attendance were enough to keep me excited for months. The gallery will be open during the month of August: Thursdays through Saturdays 11am-6pm, Sundays 12m-5pm, and by appointment. The Samson gallery is located 450 Harrison Avenue/29 Thayer Street, Boston; you can reach them at 617-357-7177 or visit www.samsonprojects.com for more details.

You can follow me @SociallyScene_ or Social Scene FB for more up to the minute events going on in the city.

March 2013 "Socially Scene" Nara Paz at Bond Boston Post Gazette Column #37

Fashion Show Follow up…. Local Fashion Designer Nara Paz reveled here 2013 Spring/Summer collection last week at Bond. The night was filled with stylish celebrities; cocktails and a classic VIP list from Boston were in attendance for this evening of high end fashion!

Nara Paz is a professional success in both graphic and industrial design in her homeland of Brazil and a summa cum laude graduate in fashion design and production in the USA, Nara Paz is now making a notable impression as a high-end fashion designer among peers in New York and beyond. Known for her exquisite designs and attention to detail, Paz has earned industry recognition being selected a finalist in Fashion Group International's 15th Annual Rising Star Awards in February 2012. Her standout gowns and eveningwear, which offer a contemporary perspective on classic silhouettes, have been featured in numerous fashion publications and blogs in the USA and have been worn at the White House, the Grammys, the Oscars, and the Country Music Awards.

The fashion design philosophy of Nara Paz is a commitment to the perfection and equilibrium of shapes, forms, colors, and textures. She is not driven by trends. She prefers to create her own interpretation of a theme or approach incorporating her intuitive artistic vision with wearability, but with an appreciation of what is the acceptable fashion mood of the times. The result is a balanced but evocative approach to design and construction – a reflection of her passion for fine art feminine beauty. She uses unusual textiles, luxurious fabrics and pays extreme attention to details and quality of finish – a level of artisanship that gives her designs an exotic flair and distinctive difference. "I want to become known as someone who designs high-class, high-value clothing for discerning women who have a sense of who they are … to bring out the best in every woman who chooses to wear them." High-Class, High-Value Clothing For the Real You!

Nara's show was held to introduce her current line; Inspired by the lush flora and fauna of Hawaii, Paz translates its tropical hues and rich textures into her Spring/Summer 2013 "Wonderful World" Collection. Citrusy lemons, ginger reds and coral pinks stand out against crisp white cottons and white sheer chiffons accented with gold mini-metallic daisy appliqués. The combination of delicate lace and soft lambskin is seen throughout the collection in ladylike pencil skirts, luxurious tailored Metalassé Lamé dresses, jackets, and separates; necklines and shoulders are touched with youthful grosgrain. A relaxed yet sophisticated maxi-jumpsuit in Georgette Silk allows for an effortless day-to-nighttime transition and is joined by vibrant pink and red Dahlia-print dresses with sheer chiffon overlays.

When I spoke with Nara, I asked where here focus was and what the highlight of the show was for her personally. "Our "Spring Wonderful World Fashion Show" and Pop-Up store was a combination of a sample sale and exhibition of our finest Couture Collection. We wanted to have a very intimate and sophisticated atmosphere and were very happy with the outcome clients such as Kayla Harrison Judo Olympic gold medalist and socialite Yolanda Cellucci shows their support as well enjoyed the show." She mentioned, "Also Book author of "Fashion Design, Referenced "- Emily Banis - who also was present at the show said "The show was fantastic and so in touch with fashion's zeitgeist". The high lights of the show were the exclusive NARA PAZ Flower print inspired by the lush Flora and Fauna of Hawaii - MAXI- JUMP a combination of Maxi dress and Jump suit one of NARA PAZ spring best sales." Nara also expressed her gratitude that, "The show could not have been done without our sponsors; Beucage Salon, Fashion Moi, Beauty Refined, Bond Restaurant and Lounge and Langham Hotel."

Nara Paz Design International is the design house co-owned by designer Nara Lucia Paz-Gain (Nara Paz) and her husband Dennis Terrance Gain (Dennis Gain) for the design and manufacture of high-quality high-value women's clothing under the brand-name Nara Paz. Nara Paz Design International is a wholly owned operating unit of Vision First Corporation, a family owned company that also specializes in consulting for startups, turnarounds, and international business development.

Nara's line is versatile and making its way around the world. Some of the high end boutiques where her styles can be seen are; NEW YORK, Anik 1122 Madison Avenue, New York, NY www.anikny.com. LONG ISLAND, Fifth On Main 125-131 Main Street, Bay Shore, NY www.fifthonmain.com. AU/SYDNEY and NZ/AUCKLAND.

NARA PAZ High End Designs first Annual sale will be running until June 1st only by appointments in her Boston studio located 10 Tower Office Park, Suite 401, Woburn MA. To view more of Nara's luscious looks for this season and one's past you can visit her website at www.narapaz.com, follow her on FB at Facebook.com/narapaz, Twitter at twitter.com/NARAPAZDESIGN or contact her at the store for a private show of your own at 617-365-7948.

January 2013 "Socially Scene" Mario Testino Shows in Boston Boston Post Gazette Column #18

Fashion Icon in Boston…. With the holidays in the past and new year begun a 2013 spring collection will be upon us shortly and what a better way to get into the spirit than visiting an exhibit by a fashions most celebrated snapper. His career spans more than 30 years and has shot hundreds of covers for various magazines including Vogue, and worked with the likes of Kate Moss, Gisele Bundchen and Naomi Campbell before they gained celebrity status. He has brought his first ever U.S. exhibit "In Your Face" to The Museum of Fine Arts here in Boston where his photography will be on display through February 3rd.

Mario Testino, a Peruvian fashion photographer, whose work has been featured in magazines such as Vogue and Vanity Fair, eclipsed when he was chosen by Princess Diana for her 1997 Vanity Fair photo shoot. His US debut brought top of the line in the fashion industry, all in one place to honor his work. "It's very interesting for me to come to a city like Boston because it's not a city that I go to very often" said Testino, "And to see the queues of cars outside and the whole enthusiasm about coming to my show, it's quite touching." For the opening in back in November Testino was joined by Vogue's Anna Wintour, A-list model Gisele Bündchen, Victoria's Secret model Alessandra Ambrosio and more as they took in the museum's "In Your Face" and "British Royal Portrait" photos. While everyone was full of anticipation for the new exhibit, Gisele was more than most. The glowing and radiant Bündchen couldn't have been more excited to have Testino's exhibit in her new hometown. "You know, I love Boston. I've been living here for quite some time now and when Mario reached out to me and said, "I'm going to do an exhibit in the Museum of Boston and you have to come," my reply was simple, I'm there!"

Queen of fashion and Vogue's Editor in Chief, Anna Wintour has worked with Testino for most of her life. "He just loves life and I think that really comes through in his pictures." At the opening of Testino's exhibition, Wintour explained what made him one of her go-to photographers. She told Fashionista, "I think that for celebrities and people they can sometimes be insecure about the way they present themselves. I think that one of his great skills as a photographer is making people look as beautiful and extraordinary as they possibly could." To prove her point she mentions, "unflattering passport photos will haunt most of us for a decade" so to ensure hers was picture-perfect the Vogue editor-in-chief, recruited "Testino" to shoot hers.

With such a worldly and decorated photographer visiting this exhibit one can only imagine the beauty it will bring. The Mario Testino exhibit will be on display through February 3, 2013 at the Museum of Fine Arts Boston located at 465 Huntington Avenue Boston. You can contact the front office at 617-267-9300 for hours and prices.

Chapter Thirteen – 2012

"A Women should be two things, classy and fabulous" —Coco Chanel

10-17-2012 "Socially Scene" Style Fixx Preview Boston Post Gazette Column #10

Come and Get Your Style Fixx…. Just when you thought all of this seasons fashion shows had come to an end, Boston went and saved the best for last. Now celebrating 11 Years of events Style Fixx will be having their annual beauty boutique on October 24-25th at the Boston Center for the arts. With fashion, beauty, fitness, cocktails, and home decor it is definitely a show you don't want to miss.

Guests are invited to dive into the new interactive boutique experience at StyleFixx 2012! They will be introducing "Indie Incubator," their independent designer marketplace. You will have the opportunity to consult with fifty-five independent professional designers and shop their fall 2012 lines. Also receive a famous STYLEFIXX Swag Bag Tote® stuffed with spectacular products including; Tei Spa Essentials, Zico & more, Sip complimentary Barefoot Wine & Champagne. For all you single or soon to be off the market ladies there will be a Jeweler's Building Lounge where you can design you dream engagement ring. What's a little shopping without some relaxation, you can enjoy a complimentary massage by Massage Envy along with hair and facial treatments by Jose Eber and Dermalogica. All this cachous can wear you out but not to worry there are treats, Sample Haru Sushi, and delicious cupcakes compliments of Bad Kat Kupkakes. This busy event is offering shoppers an evening of product sampling, hair & beauty treatments, complimentary champagne, appetizers, music and more.

As so often fashion goes hand in hand with charities this show follows the trend. Proceeds will benefit, One Angel Foundation & Susan G. Komen. "The quality of the shoppers was outstanding. I nearly sold out my line on the very first night!" –Kara Janx, Project Runway Designer. With things calmed down from Boston Fashion Week, it's time for Boston's largest fashion and beauty event. StyleFixx is here!

So mark your calendar for Wednesday October 24th and Thursday October 25th. Style Fixx will be taking place at the Boston Center for the Arts on 539 Tremont Street. Shopping hours will be from 5-10pm. For more information or to purchase tickets, visit www.stylefixx.com.

10-29-2012 "Socially Scene" Style Fixxed Boston Post Gazette Column #8

I Got Style Fixxed…. A few weeks back I wrote a preview to an event being held at the Boston Center for the Arts on Wednesday and Thursday of last week. The event coordinator Ana Walker was so gracious to extend an invitation. When I arrived there was a classy red carpet walkway with a brand new car being given away, it was then I knew this was going to be a great time. The shopping hours were from 5-10pm and I figured if I was there by six, all should go well. They labeled it a shopping extravaganza and that it was. With what I thought was a nice quite time to arrive the lines were already wrapping around corners and ladies jumping from booth to booth. Through most the night I found the longest of lines to be for the complimentary glass of wine or champagne from Yellowtail Vineyards and of course the onsite salons offering free services. Iconic member of the salon industry Johnny Marchio from Rock Paper Scissors Salon was on hand doing hair himself to promote his new venture on Newbury street. Hairo, is an innovative wash and blow-dry only salon. It has become a high demand and such a great idea for that quick fix. I couldn't pass up the opportunity to get my hair done by such a well-known stylist that while waiting I got a chance to chat with his receptionist, Michele. She mentioned, "The concept of a blow-dry bar is awesome. Being right on Newbury we have women who are in town on business and come in for a blow-dry that will last them through the meetings. We even have a great following of women who will come in for a session that will last them a week." She explained to me the little ticks of the trade on making it to the gym and keeping that luscious blow-dry intact. Sorry ladies can't reveal those secrets here but Johnny and his Hario team will be happy to. You can find them at 135 Newbury, call to book an apt 617-266-1199, or check all they have to offer at www.washandblowdry.com. As I continued to travel through the room each booth I passed seemed to offer so much. L'ecole Nuit was a couture lingerie line, The European Wax Center was offering free eyebrow service, and Finale desserts were there tempting with their flowerless gluten free chocolate as well as Bad Kat KupKakes and in my opinion the best in Boston. Classic designer studious like Candice Wu on Albany Street Boston had their finest to offer yet not everyone was Boston based there was Jarm knitwear designs all the way from Russia and Confabulous Cases for all your cell phone needs that are web based only. With over fifty-five independent designers, the fantastic StyleFixx tote you receive, the free facial, hair and make-up services available and most importantly proceeds benefiting One Angel Foundation & Susan G. Komen it's an event you don't want to miss next fall in Boston. Although the show has set sail to LA, Style Fixx will return for its 12th consecutive show to Boston next year. You can check dates or even see if you can catch it in another major city at www.stylefixx.com.

October 2012 "Socially Scene" Wrapping Up bosFW Boston Post Gazette Column #6

Wrapping up Boston Fashion Week.... With all the past week festivities and sneak peeks into the hottest lines the ICA will close the show with their presentation of "Fashion Forward" on Friday Oct 5th from 5-10pm. It will be an amazing evening of art and creativity showcasing some of Boston's most magnificent boutiques, stylists, and designers. View lavish styles by Louis Boston, Riccardi, Serenella, Turtle, and Uniform—all inspired by the rich color and vibrant pattern found in the work of Brazilian artists Os Gemeos. Hair and make-up will be created by industry icon Salon Mario Russo.

Fresh from their debut of new collections at Boston Fashion Week, designers Michael De Paulo and Tonya Mezrich of mike&ton and designer Daniela Corte join ICA First Fridays: Fashion Forward to introduce styles from their Spring/Summer 2013 collections. Editors from the culture magazine Bad Day will also be making an appearance to promote the launch of their latest issue, featuring the designer agnès b.

A local favorite will be on site putting the finishing touch on each outstanding style. Salon Mario Russo will be using their expert technique to compliment theses designer concepts. Mario Russo has been a part of the New England beauty industry since 1990 when he opened his first salon right here in Boston on Newbury Street. Mario's focuses on attention to detail that will create a life of sophistication and glamour. "Everyone has the potential to be beautiful with the right cut and color. It is a matter of selecting a stylist who is intuitive and has been trained to craft a hairstyle that expresses your personal style along with complimenting your lifestyle." – Mario Russo

The runway comes to the ICA for ICA First Fridays in the opener of where art goes overtime. On the first   Friday of the month there can be guest DJs, live performance, gallery talks, specialty drinks, and more. For more information, visit http://www.icaboston.org/programs/first-fridays/. Tickets for the fashion show on Oct 5th can Tickets can be purchased at https://buy.icaboston.org or by called the ICA Box   Office at 617-478-3103.

September 2012 "Socially Scene" Boston Fashion Week Preview Boston Post Gazette Column #5

Boston Fashion Week….. Beginning Thursday September 27th and continuing through Thursday October 6th the spotlight will shine on local designers as the most fashionable Bostonians celebrate "The Tent" at Boston Fashion Week. During an Opening Night Gala attendees will be sipping themed cocktails, basking in canapés and food stations from Executive Chef Rachel Klein of Mandarin Oriental, Boston. Guests can also enjoy a special appearance from Fern Mallis, widely credited as the creator of New York Fashion Week. The program will honor Fern Mallis' role as an industry icon as well as the work of Big Brothers Big Sisters of Massachusetts Bay for their contributions to the incredible work of mentoring local youths. The tent will be located outside the Mandarin Oriental Boston just off Newbury Street. To purchase tickets, travel directions and show times visit http://thetent.eventbrite.com There will be multiple events daily around the city and you can go to bostonfashionweek.com to see the full listing but here are a few highlights scheduled;

WAR and FEMALE DRESS…Now through October 10, 2012, Produced by the Lasell Fashion Collection. During WWII rationing was a serious issue and fashions evolved around this concept. Patriotism and austerity were two of the most important aspects of dress. Restrictions were considered supportive of the war effort and one could use clothing to show devoted patriotism. Featuring British CC41 & American 1940's Dress. Hours: Monday-Friday, 9am-5pm Lasell College 1844 Commonwealth Ave For more information: jcarey@lasell.edu

COLLEGE FASHION WEEK….Saturday, September 29 6m at The Estate 1 Boylston Place (The Alley), Boston MA. It will be sponsored by HerCampus.com and U by Kotex. This high-impact show focuses on student styled designs modeled by actual students, featuring unique looks that define their vision in the classroom, the gym, for the weekend and in formal attire, including student designers from local colleges and universities. For more information: windsor@hercampus.com this event is free.

THE LAUNCH.... Sunday September 30th in the Tent at 2pm. Fashion Group International of Boston in partnership with Boston Fashion Week is the power behind THE LAUNCH, an event that puts the a force of established industry professionals alongside five new designers to watch. Each designer chosen is a recent graduate from one of the many well-known fashion design programs in the region and will show a capsule collection as part of this group presentation. Learn more about this production visit http://thetent.eventbrite.com

Monday, October 1

On the COPLEY CATWALK ..... Monday, October 1 6pm door will open at Copley Place - Center Court 100 Huntington Avenue, Boston MA. At 6:15pm things will get underway with the Student Show: School of Fashion Design a -Retail fashion show highlighting this seasons latest trends! Copley Place hosts back to back fashion shows featuring high end retailers, and special student design runway presentations by local fashion design schools. This is open to the public.

THE ART of DRESSING WELL: DENISE HAJJAR .... Tuesday October 2nd at the Fairmont Copley Plaza-Oval Room Boston 138 St. James Avenue Boston, MA 02116. The show will start at 6pm yet a VIP reception is scheduled for 5:45 to prepare for the fantastic unveiling of Denises creations. Her 2012 Fall Fashion Show is to benefit Dress for Success is sponsored by Cunard Liner and the Fairmont Copley Plaza Hotel. The mission of Dress for Success is to promote the economic independence of disadvantaged women by providing professional attire, a network of support and the career development tools to help women thrive in work and in life. To help celebrate this occasion the event will have some celebrity faces. Hosting will be Shayna Seymour of WCVB-TV 5's "Chronicle." Special guest models include: Lois Cornell, Carol Fulp, Joanne Jaxtimer, Karen Kaplan, and Laura Lamere. With proceeds from the show going to the dress for success organization there is also a chance for guests to walk away with more than just the newest trends. A drawing of the raffle will take place at approximately 7:50 to win the GRAND PRIZE provided by Cunard Ocean Liners, A SEVEN-DAY TRANSATLANTIC CROSSING ABOARD QUEEN MARY 2. Additional Raffle Prizes and Donors Include: AAA Southern New England - Samsonite Luggage Package & AAA

Gift Bag, Antico Forno - dinner for 4, Beantown Bootcamp - week of free classes, Clarisonic - sonic cleansing machine, Ensemble - gift certificate, J.McLaughlin - Aken tote bag, Local Charm - gift certificate, Sara Campbell - gift certificate, Sedurre - gift certificate, Skin Innovations Skin Care & Spa - gift certificate, Stages of Beauty - starter kit of skin care products, Terramia Ristorante - dinner for 4...and more! The prizes are top of the line so make sure to buy your tickets for a chance to win. You can purchase tickets online to save time, or they will be available at registration the night of the event.

Tickets for the show can be purchased at http://dfsbfashionshow2012.eventbrite.com. Students will have Standing room only and must present valid student ID at door – Free.

SHOP for GOOD with JIMMY CHOO and STILISTA|BOSTO...... Thursday, October 4 Copley Place 100 Huntington Ave. #107 Boston, MA. The entertainment will begin at 6pm and is presented by Jimmy Choo and Stilista|Boston. This is a one of a kind private shopping event with complimentary stylist services by Stilista|Boston's styling team, with 10% of all sales benefitting Boston Medical Center's Women's Cancer Survivorship Programming. Guests are invited to enjoy cocktails and catered refreshments while you browse the sensational fall / winter shoe and handbag collection. This is a private fund-raising event that is by invitation only. To request an invite, please contact info@stilistaboston.com or 617.965.2500.

CELEBRATING WOMEN FASHION...... Thursday October 4th, 8pm at 3025 Washington Street, Boston MA. The Celebrating Women Fashion Show will air live on channel COMCAST23/RCN 83. We will feature 5 local designers and is presented by LookingFabz. Space is limited. RSVP Required: contactus@lookingfabz.com

LISTEN TO YOUR BODY FASHION FUNDRAISER....... Friday October 5th, 6pm Ray and Joan Salvation Army Kroc Center, 650 Dudley Street, Boston MA. This show will be presented by Musu-kulla Massaquoi and Breast Cancer Awareness Benefit to Raise Funds for the Dana-Farber Cancer Institute's Mammography Van which Services the Boston Metro Area. There will be Fashion, Poetry, & Silent Auction also featuring designers Aminata Dakowa, Babatunde Ajiboye, Nadrah Ra Bey, Natural Solutions,

Nigel Ramsay, Pelenge, and Ty Scott. To purchase tickets for the presentation visit http://thebeginningoflove.eventbrite.com

Performer.com Models & Talent Magazine's SHOWCASE & PHOTO SHOOT……. Friday October 5th, 10pm at Cure Lounge 246 Tremont Street, Boston MA. This exceptional show is presented by Boston Fashion Awards 2013 and will include live indoor/outdoor photo shoot with luxury vehicles (weather permitting) & designer showcase. It will also be featuring designers Samuel Vartan, and Isabel Originals with hair & makeup provided by Indra Salon. It will be free before 11pm and for more information contact: info@Performer.com or visit the website: http://www.bostonfashionawards.com

6th ANNUAL BOSTON FASHION WEEK CELEBRATION PARTY…….. Saturday October 6th, 10:30 pm at Bar 10 at Westin Copley Hotel 10 Huntington Avenue, Boston MA. This social affair will be one of the closing for Boston's fashion week and is sure to be a compliment to all the festivities the 2012 event has held. It will celebrate this year's most stylish Boston Fashion Week party with the runway models, fashion designers, stylists and photographers that made Boston Fashion Week 2012 possible. To purchase tickets, see listing for and directions you can visit http://bfwparty12.eventbrite.com.

10-10-2012 "Around Town" Bling in Boston, Sondra Celli Boston Post Gazette Column #4

Bling in Boston…… Sondra Celli a Boston-based fashion designer who is taking over the spotlight with her newest show "Bling it On" premiering September 20th at 10/9c. Famous for her animated designs on TLC's "My Big Fat American Gypsy Wedding" this series focuses on the not so conservative side of New England as all three episodes are based here in Massachusetts.

With a spin off series she thought could never be yet due to the huge response from her first show, Sondra welcomes viewers into her business. Living in a Waltham world which is all about fashion, design, and bling, Sondra and her team create the most lavish of designer dreams. When speaking with Saundra she was very passionate about saying," It's not being materialist with the cloths; (since most use Swarovski crystals) it's about being happy, loving their cloths. Bling makes people feel great!" She also had a lot of enthusiasm with the fact it's not just gypsys this time around. Stepping into the world of bling are; a rhinestone baby carriage, drag queen, ballroom dancer, an order for a neon wedding dress, also Brittney Bang and pup who is an owner of a Newbury street dog store. Yet the most exciting and challenging was the chance to bling her very own mother, Yolanda.

With Celli being such a perfectionist and always believing that more is a must, makes sure every outfit that comes through her doors is absolutely immaculate, down to every last detail. Always welcoming the fascinating orders with an open mind Celli takes viewers into her workroom to experience her visions, challenges, and successes from every outfit. Sondra, along with her seamstresses and clever "blingettes" manage to pull it together and get every job done regardless of the difficult designs and stiff time restraint.

With the show airing every Thursday here is a little bit to look forward to from each episode courtesy of TLC; "A Neon Wedding Dress!", premieres September 20 at 10/9c. Dressmaker Sondra Celli and team work around the clock to make a steampunk vision come to life, a blinged out birthday dress fit for a princess, a classy yet playful look for pet store owners and their dog, and a neon wedding dress for a Vegas bride! "The Zipper Just Split!" premieres September 27 at 10/9c. Sondra Celli's skills are tested when a self-proclaimed tomboy wants design control over her gown; a cancer-survivor is pretty in pink when she asked to be blush; a blinged-out gypsy stroller is ready to roll; a drag queen diva has a wardrobe malfunction! "The Craziest Request Yet!" Premieres October 4 at 10/9c. Designer Sondra Celli finds herself trying to please some very opinionated clients: a bride-to-be and a pushy maid of honor, an aspiring singer with her shot in the spotlight, a ballroom dancer with an overly critical partner, and her pickiest client of all - her mother!

Reality television can be such an extraordinary thing when it gives you the opportunity to dive into a world like this. Sondra and team take fashion and the trails of a designer to a whole new level. Be sure to tune into the premiere on Sept 20th and support our local rising star.

September 2012 "Around Town" Fashion Night Out Follow Up Boston Post Gazette #3

Fashion Night Out Follow Up……. September 6th from Manhattan to Milan, Atlanta to Australia, the afterhours shopping extravaganza Fashion's Night Out, with stores in over five hundred cities nationwide, Newbury Street had a show of its own. Boston participated in its second year of the event and after being voted "worst dressed city" by GQ magazine the city decided it was time to show the world what the Hub has to offer.

Mayor Menino kicked off the event on center stage at six. With live bands like Sweet tooth and the sugar babies, DJs like Boston's own Frank White spinning out-front Converse also herb chambers displaying over 80 dream cars through six blocks of Newbury there was more to see than just a shopping spree. Some of the sponsors included Kimpton Hotels "Nine Zero," City Sorts, Reebok cross-fit and fix your feet to name just a few.

Most every store had some sort of deal or giveaway to promote during the festivities. Bella Bridesmaid was handing out a cocktail to anyone searching for that perfect gown; Salon Acote gave a free $30 gift card with a purchase of a $100 one. Ben Sherman went over the top with "shirteliers" roaming the streets in a classy top hat look letting guests know they were not only offering a surprise gift but also a complimentary cocktail. Now the longest line I saw that just continued to grow was for Georgetown cupcakes, it was a mob for the runway velvet cupcake that was being given away.

Not all in show were actual stores on Newbury Street; there were online shops as well. Pretty Divas had one of a kind dresses and is an online store based out of Leominster. Style fix another online business where both "subletting" for the night through spaces like real estate companies willing to help out with the event.

After strutting the street, chatting with the businesses, and seeing the fun filled entertainment it's safe to say Boston's Fashion Night Out was a success.

September 2012 "Around Town" Denise Hajjar Preview Boston Post Gazette Column #2

Fashion for a Cause....... Local fashion designer Denise Hajjar's presents her 2012 Fall Fashion Show "The Art of Dressing Well" Tuesday October 2nd, 2012 Fairmont Copley Plaza Hotel 6:00pm / Oval Room. In her well-known style, the proceeds from the show are going to local Boston charity "Dress for Success."

Boston native with her studio right where she grew up in the South End, Hajjar has spent thirty plus years "donating" to fashion. Coming from a background in the field, her grandmother was a designer in Damascus, Syria, and her grandfather a patternmaker and dress factory owner from Beirut, Lebanon. Denise has established herself as a top designer and March of 2006, was approached by the Fairmont Copley Plaza Hotel, who was looking for someone "authentically Boston" to be their "Designer-in-Residence".

 Denise's philosophy, "Giving back should be the rule, not the exception." Hajjar's fashion shows are always tied in with a charity of sorts. Prior events were linked with St. Jude Children's Research Hospital and this one coming up Dress for Success. When I asked Hajjar what she was working on next she giggled and said, "Getting the show done. So much work goes into these, hair make-up, models, music." With her status rising in the industry year after year, Boston is a lucky city to have a local work so hard and give so much back.

The mission of Dress for Success is to promote the economic independence of disadvantaged women by providing professional attire, a network of support and the career development tools to help women thrive in work and in life. Founded in New York City in 1997, Dress for Success is an international not-for-profit organization offering services designed to help our clients find jobs and remain employed. Each Dress for Success client receives one suit when she has a job interview and can return for a second suit or separates when she finds work. Dress for Success has served more than 650,000 women around the world. All Dress for Success organizations are not-for-profit entities. You can learn more about the program at www.dressforsuccess.org/boston.

Tickets for the fashion show on Oct 2nd 2012 can be purchased on Denise's site at www.denisehajjar.com or you can stop by her store for more details at the Fairmont Copley Plaza 138 St. James Avenue, Boston or call 617-927-5990.

October 2024- Denise Hajjar Sets the Standard for bosFW Scene&Style Magazine Issue #91

November 2024 Boston Fashion Awards – May 2025 Scene&Style Magazine Issue #98

November 2024 Mass Fashion Week Finale – April 2025 Scene&Style Magazine Issue #97

November 2024 Boston Fashion Icon Awards Show – March 2025 Scene&Style Magazine Issue #96

October 2024 Boston Caribbean Fashion Week Closing Show – February 2025 Scene&Style Magazine Issue #95

October 2024 bosFW Closing "Glam Slam" Scene&Style Magazine

October 2024 bosFW Everybody Belongs – January 2025 Scene&Style Magazine Issue #94

October 2024 House Fashion Week Closing Show – December Scene&Style Magazine Issue #93

October 2024 NH Fashion Week Debut– November Scene&Style Magazine Issue #92

October 2024 VAVA Fashionably LATE bosFW Preview Scene&Style Magazine

October 2024 Fashioning Success: The Intersection of Entrepreneurship and Design Scene&Style Highlight

9-20-2024 Our Girl Linda Celebrates Cellucci 10-11-2024 Boston Post Gazette

September 2024 - An Infinite Evening of Coco Chanel Scene&Style Magazine Issue #90

August 2024 Swim Boston on Rooftop Runway - Scene&Style Magazine Issue #89

July 2024 bosFW and Boston Bid Present an Open Runway - Scene&Style Magazine Issue #88

June 2024 Hajjar's Seasonal Must Haves Hit the Marina Bay Runway - Scene&Style Magazine Issue #87

April 2024 Living Arts Boston, Fashion's Finest on the Seaport Runway - Scene&Style Magazine Issue #86

March 2024 Retiring Off the Mic, the One and Only DJ Sterling Golden Scene&Style Magazine Issue #85

February 2024 Ferrari Red Set the Tone for Fashionably Late Scene&Style Magazine Issue #84

January 2024 Simpson's Collection Shows Vibrant Color Pops - Scene&Style Magazine Issue #83

Chapter Two – 2023

"What you wear is how you present yourself to the world, especially today, when human contacts are so quick. Fashion is instant language."
—Miuccia Prada

December 2023 Joe Malaika's Focused Fashion for the Everyday Warrior - Scene&Style Magazine Issue #82

November 2023 Denise Hajjar Collection Dons Winter Must Haves - Scene&Style Magazine Issue #81

October 2023 United in Style, Fashion for a Cause Hit the Runway - Scene&Style Magazine Issue #80

September 2023 Our Girl Linda Dance Party - Scene&Style Magazine Issue #79

August 2023 Boston Barbie Glittered the Omni Rooftop Runway - Scene&Style Magazine Issue #79

July 2023 Caribbean Catwalk Showed Bold and Bright - Scene&Style Magazine Issue #78

June 2023 Fashion's Future Dashed the Open Runway - Scene&Style Magazine Issue #77

May 2023 Yolanda Cellucci The Glitz and Glam of Fashion - Scene&Style Magazine Issue #77

April 2023 / December 2022 Show Date, Designer Joe Malaika Drops SS23 Collection - Scene&Style Magazine Issue #76

March 2023 A Fashionable Legend Honored - Scene&Style Magazine Issue #75

February 2023 BogoSplit Showcasing Across Boston - Scene&Style Magazine Issue #74

January 2023 / September 2022 bosFW AGEISM: CULTIVATING CONVERSATION - Scene&Style Magazine Issue #73

Chapter Three – 2022

**"Give a girl the right kind of shoes and she can rule the world." —
Marilyn Monroe**

December 2022 Slope Style Revealed Fashionably Late at the Liberty - Scene&Style Magazine Issue #72

November 2022 bosFW Hajjar's Preview to Fashion Week Set a Standard - Scene&Style Magazine Issue #71

October 2022 Deep Camel Leather Stuns at Boston Caribbean Fashion Week - Scene&Style Magazine Issue #70

September 2022 Our Girl Linda's Runway Charity Show Lit Up the Dance Floor - Scene&Style Magazine Issue #69

Chapter Four- 2021

"One is never over-dressed or under-dressed with a Little Black Dress."
—Karl Lagerfeld

December 2021 Malaika Dons Excessive Fashion - Scene&Style Magazine Issue #54

November 2021 Vartan W21 Collection Debuted at Henderson House Scene&Style Magazine Issue #53

October 2021 bosFW Bianchi Showed an Essence of Spray Style - Scene&Style Magazine

October 2021 bosFW Hajjar Hosts First Ever Boston Fashion Week Show on the Bay Scene&Style Magazine Issue #52

September 2021 bosFW THE CUE Opens Fashionably Late - Scene&Style Magazine

September 2021 Vartan Reveals Deep Bold Expression in his Latest Collection - Scene&Style Magazine

September 2021 New England Fashion Week - Scene&Style Magazine Issue #51

August 2021 Shaco Couture Collection Highlights Wilderness Looks Scene&Style Magazine Issue #50

July 2021 DreamRose - New England Runways Have Re-Opened

July 2021 Hajjar's SS21 Collection Hits the Boardwalk Scene&Style Magazine Issue #49

June 2021 Kreyol Presents "Freedom : Standing on Legacy Scene&Style Magazine Issue #48

February 2021 Gucci Shows Logo Canvas with Retro 70s looks Scene&Style Magazine Issue #44

January 2021 Spring Fashion in Store from Versace Scene&Style Magazine Issue #43

Chapter Five – 2020

"Don't be into trends. Don't make fashion own you, but you decide what you are, what you want to express by the way you dress and the way to live." —Gianni Versace

December 2020 Support Local this Holiday Season with our Gift Guide Scene&Style Magazine Issue #42

10-4-2020 "A Night Reminiscent of Paris" Denise Hajjar Scene&Style Magazine Issue #41

August 2020 Italian Eye Wear, an Everyday Accessory SCENE Magazine /Scene&Style Magazine Issue #40

June 2020 Italian Time Pieces Lead the Way SCENE Magazine / Scene&Style Magazine Issue #39

May 2020 Fashions Front Line Hero's Aspiring Magazine Scene&Style Magazine Issue #38

April 2020 Thog Street Style Is the Supreme Brand of OKC Scene&Style Magazine Issue #37

February 2020 A Fearless Leader in Boston Fashion Scene&Style Magazine Issue #36

January 2020 Snow Style from the Lodge to the Mountain – Scene&Style Magazine Issue #35

Chapter Six – 2019

"Style is something each of us already has, all we need to do is find it."
—Diane von Furstenberg

November 2019 / December SCENE Winter Issue How Italy has Influenced the World of Fashion – Scene&Style Magazine Issue #34

October 2019 "A Fashion Finale Like No Other – Denise Hajjar" Scene&Style Magazine Issue# 33

October 2019 bosFW "Boston Fashion Week Opening Celebrating 25 Years" Scene&Style Magazine

September 2019 bosFW 9-24-2019 "Boston Fashion Week Opening Celebrating 25 Years" Scene&Style Magazine Issue #32

August 2019 Rooftop Fashion Rocks the Revere Scene&Style Magazine Issue #31

July 2019 Angela Timas Heats Up Summer at Steeped in Style Scene&Style Magazine Issue #30

May 2019 Get dolled up for Queer Me Out with Carmen Carrera Scene&Style Magazine Issue #27

May 2019 Scene&Style Magazine - FGI Boston Set Up Camp for the Annual MET Gala

April 2019 The Dance Party of the Decade for "Our Girl Linda" Scene&Style Magazine Issue #26

March 2019 The Space is Set for Designer Denise Hajjar at her new location Scene&Style Magazine

Issue #25

February 2019 Scene&Style Magazine - Denise Hajjar to Host Cocktail Celebration in New Location

February 2019 Scene&Style Magazine - Hajjar Hits the NYC Fashion Week Runway

January 2019 Scene&Style Magazine Issue #24 - Boston Fashion Celebrates Their Finest

Chapter Seven – 2018

"Dress shabbily and they remember the dress; dress impeccably and they notice the woman." —Coco Chanel

November 2018 Scene&Style Magazine Issue #23 - Slope Style in the She Shed

November 2018 Scene&Style Issue #22 (10-6-2018) bosFW "The Real Oliver Thomas Shows Fashionably Late -Styled by KB Fashion Productions Collaborating; Angelica Timas, Simone Simon, Irina Gorbman, Lindsay Tia, were Jevela Jewelry, T. Jazelle, Tracy Belben"

October 2018 bosFW Scene&Style Magazine - Roxbury Faith Restored Through Fashion

10-5-2018 bosFW Scene&Style Magazine "Reina Valentina Makes a Fashionable Debut"

December 2018 Scene&Style Magazine Issue #21 (10-3-2018) bosFW "Hajjar Ruled the Runway Once Again" – Denise Hajjar

10-3-2018 bosFW Scene&Style Magazine "Lasell's Fashion Creativity was Put to the Test- Presented by KB Fashion Productions"

10-1-2018 bosfw Scene&Style Magazine "Boston Fashion Week Opening-The Power of Women, The Future of Boston Fashion Featuring; Gina deWolfe of deWolfe Leather Goods, Cecile Thieulin of Simone Simon, Meghan Doyle Tallulah and Poppy, Joelle Fontaine of I Am Kréyol, Graciela Rivas Leslin of Graciela Rivas Collection, Melina Cortes-Nmili of lalla bee"

9-31-2018 bosFW Scene&Style Magazine "MadeINcubator, Panelists; Gretta Monahan, Leah Gardner, Kathy Benharris, Elisha Daniels, David Josef, Anna Foster, Janet Howard"

9-30-2018 bosFW Scene&Style Magazine "Fashion on Fire Featuring; Madeline Ventresca, Lalla Bee, Jaclyn Robichaud Doyle, Em Watson, Yetta Procope, KHANGLE"

October 2018 bosFW "Bianchi Gets Steeped in Style" Scene&Style Magazine Issue #21

September 2018 bosFW Scene&Style Magazine TANGOELLA gets Steeped in Style

September 2018 Boston Fashion Week Honors Linda Cole - Petrosian Scene&Style Magazine Issue #20

August 2018 Caribbean Fashion Week Lights up the Ink Block Scene&Style Magazine Issue #19

June 2018 Men's European Fashion Comes to Boston's Newbury Street Scene&Style Magazine

Issue #18

May 2018 Peach and B/SPOKE Teamed Up for Fashionable Charity Ride Style Scene&Style Magazine Issue #18

April 2018 Denise Hajjar Shows at Steeped in Style Scene&Style Magazine Issue #17

March 2018 LaFauci and Sarian Pair Up for a Seductive Fashionably Late Scene&Style Magazine Issue #16

February 2018 Love Fashion and Song in an Operatic Evening Scene&Style Magazine Issue #15

January 2018 Consolidation is the New Black Scene&Style Magazine Issue #14

"My relationship with fashion has always been that each of us stars in our own movies and costumes ourselves to play the part we want. You take blouses and jeans and dresses, and you put them together, and they tell your story." - Marc Jacobs

December 2017 SKEA Hit the Fashionably Late Slopes with Ski Wear Scene&Style Magazine Issue #13

December 2017 Scene&Style Magazine Boston Fashion Awards 2017

November 2017 David Josef, Fashion to the Rescue Scene&Style Magazine Issue #12

October 2017 Scene&Style Magazine bosfw LaFauci Shines on Color in Couture Runway

October 31st 2017 Scene&Style Magazine Annual Halloween Gala was Boston's Best Bash

10-26-2017 Scene&Style Magazine "Vogu Featuring; Josefa Disilva, Allexandra Bianchi, Shaco Couture, Janabay, Yannery Burgos, Ann Marie LaFauci"

10-26-2017 Scene&Style Magazine "Fashion on Fire Featuring; Maddy Ventresca, LaFille Colete, Tina Melo, Marilla Designs, Daniel Hernandez, Solo Jubin"

10- 19-2017 Scene&Style Magazine "THE CUE Collection Marveled the Liberty Runway" - Lindsay Tia Styled by KB Fashion Productions

10-13-2017 Scene&Style Magazine "What They Didn't Teach You in Fashion School, Presented by Jay Calderín"

10-12-2017 Scene&Style Magazine "Carbon Concepts" showing the "Elements of Fall Beauty – Styled by KB Fashion Productions"

Chapter Nine – 2016

"After all, computers crash, people die, relationships fall apart. The best we can do is breathe and reboot" - Carrie Bradshaw

December 2016 In Depth With Angelica Timas Scene&Style Magazine Issue #1

November 27, 20242016 Scene&Style Magazine - Benharris Brings the Runway Back to the Boston.com Ski and Snowboard Expo

10-16-2016 Scene&Style Magazine - Anne Fontaine Brought Brazilian Style to Boston by KB Fashion Productions

10-14-2016 Scene&Style Magazine - Official Boston Fashion Week Opening Hosted by A Mavens World Hosted by Gustavo Leon and Eve Marcelli

10-5-2016 Scene&Style Magazine - Kelly Dempsey Kicked off Boston Fashion Week 2016

9-28-2016 Scene&Style Magazine - Angelica Timas Closes Boston Fashion Week

7-2016 boscFW Caribbean Dreams at the ICA Boston Post Gazette Socially Scene Column #133

June 2016 Scene&Style - Modeling Against Bullying is Back at Emerald Lounge Boston Post Gazette Socially Scene Column #132

June 2016 Scene&Style - Date Night Rentals with Date My Wardrobe

6-2016 T*Racy Shows Fashionably Late Boston Post Gazette Socially Scene Column #130

June 2016 Bravery Brand Honors Local Hero's Boston Post Gazette Socially Scene Column #129

April 2016 Scene&Style - Josef's Runway for a Rescue Boston Post Gazette Socially Scene Column #128

3-2016 Project Runway Sensation Takes Over Apple Boston Post Gazette Socially Scene Column #128

March 2016 Scene&Style - Angelica Timas Shows Spring Collection Boston Post Gazette Socially Scene Column #127

3-11-2016 Fashion Power Play by KB Fashion Productions Boston Post Gazette Socially Scene Column #126

2-2016 Designer Candice Wu Opens New Boutique Boston Post Gazette Socially Scene Column #125

1-2016 SKEA Slopes Down Fashionably Late Socially Scene Column #124

Chapter Ten – 2015

"Never use the word 'cheap.' Today everybody can look chic in inexpensive clothes—the rich buy them, too. There is good clothing design on every level today. You can be the chicest thing in the world in a T-shirt and jeans—it's up to you." - Karl Lagerfeld

12-11-2015 Fashion's Finest Gather at DVF on Newbury Boston Post Gazette Socially Scene Column #123

11-27-2015 Slope Style Hits the Ski&Snow Expo Runway Boston Post Gazette Socially Scene Column #122

11-13-2015 Frank&Oak Opens on Newbury Boston Post Gazette Socially Scene Column #121

10-16-2015 Socially Scene Column Boston Post-Gazette Boston Fashion Week Reviewed Column #120

9-25-2015 bosFW Preview Boston Post Gazette Socially Scene Column #116

8-14-2015 Miss Central Massachusetts was Crowned Boston Post Gazette Socially Scene Column #115

7-10-2015 BMC Catwalk for a Cure Boston Post Gazette Socially Scene Column #114

6-26-2015 High Society Fashion Boston Post Gazette Socially Scene Column #113

6-26-2015 Denise Hajjar Celebrates Two Years in Residence at the Intercontinental Boston Post Gazette Socially Scene Column #113

January 2015 Scene&Style - East Coast Alpine Arrives Fashionably Late

Chapter Eleven – 2014

"Fashion fades, style is eternal" - Yves Saint Laurent

December 2014 Scene&Style - Timeless Tuesday "Skea" Styled by Kathy Benharris

November 2014 "Socially Scene" Bosfw Closing "Expressions the Faces of Boston Fashion" Boston Post Gazette Column #112

October 31st 2014 "Socially Scene" Denise Hajjar, David Josef, KRÉYOL, Julie Kontos / KB Fashion Productions Reviewed Boston Post Gazette Column #111

October 24th 2014 "Socially Scene" JJP Collections and Revs Reviewed Boston Post Gazette Column #110

October 10th 2014 "Socially Scene" BosFW Denise Hajjar Review Boston Post Gazette Column #109

October 2014 bosFW "Socially Scene" Fashion Meets Science Boston Post Gazette Column #108

10-3-2014 "Socially Scene" BosFW 2014 Break Down Boston Post Gazette Column #107

9-26-2014 "Socially Scene" Looking Forward to BosFW 2014 Boston Post Gazette Column #106

8-15-2014 Alistair Archer Painted the Bond Runway Socially Scene Column #99

8-8-2014 "Socially Scene" Seaside Allure Revere Rooftop Review Boston Post Gazette Column #98

7-25-2014 "Socially Scene" Miss Central Massachusetts Review Boston Post Gazette Column #96

7-11-2014 "Socially Scene" SDF at the Langham Review Boston Post Gazette Column #93

7-4-2014 "Socially Scene" BMC Catwalk for a Cure Review Boston Post Gazette Column #92

6-27-2014 "Socially Scene" StyleWeek Swim Review Boston Post Gazette Column #91

6-6-2014 "Socially Scene" South Shore Swim Review Boston Post Gazette Column #89

5-2-2014 "Socially Scene" Mass College Fashion Timeless Tuesday Review Boston Post Gazette Column #84

4-25-2014 "Socially Scene" StyleWeek Favorites Show at Timeless Tuesday Boston Post Gazette Column #83

4-18-2014 "Socially Scene" Miss Massachusetts Pageant Review Boston Post Gazette Column #82

March 2014 "Socially Scene" Body By Blo Review Boston Post Gazette Column #80

March 2014 "Socially Scene" Candice Wu Couture Boston Post Gazette Column #78

February 2014 "Socially Scene" Venni Caprice Fashionably Late Show Boston Post Gazette Column #76

2-21-2014 "Socially Scene" Denise Hajjar Valentines Show Boston Post Gazette Column #74

2-7-2014 "Socially Scene" Style Week Boston Post Gazette Column #72

1-24-2014 "Socially Scene" CKP Fashion Show Boston Post Gazette Column #71

1-3-2014 "Socially Scene" TWOB Collaboration Fashion Show Boston Post Gazette Column #68

11-29-2013 "Socially Scene" Diane von Furstenberg Boston Post Gazette Column #63

11-15- 2013 "Socially Scene" Style Fixed Boston Post Gazette Column #61

Chapter Twelve – 2013

"Fashion is part of the daily air and it changes all the time, with all the events. You can even see the approaching of a revolution in clothes. You can see and feel everything in clothes." —Diana Vreeland

10-18-2013 "Socially Scene" Firas Yousif Reviewed Boston Post Gazette Column #57

10-11 2013 "Socially Scene" BosFW Closes Boston Post Gazette Column #56

10-4 2013 "Socially Scene" BosFW Reviewed Boston Post Gazette Column #55

9-27-2013 "Socially Scene" BosFW Preview Boston Post Gazette Column #54

August 2013 "Socially Scene" Revere Roof Top Review Boston Post Gazette Column #51

August 2013 "Socially Scene" Revere Roof Top Fashion Boston Post Gazette Column #49

August 2013 "Socially Scene" - Rose Cherubini Boston Post Gazette Column #39

March 2013 "Socially Scene" Nara Paz at Bond Boston Post Gazette Column #37

January 2013 "Socially Scene" Mario Testino Shows in Boston Boston Post Gazette Column #18

Chapter Thirteen – 2012

"A Women should be two things, classy and fabulous" —Coco Chanel

10-17-2012 "Socially Scene" Style Fixx Preview Boston Post Gazette Column #10

10-29-2012 "Socially Scene" Style Fixxed Boston Post Gazette Column #8

October 2012 "Socially Scene" Wrapping Up bosFW Boston Post Gazette Column #6

September 2012 "Socially Scene" Boston Fashion Week Preview Boston Post Gazette Column #5

10-10-2012 "Around Town" Bling in Boston, Sondra Celli Boston Post Gazette Column #4

September 2012 "Around Town" Fashion Night Out Follow Up Boston Post Gazette #3

September 2012 "Around Town" Denise Hajjar Preview Boston Post Gazette Column #2

www.ingramcontent.com/pod-product-compliance
Lightning Source LLC
Chambersburg PA
CBHW051547250726
48653CB00004BA/1034